W9-BNT-340

# of Behavioral Strategies
for Individuals with Autism

Beth Fouse, Ph.D. and Maria Wheeler, M.Ed.

A Treasure Chest of Behavioral Strategies for Individuals with Autism

All marketing and publishing rights guaranteed to and reserved by

721 W. Abram Street
Arlington, Texas 76013
800-489-0727
817-277-0727
817-277-2270 (fax)
E-mail: info@FHautism.com
www.FHautism.com

© Copyright 2005, Beth Fouse, Ph.D. and Maria Wheeler, M.Ed.

Cover design and book layout: Matt Mitchell, www.mattmitchelldesign.com

All rights reserved.

Printed in the United States of America.

No part of this book may be reproduced in any manner whatsoever without written permission of Future Horizons, Inc. except in the case of brief quotations embodied in reviews.

ISBN 1-885477-36-8

Dedication by Beth Fouse

I dedicate this book to my family—my husband, William D. Fouse, my four sons, Lynn, Mick, Alan, and Doug Lee, their wives, and my six grandchildren. Over the years, they have given up time and attention so that I could pursue career goals and work on projects such as this book. Without their support and understanding, I would not be able to accomplish my personal goals. For that, I give them my love and gratitude.

Acknowledgments by Beth Fouse

I wish to express my appreciation to the members of the East Texas Chapter of the Autism Society of America for allowing me to work with them and be a sounding board for ideas. They are always willing to "lend" their children for special projects.

I would also like to thank the Upshur County Special Education Cooperative for the opportunity to work with special children in the school districts they serve. Being on public school campuses on a weekly basis keeps me grounded and realistic. The special education support staff and classroom teachers with whom I have worked are true professionals who care about students.

I also want to thank some special parents and children with whom I have worked for several years for allowing me to share knowledge and experiences about children and autism. These special mothers and their children are:

Charlotte and Josh;

Michelle and Ellias;

Betty and Nick; and

Sherry and Phillip.

Finally, I express my appreciation to Dr. Consuelo Bossey from Our Lady of the Lake University and Veronica Zysk Palmer of Future Horizons, Inc. for their help in editing this book.

Dedication by Maria Wheeler

I dedicate this book to the memory of my father, Walter Wheeler, a psychologist who was devoted to making a difference in the lives of children with learning and behavioral difficulties. Throughout the years we shared, he gently guided me with wisdom, patience, knowledge, and understanding, while allowing me the freedom to follow my heart. His insight and compassion have given me the courage and commitment to make a difference in the lives of children.

Acknowledgments by Maria Wheeler

I wish to extend my sincerest appreciation to the families and educators who have provided the experiences and foundations for this book. Their perspectives hold the key to making a difference and providing quality opportunities for persons with autism and other behavioral disorders. Their sincere dedication makes a difference in all our lives.

I express my appreciation and affection to Jim for believing in me. His caring support is inspiring.

I wish to express a special thank you to Wayne Gilpin and Veronica Zysk Palmer of Future Horizons, Inc. for their expert guidance and assistance in this endeavor.

I especially wish to thank Sara, Chris, Brian, and all of the other children and adults who have honored me with the privilege of viewing autism from their eyes and hearts. I am often guided by Brian's heart-wrenching plea: "I just want to be a real boy."

Authors' Note

The names of individuals were
changed to protect their
confidentiality.

Table of Contents

About the Authors

Beth Fouse, Ph.D. is an Associate Professor in the Department of Special Services, School of Education and Psychology, at The University of Texas at Tyler. She teaches courses in special education and gifted education. Special education courses include topics in various disability areas including autism, communication disorders, behavior disorders, and inclusion. She has over twenty years experience in the public schools as a classroom teacher and school administrator.

She works one day per week with a special education cooperative providing family training, school/home liaison services, and classroom curriculum consultation for teachers of students with autism and other behavioral disorders. She also provides parent training, on-site classroom curriculum consultation, and in-service training for other school districts and educational agencies in the northeast Texas area. She has Texas teacher certificates/endorsements in elementary education, serious emotional disturbance and autism, learning disabilities, mental retardation, early childhood handicapped, deficient vision, gifted education, educational diagnostician, school counselor, supervision, special education supervision, and mid-management. She is also a certified instructor in Nonviolent Crisis Intervention through the Crisis Prevention Institute and has been certified by Dr. Guy Berard as an auditory integration practitioner. She has published several articles in special education and gifted education. She is co-author of a Phi Delta Kappa Fastback and FastTrack, *A Primer on Attention Deficit Disorder*, and author of *Creating a Win-Win IEP for Students with Autism*.

Maria Wheeler, M. Ed. has spent twenty-two years of her professional life in the fields of Psychology and Special Education, with an emphasis on Neurobehavioral Disorders, Applied Behavior Analysis, and Specific Learning Disabilities. She has held positions in Florida and Texas as a special education classroom teacher; behavior specialist; consultant for emotional disturbance and behavior disorders; and director of behavioral services for residential treatment centers serving adults and children with neurobehavioral disorders and developmental disabilities. She has Texas teacher certificates/endorsements in serious emotional disturbance and autism, special education, and psychology. She received her education and training in Florida.

Maria works as a consultant serving various school districts, educational agencies, and families throughout Texas. She provides on-site behavior management and classroom curriculum consultation for teachers of students with autism and other behavioral and learning disorders. She also provides on-site coaching for in-home trainers and tutors, parent training, and professional development training.

About This Book

The authors' purpose in writing this book was to provide a resource manual that applies theory and best practices in behavior management to individuals with autism. The goal was to write a book parents and educators would find as an easy reference for using behavioral interventions with individuals with autism. To this end, certain visual symbols were used throughout the book to cue the reader to important information. The visual cues which follow the treasure chest theme are described below.

 The key is used to indicate single important concepts.

 The gems are used to indicate major concepts with lists relating to the major concept.

 The crossed swords are used to draw the reader's attention to cautions related to the behavioral interventions being discussed.

 The treasure chest cues the readers to case examples that illustrate the concepts presented.

Chapter One introduces readers to the autism spectrum and general concepts related to characteristics associated with autism. This introductory chapter also discusses the impact of these behaviors and characteristics on school and home environments.

Chapter Two looks at the relationships that exist between communication and behavior. Suggestions for addressing behaviors through effective communication programs are provided.

Chapter Three addresses sensory issues and the relationship with behavior. Specific concepts discussed are: alertness, hypersensitivities, hyposensitivities, specific types of dysfunctions, and appropriate interventions for sensory difficulties.

Chapter Four examines physical issues that can impact behavior. Some of the issues considered are medical issues, medications, diets, allergies, and vitamin therapy.

Chapter Five considers the impact of social-emotional issues on behaviors and discusses needs for social skills instruction. Social Stories and Social Review, the use of books, and peer assisted interventions are also discussed.

Chapter Six presents information related to structuring the environments in which the individual with autism must function. Suggestions are provided for the physical environment, routines and rituals, visual cues, schedules, and a sensory diet.

Chapter Seven addresses methods for increasing desired behaviors. These include functional analysis of behaviors, antecedent control, self-regulation, use of consequences and reinforcement, and guidelines for setting up "safe" areas.

Chapter Eight provides strategies for decreasing unwanted behaviors. These strategies include reinforcement, punishment, negative consequences, behavior momentum, and various forms of time-out.

Chapter Nine considers crisis management and other special problems related to individuals with autism. Early warning signs, meltdowns or "catastrophic reactions", physical aggression, and temper tantrums are discussed. Suggestions are also provided for self-stimulating behavior, running away, dramatic exits, safety issues, pica, climbing, toileting, stripping and disrobing, masturbation, and sleep disorders.

Chapter Ten considers information related to writing behavior management plans. Changes from The 1997 Amendments to IDEA are included. Sample behavior management plans are included in Appendix A.

Chapter Eleven provides the reader with instructions related to data collection. Specific forms related to the chapter are included in Appendix B.

Chapter Twelve presents stress management strategies for caretakers of individuals with autism.

Chapter Thirteen presents conclusions that may be drawn from information presented in this book. This is followed by appendices, a glossary and references.

CHAPTER One

Impact of Autism Characteristics

Autism as defined by the Autism Society of America is a neurological disorder. (ASA, 1997). This means that it is caused by dysfunctions within the body, particularly in the brain. Any parent of a child with autism can describe the manifested characteristics. However, the descriptions from different parents may differ drastically because autism is a spectrum disorder. It occurs at all intellectual levels and resultant characteristics, difficulties in communication, social interaction, and behavior, are as unique as the individual.

Although communication, social interaction, and behavior can be discussed in isolation, the impact on home, school, and community environments is more important when looked at from an integrated perspective. The problems in communication and social interaction frequently lead to expressions of feelings through behavior. For example, the lack of a consistent means of communication may be expressed through a temper tantrum or other displays of frustration when the individual is not able to express the thoughts through typical oral or written channels. Difficulty understanding oral language may result in what appears to be noncompliance when, in reality, the person has not complied with specific requests because the commands were not understood.

The wide variance in the spectrum of autism may also be confusing to persons attempting to understand a specific individual's problems. Anxiety, for instance, can be exhibited in some individuals by nervousness, fidgeting, muscle tension, giggling, etc. In individuals with moderate functioning, anxiety may be exhibited through loud or unusual noises, increased activity and arousal levels, and inappropriate or uncontrollable laughing or crying. At the severe end of the spectrum, individuals may exhibit anxiety by "shutting down," screaming, running wildly through the room, becoming violent, or other tantrum type behaviors. Table 1.1 illustrates challenging behaviors that might result at the mild, moderate, and severe levels of functioning because of problems in the areas of communication and social interaction.

Table 1.1. The Spectrum of Autism

Behaviors that may be exhibited		
More Severe	Moderate	Less Severe
Temper tantrums	Noncompliance	Language problems
Nonverbal	Echolalic	Verbal
Screaming	Unusual noises	Giggling, fidgeting, & muscle tension
Withdrawl	Observes others	Interacts with others
Severe sensory dysfunctions	Moderate sensory dysfunctions	Mild sensory dysfunctions
Aggressive behaviors	Running away	Panic attacks

As we work with parents and educators, we find that challenging behaviors result in frequent feelings of inadequacy and frustration for caretakers of individuals with autism. Because we do not think or feel like individuals with autism, it is difficult to understand why certain behaviors are exhibited. We can be likened to detectives looking for a hidden treasure. Sometimes we find a treasure, but don't have the key to open the chest. Other times, we don't even know where to look. The purpose of this book is to help parents and educators know where to look for answers to challenging behaviors and to provide some guidelines and procedures to use.

This book, our treasure chest, is full of positive intervention techniques and strategies for dealing with the challenging behaviors of individuals with autism. Sometimes you may reach into the treasure chest and pull out the wrong technique. Then you will have to try again. Other times, your key might not fit the treasure chest and you will have to look for another key. Through this book we offer multiple keys and gems for helping readers fill their own personal chests with positive intervention strategies for working and living with individuals with autism.

Critical Characteristics Impacting Behaviors

Although each individual is unique, there are certain factors that appear to impact many people with autism. Limited communication or the lack of communication is a major factor impacting behavior of these individuals. Nonverbal persons may exhibit inappropriate behaviors to indicate their needs or desires.

Some individuals who have no consistent means to communicate use temper tantrums or other inappropriate social behaviors to indicate their wants and needs. One 12-year-old drops to the floor, refusing to move, when he does not want to go somewhere. He continually goes to the door in the classroom to indicate that he wants to go outside. When he doesn't like something, he will make loud noises. Dr. Temple Grandin (Grandin & Scariano, 1986, p. 21.) reported that "Screaming and flapping my hands was my only way to communicate."

Sensory Issues

Another major factor impacting the behavior of individuals with autism may involve the senses of touch, sight, hearing, taste, and smell as well as vestibular and proprioceptive input. Tactile defensiveness in individuals with autism is well noted in the literature (McKean, 1994, 1996; Grandin, 1995; Grandin & Scariano, 1986; and Miller, 1993). Light touch may be very uncomfortable. Different textures and touches may cause violent reactions in some individuals. (Willbarger & Willbarger, 1991).

Auditory Processing Problems

Other individuals have extreme auditory processing problems. Donna Williams (Hayward, 1994) reports that auditory information may be inconsistent resulting in distorted comprehension. In a program aired on *Eye to Eye with Connie Chung*, she stated that children who scream, "I can't hear you," may actually mean, "I can't understand you consistently." Central auditory processing problems definitely impact the individual with autism. Additionally, according to Dr. Guy Berard (1993) and others (Rimland & Edelson, 1994; Veale, 1994), many individuals with autism have hypersensitive or painful hearing. They hear certain frequencies of sounds very intensely. If the sound levels are such that they cause pain, the individual may either shut down to tune out the "painful sounds" or exhibit aggression or rage behaviors as a reaction to the pain.

Social-emotional Characteristics

Social-emotional characteristics include high anxiety, low frustration tolerance, excessive fears, panic attacks, and limited social interaction. High anxiety, fears, and panic attacks may result in withdrawal into self or running away. Low frustration tolerance may result in extreme anger or rage that causes the escalation of physical or verbal aggression. All of these characteristics may limit social interaction. Abnormal fears, anxiety, and panic may inhibit the individual from interacting with others. Exhibitions of physical and/or verbal aggression will cause others to limit their interactions with persons exhibiting such behaviors.

Behavioral Characteristics

A short attention span, impulsivity, distractibility and hyperactivity make it difficult to focus on tasks which result in troublesome situations. Impulsive persons frequently act without regard for consequences. Obsessions and compulsions are problematic for the compulsive individual as well as others in the surrounding environment. There frequently are no logical reasons for the obsessions and compulsions. When compulsive or ritualistic behaviors continue, the individual is viewed as strange or bizarre by others.

Impact on Home Environment

The characteristics of autism also affect home environments in many ways. Some families are able to deal with certain challenges better than others. The individual with autism may not exhibit as many problem behaviors or the family may have better resources for coping. However, it is typical for families of individuals with autism to experience more stress and frustration in their daily lives than most families. Parents of these children have higher divorce rates as a result of demands placed on time, energy, and finances. Frequently, there is no time or energy left for maintaining a "couple relationship" because the focus is always on the child's needs.

In some cases, siblings or family members feel jealousy or embarrassment associated with the family member with autism. Some family members may still be recovering from the grief and loss felt when the "actual child" turned out to be very different from the "anticipated child." Family members may express these feelings through anger, resentment, and/or guilt.

Autism also impacts family finances. Many children with autism have other disabilities that necessitate special treatments. Parents often spend exorbitant amounts of money looking for "miracle cures" and tracking down the latest treatments and programs that appear promising. This may result in feelings of resentment if purchasing other desired items is limited due to money spent on treatments and resources related to autism.

Additionally, working on a daily basis with children with autism can be very physically demanding. Some parents lift weights and do other exercise programs to maintain their strength and endurance for responding to the physical challenges exhibited by some individuals with autism. They may also develop a lack of confidence in their parenting skills because the methods and techniques that they read and hear about don't work with their child. Parents may also become isolated from family and friends because the child's behavior causes others to shy away from interaction with the family.

Impact on School Environment

At school, even skilled teachers can develop stress and frustration when typical methods don't work with a specific student. Programs for students with autism can be physically and emotionally demanding and frequently have high rates of staff turnover. When methods don't work or stop working, a lack of confidence in teaching skills may result. Because there may be only one teacher on a campus working with students with autism or other developmental disabilities, teachers may feel isolated and alone. There is no one to support them when they have really bad days. Co-workers may not understand the situations with which they are dealing. For optimal success, both parents and teachers should receive extra support for coping with the special problems of individuals with autism.

CHAPTER *Two*

What Does Communication Have To Do With Behavior?

Communication, a major area of difficulty for individuals with autism, and behavior are closely related. Behavior does not occur in a vacuum. It cannot be viewed in isolation. When addressing behavioral concerns and planning strategies for intervention, it is critical to analyze the communicative function from the individual's perspective. Is the behavior performing a function for the individual with autism? Is it a reaction to something in the environment? Is the behavior being exhibited to say, "I don't want to do something"? What will happen if we try to stop the behavior? Rather than simply working to eliminate problem behaviors, the focus for change should be teaching acceptable behaviors for communication through the use of long-term positive behavioral supports. It is helpful to always remember, ***behavior is communication***.

Communication Characteristics

How do we know what his behavior means when he can't talk?

All persons need a method of communication. When an individual attempts to express a want, need, thought, or feeling, inappropriate behaviors may occur if an effective, socially acceptable means for communicating is not available. Sometimes individuals devise their own means for communicating, as improper behaviors. Others must then interpret the behaviors. For example, a parent might know that pacing around the room means "I need to go to the bathroom," or going to the sink means "I need a drink." However, individuals unfamiliar with the person may not recognize the behaviors as communication, resulting in troubling behaviors or frustration at the inability to get needs met.

Consequently, using an effective communication system can eliminate many problem behaviors because it enables a person to obtain wants and needs. If the individual points to a symbol for toilet, most people understand the person needs to go to the restroom. Those same people may not interpret constant pacing as a need to go to the restroom.

Caretakers in the immediate environment learn what the behaviors mean because of repeatedly observing the association between the person's behaviors and related wants and needs.

Why can't my child communicate?

Social behavior, communication, and learning patterns are significantly influenced by abilities to perceive, organize and process incoming information. Most people can speak fluently without consciously thinking about how to say something. Others may sometimes have to search for the right word to describe what they are thinking. It is not uncommon for people to visualize something and be able to describe it, but not be able to "pull up" the right word. This generally occurs so seldom that it's not a problem. However, nonverbal persons may have additional problems. For some, speech is not automatic.

Motor planning difficulties can significantly interfere with expressive communication and behavior. It is theorized that motor problems exist that inhibit development of speech. These persons must consciously think about what they want to say **and how to say it**. They must consciously think about how their mouth moves to form certain letters and how to blend the sounds together. If they are actually able to say the word, it generally takes much longer. At times, you can actually see the person moving the mouth in different ways to try to pronounce the sounds correctly. Others simply cannot get the muscles necessary for speech to work properly so they can speak. Consequently, these individuals are unintelligible or nonverbal. They may be extremely frustrated and angry because they know what they want to say, but cannot get the sounds out so others can understand.

 **Frequently, individuals with autism have no "screen" to filter out extraneous incoming information.**

Incoming information from the environment may result in the individual "tuning out" information that may be overwhelming. Other persons with autism may react in very different ways. Instead of withdrawing by "tuning out," an individual may be so overwhelmed by environmental sounds and other stimuli that inappropriate behaviors may be displayed. Behaviors commonly seen under these conditions include running away; loud, unusual noises; screaming; covering ears; tantrums; self-stimulation; physical aggression; and self-injurious behaviors.

 **Characteristics of autism such as disorganization, distractibility, difficulties in auditory processing, and focusing on details may interfere with the individual's ability to communicate.**

Disorganization and distractibility may draw the individual away from conversation, resulting in lack of attention to the conversation. Disorganization may also impact communication abilities as the individual may have difficulty in planning and staying on topic. Difficulty in sequencing and inconsistent auditory responses may result in problems with processing information accurately. Tendencies to focus on details or an inability to differentiate relevant from irrelevant information may cause the individual to focus on unimportant parts of the conversation or communication. Consequently, the person misses the important parts of the communication.

 **Individuals with autism frequently exhibit poor understanding and interpretation of nonverbal social cues (body language, voice pitch, tone, inflection, loudness, facial expression, and eye contact).**

A lack of understanding of nonverbal social cues creates many problems for individuals with autism. Difficulties reported by some adults related to interpretation of nonverbal social cues include problems with reading facial expressions and interpretation of body language. For example, I might look at a person and see a frown. This cues me to ask "What's wrong?" or give the person time and space to work through a problem. A person with autism, not recognizing the frown as a visual cue proceeds as usual, thus, creating a worse situation.

At the Autism Society of America (ASA) Networking Luncheon (1996), Sara Miller stated, "I observe people around me and make proper social responses by imitating people I trust. If I don't see someone to imitate, I imagine what my best friend would do in a similar situation." She rehearses acceptable responses to situations so she can respond appropriately in similar situations. Grandin (Donnelly, Grandin, Bovee, Miller, & McKean, 1996) also makes social mistakes because of difficulty interpreting social cues and facial expressions.

 **Some individuals with autism have limited or no usage of nonverbal communication. Others may use gestures and other forms of communication in an excessively exaggerated or dramatic manner.**

The words we speak account for only 7% of the message that is communicated. The rest of the message is conveyed through body language, facial expression, and other paraverbal or nonverbal means such as tone, volume, and cadence of our voice. (Houston Mediation Center, 1990). Individuals with autism who have speech may use a monotone voice or unusual pitch when speaking. The use of typical nonverbal communication, such as hand gestures or facial expressions, may not accompany their speech. Consequently, individuals may have difficulty interpreting communicated messages when no cues other than the spoken words are available. In turn, individuals with autism may exhibit frustration or anger when not understood.

Many individuals with autism have limited or no understanding of the PROCESS of communication. There may be minimal or nonexistent conversational skills along with limited understanding of reciprocity or turn-taking.

Some individuals do not understand turn-taking is a part of social conversation. Behaviors may include talking all the time or only responding to questions. Those who only respond to questions are exhibiting difficulties in topic maintenance. Responses are very rote with minimal expansion on concepts.

They don't know how to add information to their basic answers. For example, one young man had learned to greet people by saying "Hello" and "Where are you from?" However, he often moved on to other persons before waiting for the previous person to respond to his greeting. Those who talk constantly may only talk about certain obsessions or specific areas of interests, with little concern for the interests of their communication partner. In some cases, the individual simply doesn't understand that others may not share their interests in weather, wheels, plumbing, numbers, etc. Consequently, these problems commonly result in behaviors that other people find offensive or irritating such as interrupting, failing to respond, "hogging the conversation," and talking nonstop.

 Some persons with autism exhibit immediate or delayed echolalia.

Immediate echolalia usually takes the form of repeating the last part of a sentence or phrase that someone has just said. In response to "What did you do today?" a common echolalic reply would be "do today." Delayed echolalia involves repeating words or phrases that may have been heard yesterday, two weeks previously, or even months before. For example, one young teenage boy only says, "Don't hit your head." Because he repeatedly hits his head, this is a phrase that he has heard regularly. Some professionals, such as Prizant & Wetherby (1987), believe that echolalia can serve a communicative function. In some cases, echolalia appears to be an attempt to control or regulate behavior. In the above example, the young teenager usually says "Don't hit your head" just prior to exhibiting the behavior.

 Many individuals with autism exhibit very literal interpretations of language with little or no understanding of non-literal uses of language.

A young teenager on a panel of young adults with autism talked about an experience at school. One of her teachers angrily turned to the class and said, "Don't even breathe." She described her thoughts to the audience. "I was very upset with my teacher. Doesn't he know that we can't hold our breath much over a minute? Is he trying to kill us?" When she arrived home, her mother explained the teacher really meant, "Be quiet; don't talk." (Donnelly, 1995).

Idioms in language are abstract concepts and very difficult for many individuals with autism to understand. In working with individuals with autism, we must constantly be aware that language contains many idioms that convey messages that may be interpreted very differently by persons with concrete thinking. Dr. Gary Mesibov (1995 TEACCH Training) asked a young man with autism "What does 'Don't cry over spilled milk' mean?" The response was, "If you spill your milk, don't cry." The same young man responded that "A penny saved is a penny earned." means "If you find a penny, put it in your bank."

Concrete thinking leads to behavioral responses based on the individual's interpretation of language. What appears to be inappropriate behavior may actually be a very appropriate response, based on a literal interpretation of what was said.

CASE EXAMPLE

A young man residing in a group home was rearranging the furniture in his room on a weekly basis. This was a problem because the room was small and only one room arrangement was feasible. Careful analysis of the behavior showed that it only happened on Wednesdays. In looking at events preceding the behavior, staff realized that the young man was told to "change your bed" when they meant "change the sheets on your bed." The only way this young man knew to change his bed was to move it to another place in the room. He couldn't understand why staff members were getting angry at him when he thought he was complying with their request.

 **Individuals with autism may use words without attaching meaning.**

Strange as it seems, many people can actually use words correctly without truly understanding the meaning of the word. In fact, one young student passed a test covering fossils and dinosaurs. About a week later, he asked his mother what a fossil was. This creates a problem because people assume that the use of a word indicates understanding, whether the word is used in conversation or in directions. When used in directions, misunderstandings may appear as noncompliance. When present in conversations, misinterpretation can impact related social behavior.

How will communication issues affect his life?

If a child with autism acquires effective communication skills before the age of 6, there is a better chance that the individual will develop speech and become a higher functioning adult. (Frost & Bondy, 1994). Individuals having more severe limitations are generally nonverbal or display limited verbal skills that may be mostly echolalic language. Individuals functioning at higher levels may exhibit verbal skills, but still have problems in auditory processing, understanding meanings of words and phrases, and in vocabulary development. Speech may appear to be odd, unusual, awkward, or rigid. At any level, an individual's quality of life, social behavior, learning patterns and emotional health can be positively influenced by developing effective methods of communication. Therefore, when planning intervention strategies, language and communication issues must be a high priority.

In considering communication issues and the relationship to behaviors, remember that every interaction can become stressful when the conversation of others presents a flood of incomprehensible information. Even with higher functioning individuals who generally understand most incoming information, stress may be created due to inconsistent interference from processing deficits or due to *anticipation* of such lapses in processing. In response to these stresses, the individual develops a system of protection—usually relying on withdrawal, avoidance, tantrums, or aggression. Once developed, these behaviors can limit the person's ability to benefit from experiences in many situations.

I think he just chooses to disobey.

Most behaviors are directly related to organizing and understanding incoming information, as well as subsequently producing a response. Noncompliant behavior, often an exhausting problem, is directly related to understanding cues, in addition to planning, and producing responses. Frequently, behaviors that appear on the surface to be deliberate defiance may be an attempt to control and influence the environment. Usually it is an expression of a desire for sameness. Individuals with autism generally do not like unexpected changes in routine or surroundings. These expressions, which are an attempt to communicate a feeling, are frequently misinterpreted as behavior problems.

Other behaviors such as compulsions and obsessions seem to be internally driven. They may not appear to have a purposeful function. However, addressing related communication issues can reduce the stress that may elicit such behaviors.

Suggestions for Addressing Behavior Through Effective Communication Programs

In light of the unique needs of persons with autism, it is of utmost priority to teach an effective means of communication that can be used with a wide audience of people in different settings. Preferably, individuals should develop a variety of methods in order to have a total communication system that functions effectively across different settings.

Communication systems for individuals with autism should allow the individual to communicate wants, needs, thoughts, and feelings across a variety of settings, persons and tasks. The ultimate goal is to enable the individual to be as independent as possible. The system should encourage and support self-initiated, spontaneous communication.

Devise an array of strategies to communicate across all persons, settings, and tasks.

- Prompt pointing or other motor responses required.

- Incorporate visual cues into the communication system.

- Establish routines for the individual to follow.

- Build in generalization and carryover by varying materials, persons, and environments.

Encourage communication in natural, meaningful situations.

- Set up situations where the individual is required to make choices; begin with choices between desired and hated objects.

- Establish communication goals as part of every activity.

- Build in child-to-child and group interactions whenever possible.

- Encourage turn-taking.

Focus on a communicative-interactive approach with all caregivers as facilitators.

- Validate every communication. Respond to and build upon any intentional behavior (i.e., reaching for objects, speaking single words, and purposeful, echolalia).

- Encourage active involvement with materials, physical activities, movement, music, etc. Avoid passive participation. Incorporate music and movement into as many activities and tasks as possible.

- Encourage initiation of communication. Hold back; don't always anticipate needs. Control access to preferred items.

- Avoid overreaction to new or "cute" communication attempts as the person may be overwhelmed by the reaction and "shut down."

Alternative Communication

 Motor planning problems resulting in a lack of useful speech generally indicate a need for an alternative system of communication. Such systems are not designed to replace spoken communication, but are structured to supplement and facilitate verbalizations in a consistently effective manner.

 Some of the more common types of alternative communication systems include:

- gestures and pointing,

- communication boards (objects, photos, or pictures),

- object or picture swap,

- synthesized speech such as the Wolf, Message Mate, or Dynavox,

- picture symbols with words,

- printed words or letters, and

- sign language.

The purpose of any alternative communication system is to provide the person with a communication method that is both appropriate and effective. By using an effective communication system, the learner:

• learns the process of communication;

• engages in intentional communication for expressing wants and needs; and

• experiences successful interchanges.

Gestures and pointing may be appropriate for some individuals. Simple communication boards are frequently used to begin a system of functional communication for persons who only use gestures, pointing, and other responses such as temper tantrums to indicate displeasure and other wants and needs. These simple, low-tech solutions may use objects, photographs, pictures, or picture symbols with words. (See Appendix C for sources of communication materials.) The actual appearance of a communication board or system may take on many different forms. It may be a basket of objects that the person can use or a choice box with two to four compartments to place objects. Pictures may be arranged on a sheet of paper, a clipboard, a file folder, or any number of other backgrounds.

Regardless of the communication system used, it should always be available to the individual.

Object swaps may be used for individuals who have difficulty pointing or orienting to pictures. Objects may also be used for individuals who have visual impairments and cannot see pictures. Pictures are more abstract than objects. When appropriate, objects may be changed to pictures by pairing the picture and object. For example, when using a small glass to indicate drink, a picture of a small glass may be taped to the side of the glass as a first step in moving toward photographs or pictures.

CASE EXAMPLE

Susie got desired objects by climbing on counters or opening cupboards to get things. She helped herself to everyone's drinks and snacks. Communication instruction began with teaching Susie how to exchange an object to request a drink or food. As a result, Susie began to appropriately request drinks and food instead of resorting to unacceptable behaviors. This particular behavior problem was addressed by teaching a communication strategy as part of the behavioral intervention.

For persons who can orient to a picture, but have difficulty pointing, a picture swap may be appropriate. It may be necessary to modify the picture swap system to minimize inappropriate behaviors that interfere with using the picture communication system.

CASE EXAMPLE

Eddie had significant motor problems. He had difficulty picking up the pictures. His teacher handed him the picture so he wouldn't have to pick it up. However, he began playing a game. He wanted to throw the picture. He loved to watch the picture float through the air to his desktop or the floor. This procedure was modified by cutting a 2 inch square block about one-half inch thick. The block was covered using clear transparency film and 2 inch, clear, plastic tape resulting in a picture block which could have different pictures inserted as he progressed to new pictures. Eddie's teacher modified his picture swap system to address his motor impairment and inappropriate behaviors.

When individuals with autism have their wants and needs met through functional communication, frustration is greatly reduced. The person is less likely to exhibit inappropriate behaviors because their needs are being met through an acceptable communication system.

Parents who need assistance in developing home communication programs for preschool and school-age children may contact their local Early Childhood Intervention Program or their local public school system. Referrals may be made to either of these programs for evaluation in the area of communication needs and assistive technology. Speech therapy and assistive technology services should be available through the local public school's services at no charge to eligible students. (*Individuals with Disabilities Education Act*, 1990).

Adults with communication deficits may contact their local mental health and mental retardation authorities to see what kinds of services are available in their community. Private speech/language pathologists and language therapists may also be consulted for assistance with problems in communication. A list of resources that may be helpful to parents, professionals, and other caretakers about alternative communication systems is included in Appendix C.

Assistive Technology and Communication

Assistive technology is changing so fast that one can barely keep up with new items on the market. However, technology has opened doors for many nonverbal individuals.

As defined in the Individuals with Disabilities Education Act (IDEA) (Federal Register, 1992), Assistive technology services refers to assisting any child with a disability in the selection, acquisition or use of an assistive technology device. This includes:

- the evaluation of the needs of a child with a disability;

- purchasing, leasing, or otherwise providing for the acquisition of assistive technology devices for children with disabilities;

- selecting, designing, fitting, customizing, adapting, repairing, or replacing assistive technology devices;

- coordinating and using other therapies, interventions, or services with assistive technology devices; and

- training or technical assistance for the child, the family, professionals, or employers.

Technology allows persons to participate in situations from which they may have been previously excluded. Thus, the use of assistive technology can facilitate social interaction and participation in home, school, and work environments. Being able to interact with others may also increase self-esteem. Others begin to realize that individuals with autism are like most of our population. They are real people with real feelings!

Assistive technology can be either high-tech or low-tech. Low-tech devices are simple items such as pencil grips or paper communication boards. High-tech devices can be rather simple or extremely complex. There are many devices, both simple and complex, for producing a voice output that can be used in several ways. For example, the major things that individuals request or need during the day can be programmed into a voice output device. The person is only required to touch a display board to make a communicative response. Most devices can be programmed with phrases and short sentences which provide a functional communication system by which individuals can obtain their wants and needs.

The Individuals with Disabilities Education Act including the 1997 Amendments and the 1994 Amendments to the Technology-Related Assistance for Individuals with Disabilities Act of 1988 require that needs for assistive technology be addressed for all students with disabilities. Therefore, the first step in determining whether the student has a need in this area is the evaluation for assistive technology. This evaluation will determine whether there is a need for assistive technology, the type of communication system best suited to the needs of the student, and how much training staff, student, and parents or caretakers work effectively with the individual. ***Remember, assessment is an on-going process***. Needs may change. Consequently, needs for assistive technology today may differ from needs two years or four years later.

 A complete evaluation for assistive technology must examine the needs on an individual basis and should address:

- The needs for assistive technology may be stated in a separate assistive technology report or embedded within other reports for eligibility, modifications, functional vision reports, or related service assessments.

- Is the assistive technology service and/or device necessary for the student to receive a free, appropriate public education?

- Is it a necessary related service?

- Is assistive technology necessary to provide the least restrictive environment?

- Does the child understand cause and effect relationships?

- What kind of input device is needed?

- Does the individual possess keyboarding skills?

- What kind of equipment is needed for successful functioning in the environment?

- What kind of training will be needed by the individual's parents, and other caretakers to effectively use assistive technology at home and school?

 **The goal is to motivate the person to initiate spontaneous communication.**

This will not happen if the individual does not have easy access to communication materials. Communication boards and other assistive technology devices are not designed to be pulled out for thirty minutes a day for instruction and put away at the end of the communication period. The use of any communication system should be fully integrated into every activity the person does in school, home, work, and community. There should be coordination between different environments so that the same system is used in all environments. When individuals do not have access to functional communication systems across all settings, inappropriate behaviors may increase as communication is compromised.

Sign language

Although many individuals with autism respond to sign language or to sign language paired with verbal cues, it is not always the best choice for every person. Sign language provides visual cues; however, "Manual signing is a transient signal...it moves...it is there, and then it is gone." (Hodgdon, 1995 p. 20). The individual cannot go back and refer to it. From a receptive standpoint, some individuals need visual cues that remain in place as a reference point. In those situations, sign language may be ineffective in maintaining appropriate behaviors.

However, "learning manual signs has been the introduction to intentional communication for some students." (Hodgdon, 1995, p. 20). The introduction of signs has been the beginning of oral language development for some individuals. Another benefit is that *signs* are always available. Your hands are always there. For individuals who are cognitively capable and have the necessary motor abilities, signs may offer a viable form of communication.

Some individuals may not have the motor skills to successfully manipulate their fingers to form signs that are recognizable to anyone other than their immediate caretakers. Sign language is not universally understood. Only a small portion of the population can understand sign language. The individual cannot go to McDonald's® and order a hamburger if no one at McDonald's® understands signs. However, that person can use a visual picture menu to order as this only requires pointing to the desired food. Consider the overall situation, including the individual's skills and needs, when making decisions regarding the use of sign language. If sign language meets the needs of the individual within their environment, then signs should be used. If other communication systems are more efficient, then another system should be used.

Facilitated Communication

Facilitated Communication is one of the most controversial communication methods to be introduced during the past century. Most professionals and parents who are aware of Facilitated Communication (FC) either strongly support or firmly oppose its use with individuals with autism. Some have ambivalent feelings — believing that it is possible — but, also believing that there is much abuse and misuse of the method.

FC is a method that facilitates communication by having a "facilitator" provide physical support to a "communicator" while the person is typing messages. The typing may take place on typewriters, computers, and even paper alphabet boards. The controversy revolves around who is actually communicating. Some say it is the person being facilitated; others say the facilitator is influencing the individual to type certain messages.

Opponents of this method cite numerous research studies that have failed to validate the communication as a message from the individual being facilitated. Another concern is the high level of literacy that has been reported in individuals who were previously thought to be functioning in the severe to profound range of intellectual abilities. Biklen (1993) stated these individuals had previously learned to read on their own and were only able to demonstrate their abilities because of facilitation.

Many individuals whom I have observed communicating through facilitators were not looking at the alphabet board while they were typing. In the January 1992 training in Syracuse, NY, Biklen stated that a communicator did not need to look at the board because the individual had memorized the location of the keys on the keyboard just as touch typists memorize the keyboard and type without looking at it. There is however, one big difference. In touch typing, the typist has the home keys as a reference point, and the fingers never leave the keyboard. In facilitated communication where the communicator only uses one finger to point to the letters, the finger moves away from the board after each letter.

Although I can touch type 75 to 85 words per minute, I cannot close my eyes and spell a word accurately when I have to pull my finger away from the board after each letter. I have no reference point to use for placing my finger the next time. This is particularly true if a paper board is being used where the actual letters or position of the letters cannot be felt. In later training with Biklen, he also emphasized the importance of looking at the board. In a personal conversation with Rosemary Crossley in May of 1994, she also emphasized that the communicator must always look at the keyboard.

One other troubling situation that has arisen involves the high rate of abuse reports among this population. Many families have been completely disrupted because of these reports. In some cases, children have been removed from the family for long periods of time. In other situations, children were removed, only to be returned when courts were unable to validate the reports of the facilitator.

One beneficial result reported by proponents of FC is the improvement in behaviors that result from the use of this technique. However, one must also acknowledge that the behavior of others in the environment generally changes. One definite benefit is that the professional community has begun to view autism differently. Spoken language is no longer accepted as the only indicator of intelligence. We have learned that being nonverbal does not necessarily equate with low intelligence. Persons with autism are being treated with more dignity and respect. This alone, can result in positive behavioral changes.

Additionally, because of the close relationship that must develop between facilitator and communicator, the individual usually receives much more attention than before using FC. Although the possibility of influence is generally questioned, some individuals have moved on to independent typing after a period of time when physical support was provided to the individual and then gradually faded (Biklen, 1992). Once this occurs, no one questions the source of the message. With no one touching them, the message must be their own. If you are currently using FC, or you plan to use it in the future, you should be aware of the following recommendations related to FC.

 Do's for persons using Facilitated Communication include:

- Complete sufficient training with professionals who have experience in FC. Learn the appropriate techniques.

- Don't expect high levels of literacy. Instruct the person in reading. Crossley (1984) began with pictures and taught Annie how to read. She did not instantly read when presented with the opportunity to use FC.

- Remember, the goal is independent communication, not high levels of literacy.

- Be aware of signs of influence. Constantly guard against the possibility of influence which can be so subtle that the facilitator is unaware of it.

- Always insist that the communicator look at the board!

- Regularly strive to fade back support. Move back from the hand to the wrist, the forearm, the elbow, above the elbow, the shoulder, and finally, no support at all.

- Learn appropriate methods for validating claims of abuse.

- Use different facilitators to enable the individual to generalize skills to more than one person.

CAUTION!

Be aware of the following red flags when using Facilitated Communication.

- The facilitator has little or no training.

- The facilitator is more concerned about high levels of literacy than developing independence.

- The facilitator is not trying to fade back support.

- The communicator is not looking at the alphabet board or keyboard when typing.

- The individual has been using Facilitated Communication for longer than six months with no lessening of support.

CAUTION!

If someone reports abuse through facilitation, you should:

- Validate the claim by having another facilitator work with the individual.

- Use open-ended questions to obtain more reliable information.

- Recognize that the individual may not understand the language that is being used. Check out understanding of the words.

- Recognize that individuals with autism can get mad and make false claims like anyone else. Proceed with caution.

- Follow state reporting procedures.

Communication significantly impacts behavior. There are many methods and techniques that can be used to address behaviors through effective communication systems. Regardless of the communication method used, long-term changes provided through the development of functional communication will increase the probability of behavioral improvements.

CHAPTER *Three*

Sensory Issues And Behavior

The impact of sensory issues on behavior became very evident when walking into a classroom a couple of years ago for a consultation. Jerry, one of the students, was having a bad day. He could be heard before entering the room. He was on the bean bag in the corner, wrapped in a weighted quilt, yelling as loud as he could. An immediate question was "What happened to Jerry? How long has he been like this?" The educational staff was concerned. Although he had always exhibited challenging behaviors, Jerry was having his worst year yet. We needed to find some answers for him.

Like Jerry, persons with autism frequently lack the ability to control or "filter" incoming information from their environment. It seems the individual cannot organize or use the sensory input received from the environment. Reception to sensory stimuli appears to be totally "on" or completely "off." In the above situation, Jerry was totally "on." He was overwhelmed by everything in the environment, and was not able to "tune out" or filter anything. After careful observation and valuable information from his mother, we realized the air conditioner on the roof and the fluorescent lights in the classroom were emitting constant humming sounds. The room was divided from another classroom by a pull-together curtain instead of a solid wall. At times, these sounds overwhelmed him. Additionally, he smelled everything — the markers he used for drawing, the food on his plate, etc. His system was "hypersensitive." His parents had moved just prior to school starting; his class was located on a new campus, and he had new instructional staff. In fact, although it was only November, the third teacher and aide were working in the classroom since the beginning of school. For a child who has difficulty with change, his world had been turned upside down!

Many of Jerry's behaviors could be attributed to "sensory overload." Such overstimulation can be exhibited in many different ways. Some individuals develop protective behaviors such as avoidance reactions and withdrawal. Others, like Jerry, become aggressive or tantrum. Sometimes, behavior that seems unrelated to ongoing activities can occur due to *anticipation* of sensory overload. For example, if the child has repeatedly experienced sensory overload while in the restroom, inappropriate responses may be exhibited when it nears time to go to the restroom. Responses to stimulation can vary greatly among individuals. Some are "mono-channel." For example, in a 1994 television interview for *Eye to Eye with Connie Chung*, Donna Williams talked about her difficulties in processing incoming information. She must listen or look. She cannot use auditory and visual channels at the same time. Like many individuals with autism, her visual channel is much stronger than the auditory channel. Therefore, she asked that all interview questions be sent to her in writing prior to the interview.

When the interviewer asked her a question not on the list, she answered, "That's not one of your questions." She did go on and attempt to answer the question. However, she had to resort to typing the question so that she could read it before answering it. In contrast, some people are "multi-channel" which means that an individual needs sensory input from more than one source or modality in order to process incoming information accurately. "Tuning out," becoming overwhelmed, and using single or multiple processing channels or modalities are all sensory-based responses that directly affect behaviors.

Alertness

Arousal levels greatly impact behaviors.

States of arousal usually change several times during the day. Morning people typically wake up and are alert immediately. Night people may have difficulty with arousal early in the morning, but become more alert as the day progresses. Many people have difficulty staying alert just after lunch, particularly if they are required to sit still.

Individuals with autism frequently exhibit difficulties with their state of arousal. It is either too low or too high. "A normal state of arousal is essential for impulse control." (Trott, Laurel, & Windeck, 1993, p. 15). Various kinds of movements help individuals maintain optimal states of arousal. Activities and movements that promote regulation of arousal states should be regularly scheduled into the day for individuals exhibiting these types of difficulties.

CASE EXAMPLE

Even after a daily schedule, a work schedule, appropriate tasks, and other visual cues were implemented, George was continually overstimulated at school. His behaviors escalated to the point that he needed physical restraints for prevention of property damage and injury to others daily. After doing a functional analysis of his behavior, his schedule was changed to include more sensory based movement activities. After breakfast, he went to the bathroom, and then returned to the classroom to check his schedule. After the bathroom, his first activity was riding an exercise bicycle for ten minutes. This allowed him to calm down from the overstimulation of the school cafeteria. He was much better able to regulate his behavior and exercise self-control when he did this movement activity to calm down. After group time, independent work, and one-to-one work, he jumped on the mini-trampoline for ten minutes, an activity that allowed him to reduce stress and arousal levels. After lunch, he was able to come into the room and go to his "safe area" or participate in an activity of his choice. Frequently, this was looking at a book while wrapped in a weighted quilt for deep pressure. However, if he wished, his activity could be a movement activity such as the trampoline or bicycle. After more work time, he then was scheduled to go to music and physical education. His choice of activity at the playground was generally swinging - another calming activity that allowed George to gain control of his arousal level. By building in movement activities, George was better able to regulate his arousal levels. His need for physical restraint dramatically reduced.

CASE EXAMPLE

An 18-year-old high school student's arousal level became so high that he frightened the school staff. The student, David, went outside and was jumping up and down, hopping everywhere. With his long legs, each jump was two or three feet in the air. Not knowing what to do, the school staff called the police to take him home.

After consulting with a behavior specialist, the staff realized that these behaviors were an indication of his need for movement activity and deep pressure. This behavior problem was resolved by watching for early signs of overstimulation or hyperarousal. When David began showing signs of high arousal levels, Joe, the paraprofessional working with him, would take him outside where he was allowed to do one of his favorite activities - collecting soft drink cans from the can containers on the school ground. Once collected, he then crushed the cans by stomping them with his feet - a wonderful activity for supplying deep pressure. When calmed, he was able to go back into the classroom and complete other assigned tasks.

A functional analysis should also indicate when typical high arousal periods occur during the day so that appropriate movement activities can become part of the regular schedule. (See Chapter 7 for information on functional analysis.)

Movement activities can also regulate *low* arousal states. When it is obvious that a student is having difficulty with low arousal, the teacher can assign an errand that requires the student to move around the room or go to another classroom to deliver something. Just walking will help the student to regain a higher state of arousal. For some students, it is necessary to have them stand in order to maintain arousal long enough to complete a task.

Hypersensitivities

Many persons with autism experience *hyper*sensitivity to sensory stimuli. This is evidenced by a tendency to react negatively or with alarm to sensory input that is generally not irritating or harmful for individuals in the "normal" population. I observed this kind of reaction earlier this school year.

I had been consulting with a family who has a child with multiple disabilities and autism. Because it had been several months since I had heard from this family, I assumed things were okay.

While attending a staffing about this student, I found things were not okay. When brought in to wait for the bus, he became very agitated and began to pace rapidly back and forth across the room. I had never seen him so agitated. Previously, he usually exhibited withdrawal reactions such as sitting and rocking when he was experiencing high levels of anxiety and arousal. We allowed him to continue pacing within the confines of the room, which seemed to calm him enough to allow him to sit and wait for the bus. If we tried to force him to sit before he was calm, his behavior may have worsened. Allowing him to pace prevented escalation of behavior. In some situations, staff would have interpreted his unwillingness to initially sit down as noncompliance or direct defiance. However, when a behavior stems from sensory issues, underlying causes need to be identified.

 **Individuals who are easily overstimulated frequently respond poorly to highly intrusive methods of intervention.**

 Other behaviors which might be observed that are commonly associated with hypersensitivities are:

- repeated noncompliance,
- repeated rule violations,

- attempts to run away,

- screaming and tantrums,

- increased self-stimulation,

- increased muscle tension,

- increased repetitive movements,

- aggression to self or others,

- perseverative noises,

- climbing,

- covering face, eyes, or ears,

- attempts to hide,

- anxious or pained facial expressions, and

- withdrawal.

When stressed or overstimulated, incoming stimuli is frequently confusing and overwhelming, resulting in problem behaviors. Finding activities that calm the individual will be much more effective for coping with difficult behaviors than trying to demand compliance from persons in a high arousal state.

Hyposensitivities

Conversely, some people are *hypo*sensitive to sensory input. Persons experiencing hyposensitivity to sensory information can appear oblivious to cues from visual, auditory, tactile (touch), kinesthetic (movement), olfactory (smell), and gustatory (taste) sources. This lack of response to incoming information significantly impacts the person's ability to participate in his or her world. The individual may exhibit inconsistent work performance or appear to be bored or inattentive. Low arousal levels can also present significant concerns regarding safety issues, since the person may not attend or respond to dangerous sights, sounds, tastes, or smells.

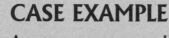

CASE EXAMPLE

Aaron, a young man I know, withdraws so totally that his teacher has to ask him to get a drink of water or move around the room before he begins his work. If he doesn't, he has a tendency to completely "shut down" and do nothing but sit and gaze or put his head on the desk and sleep. His family and educators are continually observing to determine what kinds of situations are most appropriate for maintaining his best level of arousal.

Dysfunctions in Specific Sensory Systems

Besides issues regarding levels of arousal, the way in which information and sensory perceptions are processed significantly impacts the way they are used. Sensory integration is a "process by which the brain organizes sensory information for appropriate use." (Ayres, 1979). Persons with autism often have significant sensory processing disorders that interfere with their ability to attend, learn, and relate to the environment and other people.

 Sensory integration affects the way we:

- respond to various stimuli,
- attend,
- learn,
- relate to the environment,
- perceive and use our bodies in space, and
- relate to other people.

The types of sensory difficulties associated with autism are unique and variable. The perceptual distortions can be unpredictable and changing. As a result, individuals may experience alienation, poor concentration, poor attention, ineffective social skills, low self-esteem, system overload, frustration, poor body awareness, distorted awareness of others, and responses based on faulty perceptual information.

Auditory

The auditory modality is particularly sensitive in most individuals with autism. They generally respond to sounds with *over*reactions or *under*reactions. In fact, many people with autism are evaluated for deafness as young children because they frequently act as if they don't hear anything when in fact, they may just be "shutting down."

Instead of being deaf, audiograms frequently show that individuals with autism have better hearing than most people. Sounds which may be inaudible to most persons might be heard by a person with autism. Sounds which are conversational tones for us might be painful to a person with autism. In fact, one child going to a threshold hearing test asked, "Is it going to hurt?' After testing him, I realized that school screening, which takes places at a sound level of 25 decibels, is probably painful for him. He was fearful of the hearing test that I was going to perform because of his previous experiences with school screening tests for hearing. When hearing is actually painful or irritating, the individual may overreact with anger and rage or shut down completely, becoming oblivious to his or her surrounding environment.

According to Dr. Guy Berard (1993), some individuals are sensitive to certain frequencies of sounds and not sensitive to other. This is why some noises bother them and others don't.

Noises that occur at the same frequency as their sensitivities will be bothersome. Generally, extreme sensitivities will occur in higher frequencies as opposed to lower frequencies. Some individuals will react negatively to a specific person because the sound of the person's voice is irritating to them. Usually, individuals with autism will react more positively toward males than toward females because the pitch of their voice is lower. Therefore, when working with individuals with autism, it is advisable to use low, calm voices.

Oral-Motor and Gustatory (Taste)

Many children with autism exhibit oral-motor defensiveness. This may involve both the tactile/kinesthetic system and the gustatory system. Some foods are refused because of the taste. Others are refused because of the texture and smell. One example of this type of sensory defensiveness involved Peter, an eleven-year-old, who had never eaten anything except pancakes and donuts. He ate no meats and no vegetables. Although we were not sure whether this was due to taste, tactile defensiveness, smell, or a combination of the three, it was a significant problem because of the deficiency of vitamins and nutrients in a diet consisting of nothing but pancakes and donuts.

Some may regard a child spitting out their food, particularly at the beginning of the meal, or a refusal to eat certain foods as an act of noncompliance. However, what might actually be happening is an oral-motor defensiveness which is causing this form of reaction. When individuals appear to have some forms of oral-motor defensiveness, parents or school personnel should request that an occupational therapist or speech pathologist evaluate the individual for problems in oral-motor defensiveness. Oral-motor activities such as blowing bubbles and eating chewy or crunchy foods can help individuals to process and organize information. Therefore, it is imperative that problems in the oral-motor area be addressed.

Visual

Visual information is also used "to alert and calm ourselves and to help us focus and attend." (Trott, et al, 1993). Individuals may react very differently to different forms of light. Some individuals attend and perform better in direct lighting; others in indirect lighting. One treatment technique currently being used by some individuals with autism is Irlen lenses. (Additional information about the Irlen lenses can be found in the strategies section in this chapter on page 74.) Colors even evoke positive and negative responses. Some individuals with autism are so sensitive to light that they develop visual "stims" such as flicking their hands in front of their eyes or blinking their eyes. Although it appears to be a strange behavior, we might meet the same visual sensory need by gazing at a rainbow or star or enjoying the flickering of lights in a chandelier. Everyone experiences a need for sensory input; some just meet that need in different ways.

Tactile/kinesthetic

Mr. Banks, the physical education teacher, sat discussing Joey with the multidisciplinary assessment team. We wanted to know how he was handling physical education. Did he need any modifications? We found that Joey had the motor skills to run, jump, kick, and throw that most boys his age have. However, other children generally do not interact with him socially because of his reactions. If touched slightly, he cries, "OW! That hurts!" When a ball is thrown at him, he can catch it, but he won't because "it hurts." The gym teacher then went on to say, "Of course, I know it doesn't hurt him. He's just a big, spoiled baby." Those of us who have worked with autism for a length of time know that, in fact, it might really hurt this child. For some individuals, very light touches are exceedingly painful. Others feel good when they receive deep pressure, but react in very negative ways when there is light or unexpected touch. If we are to help these individuals prepare for the world, we must help them by learning techniques to tolerate touch. We must teach people in their environment to avoid touching them unless invited to do so, or to touch them in ways that are not so irritating. We must also teach them to prepare the individual for touch. Never, even unintentionally, surprise a person with autism by touching him. The individual will probably not react with the behaviors that you expected.

CAUTION!

"Forms of deep pressure that appeal to some people may may cause fear reactions in others. (Trott, Laurel, & Windeck, 1993, p. 19.)

Proprioceptive

The proprioceptive system provides us with unconscious information from the muscles and joints. Information from the proprioceptive system enables the individual to know when and how muscles are contracting or stretching. This system also enables the brain to know where each part of the body is and how it is moving. (Sensory Integration International, Inc., 1991).

Vestibular input

The vestibular system provides the individual with unconscious information from the inner ear about the body's movement and position in space. Specifically, it integrates the neck, eye, and body adjustments to movement. It helps the individual respond to the position of the head in relation to gravity and movement.

Gravity

For purposes of this discussion, gravity refers to how comfortable people are with their heads in various positions. Young babies with gravitational insecurity will not venture out and take the risk of walking unless they are sure that there is a wall or a person to rely on for their gravitational security. Gravity receptors are located in the ears. Consequently, we generally have more energy to think on higher levels if we don't have to work against gravity to hold our heads up.

If you have ever held your head up with your hands when in deep thought, you were compensating for the effects of gravity. Sometimes, it is easier or more comfortable to read or relax in a hammock or on the couch. It relieves the person of the necessity of having to work against gravity, thus, freeing up energy to concentrate better. I frequently see children reprimanded in school because they put their head on the desk while they write or read. The teacher comes along saying, "Sit up so you can read. You're going to ruin your eyes or posture!" As a result, children sit up straight even though it might actually result in poorer focus and concentration.

How do the sensory systems affect behavior?

Professionals and parents should become aware of the differences in the sensory systems of individuals with autism and learn to use the information. Constantly working against the sensory system will eventually result in increased behavioral difficulties. This will benefit no one. We must work together. School staff, parents, and other caretakers can enhance the quality of life in individuals with autism by providing long-term, positive supports in the form of sensory-based treatments. If these supports are put into place, there will be a decreased need for discipline and behavioral interventions.

Interventions for Sensory Issues

Sensory Integrative Therapy

Once sensory issues are identifed, the question then becomes, "What can be   d o n e to treat these difficulties?" Dr. A. Jean Ayres (1979), an occupational therapist, developed a program of treatment called *sensory integrative therapy*. This program is only one of the methods that an occupational therapist may use in therapy for individuals with autism. Although Dr. Ayres' original work was with individuals with learning disabilities, it has been generalized to all populations of individuals exhibiting difficulties in sensory integration.

Although the normal population develops sensory integration naturally through play and movement in the environment, individuals with sensory integrative dysfunction are unable to process sensations from their own play. Consequently, these individuals are unable to develop the adaptive responses that organize the brain. Therapists with sensory integration training can diagnose how the individual's "sensory systems are working and then design an environment that enables the child to interact more effectively than he has ever done before." (Ayres, 1979, p. 140). The therapist assists the individual in choosing activities that will help the brain develop.

CAUTION!

Sensory integrative therapy should not be pursued without consultation or direct services from an occupational therapist or a physical therapist with training in the area of sensory integration.

Although therapy programs should not be initiated without consultation with appropriate therapists, once initiated, many of the activities can and should be followed through on a daily basis by parents, school staff, and other caretakers. One purpose of these activities is to take input the individual is receiving from various sensory sources and facilitate the development of integrative functions. According to Ayres (1979, p. 143), "The ability to organize the sensations coming from the body, and to make adequate responses to them, helps the brain to organize other functions." Some of the activities that might be recommended include brushing therapy, deep pressure therapy, vestibular and proprioceptive activities, and use of a sensory diet.

Brushing therapy

This therapy uses a small surgical brush or a corn silk brush to brush the back, arms, hands, legs, and feet of individuals with sensory defensiveness. It takes about three to five minutes and should be performed about every 90 minutes or every two hours. It is amazing to see how quickly some individuals with autism calm down after receiving brushing therapy. In some cases, as with Aaron who was *hyposensitive*, brushing therapy can help to alert the sensory system.

CAUTION!
Some individuals react negatively if therapy is not done appropriately.

- Using inappropriate techniques for brushing may create states of hyperarousal rather than calming as desired.

- If the wrong brushes are used, the brushing therapy may produce harmful effects instead of positive responses.

Deep pressure therapy

Many individuals with autism have found that deep pressure activities are beneficial for calming purposes. Grandin (1995) uses the "hug" or "squeeze" machine, which she developed, to provide a uniform amount of deep pressure. Tom McKean (1996) had special pressure bracelets custom-made to provide for his deep pressure needs. Others use weighted vests and weighted quilts for providing deep pressure. Some use joint compression, which is done by pressing the bones in a joint together, to provide the needed pressure to their bodies. Activities that naturally provide deep pressure include jumping on the trampoline, "sandwiching" the individual between two floor mats, bouncing on a large therapy ball, some martial arts activities, some ballet exercises, and hopping, jumping, and skipping.

Many people use deep pressure without even realizing it. Do you like to snuggle under a heavy quilt at night? Do you pull up an afghan when you lie down on the couch? Perhaps, you are using it because of the sensory sensations it provides — not because it is particularly cold. Heavy work such as exercising, carrying, pushing, and lifting provides positive sensations because of the deep pressure that is provided by these activities. People who garden for pleasure may feel extremely calm and relaxed after working outside for a period of time because they have been doing activities that provide deep pressure to the body.

Sensory diets

The concept of "sensory diet" is based on the idea that each individual requires a certain amount and quality of activity and sensation to be effectively alert, attentive, adaptable and skillful. Just as each individual has specific nutritional requirements for developing and maintaining optimal functioning levels (i.e. nutritional diet), each person has sensory requirements for developing and maintaining optimal functioning levels (i.e. sensory diet).

Some types of sensory-based activities seem to be very helpful for individuals who exhibit distorted sensory perception and processing. Activities that reduce the levels of arousal for periods of time also provide increased, focused sensory stimulation for individuals who do not overtly respond to sensory input.

 Some recommendations regarding implementation of sensory focused interventions or the sensory diet include:

- Recognize when the person is exhibiting a need for sensory stimulation.

- Avoid overload — use the individual's reactions to make decisions about how much and when sensory activities should be planned.

- Implement sensory activities on a daily basis as part of the individual's regular schedule.

- Incorporate reinforcers into the daily schedule of activities.

- Use arousal techniques before cognitive and language tasks as the increased arousal levels may facilitate increased development in the areas of cognition and language development.

- Provide sensory stimulation activities on request when the person recognizes an inner need for a specific activity.

- Follow arousal activities with a calming activity.

- Provide a safe area that is physically defined with boundaries, is calming, and allows the individual to do work and earn reinforcers.

Oral-Motor Stimulation

Infants and toddlers exploring the world around them frequently put objects in their mouth. This satisfies a need for oral stimulation and allows them another tool for exploring their world. Some infants and toddlers mouth everything. Others rarely put things in their mouths. It depends upon their sensory needs.

Individuals with oral motor dysfunction need to use their mouths for many purposes. Recently, during a language evaluation of Chad, a 15 year old boy, he completely destroyed a pen in about one minute! The assessment had included an evaluation of written language, but he only used the pen to write one short paragraph. Within a very short time however, he chewed on the pen so much that the top was crushed. It was very obvious that he had an intense need for oral-motor stimulation. However, in the Individual Educational Plan (IEP) meeting, his group home stated that one rule in the home was that nothing went into the mouth except at meal times. The staff were using discipline measures to address a sensory need that should have been addressed with sensory activities. Eliminating the pen chewing would not eliminate the need for oral-motor stimulation. A better procedure that was suggested at his IEP meeting was to find more appropriate objects or food for chewing.

Additionally, all persons can use oral-motor activities of sucking, chewing, and crunching to calm, organize, and alert their bodies. (Trott, Laurel, & Windeck, 1993, p. 48). Many appropriate oral-motor activities can be provided at home, school, and community.

 Some activities that will provide oral-motor stimulation include:

- Blowing, which helps children to develop breath support important for speech.
- Licking stickers and putting them in sticker books, which are fun and stimulating.
- Sucking thick liquids such as malts or puddings through a straw is calming. (Trott, et al.)
- Chewing, which is helpful in organizing the brain.
- Crunching on foods like popcorn, carrots, and celery is alerting.

Many blow toys and whistles are readily available. PDP Products and other companies also sell "whistles" with no sound for individuals exhibiting sound sensitivity. Blowing makes the rooster's feet twirl and the train slide back and forth. Children may also practice blowing by blowing Ping-Pong balls or cotton balls across the table and by blowing bubbles, a favorite activity for many.

The new dripless "sipper" cups require the child to suck much harder than other drip type sipper cups. Sucking thick malts or pudding and yogurt through straws requires hard sucking that tends to be calming to the person.

Some people chew on rubber tubing. However, this does not always look appropriate. Therefore, some other items individuals can use are chewy candy such as caramels and taffy, gum, fruit leather, dried fruit, beef jerky etc. The best bubble gum is hard to chew at first and gets easier the longer you chew. You should avoid using sugar free gum. First, it has NutraSweet® which is not good for many individuals with autism. Additionally, sugar-free gum starts out easy to chew and gets more difficult the longer you chew it. Although Trott (Trott, et al, 1993) indicates that chewing is organizing, it may also increase arousal levels.

Crunchy foods that may be alerting to you or your child include popcorn, raw vegetables such as carrots, crackers, chips, pretzels, and nuts.

 **"Flavors and textures of foods may also affect children's ability to calm, organize, and alert themselves." (Trott, et al, 1993).**

Sweet things tend to be calming. Notice how often individuals reach for chocolate candy when they are really stressed. Sour flavors such as lemon drops and sour balls are alerting. Spicy foods like Mexican salsa, fireballs, and cinnamon candy are even more alerting. Most alerting are the really hot foods like beef jerky, smoked foods, or hot and spicy Cajun and oriental foods.

 Different people have different needs.

Individuals must find the foods that are most calming, organizing and alerting to them. Individuals are unique and the foods that they respond to in certain ways may also be unique. Careful observation is necessary to determine which foods and actions create the most positive response. If there are any indications that an individual has medical or dental needs, check with a physician or dentist prior to using oral stimulation strategies.

Vestibular Stimulation

According to Ayres (1979), "The vestibular system is the unifying system. All other types of sensation are processed in reference to this basic vestibular information. The activity in the vestibular system provides a framework for the other aspects of our experiences."

 Vestibular system dysfunctions may result in difficulties in the following areas:

- tracking objects with our eyes,

- moving different body parts in unison,

- bilateral coordination,

- lack of hand dominance or ignoring nondominant side of body,

- performing skills requiring sequencing and timing,

- motion sickness,

- memory and learning basic academic skills,

- speech and language,

- ability to use body language appropriately,

- inappropriate emotional reactions and behaviors,

- gravitational insecurity, or

- hunger for new movement experiences.

Activities and suggestions for facilitating development of the vestibular system include:

- Incorporate music and motor movements into instruction as much as possible.

- Do wake-up activities before starting instruction.

- Ensure that children use recess time as a period for strenuous activity. Activities that help individuals to organize themselves include: swinging, running, sliding, hanging, and climbing.

- Do not use time-out from recess or physical education as a punishment for the child.

- Allow students legitimate reasons for movement.

- Alternate periods of sitting with periods of movement in the daily schedule.

- Activities that require intense concentration should ideally follow P.E., recess, or therapy.

- Get a rocking chair, an exercise bicycle, and a mini-trampoline for the classroom and schedule regular times for student use.

Auditory Integration Training (AIT)

Auditory integration training (AIT) is a treatment that was developed by Dr. Guy Berard in France. It is used with individuals with autism who have hypersensitivity to sounds. Although the exact mechanisms of how this treatment works in the individual's brain have not been determined, many practitioners and parents report positive results. The treatment consists of 20 thirty minute sessions of listening to music filtered through special equipment, the audiokinetron. Sessions are generally scheduled two per day for ten days although it is permissible to have a two day break between the first five day session and the second five day session. Since Dr. Berard developed the audiokinetron and trained practitioners in the United States, an American made machine was also developed which is called the BGC machine.

My personal experience in providing auditory integration training to over one hundred people is that most individuals have some subtle improvements. It does not *cure* autism. It treats sound sensitivity that may result in behavioral improvements in individuals. Much of current information is more anecdotal than research based. In our own work with AIT, an informal survey revealed that many individuals exhibited better eye gaze, more laughter and smiling, and more social interaction.

A parent I met at the Autism Society of America (ASA) national conference told me her son has had AIT three times. She felt that he improved with each treatment. Although he is not cured, he has gone from multiple daily rages to one or two per month. For her, that is enough to believe that it is a valuable treatment. One child with whom I worked exhibited very few changes after the first treatment. He appeared to be understanding what was said to him for the first time. After the second treatment, done over a year later, he seemed much calmer. The results seemed so promising that the treatment was repeated again this past spring. However, he is still nonverbal and still functions at a low level academically and developmentally. Another mother tells me that she can take her child out to eat and to Wal-mart, something she couldn't do before AIT.

 Consider the following list of recommendations when deciding whether to do auditory integration training.

- Check out the credentials of the practitioner.
- Ask who the practitioner trained under.
- Ask how long the practitioner has been doing AIT.
- Ask about the practitioner's experience with autism.
- Ask what kind of equipment will be used.
- Ask what kind of follow-up will be provided.
- Prepare your child to wear earphones which will be used to provide the music input.

- Some individuals have had dramatic improvements with AIT. Be prepared if your child does not.

- The decision to participate in it must be a personal decision of the family and individual. No one else can or should make it for you.

 **CAUTION!**

The equipment used in AIT is still under review by the Food and Drug Administration (FDA).

- The audiokinetron and the BGC machine have been declared to be medical devices. Consequently, no new equipment has been allowed into the United States for approximately three years.

- At this point in time, it is still considered an experimental procedure with no guarantees as to the benefits.

- Beware of practitioners making claims that can't be validated such as "This will cure your child!"

- At this time, there are no research results that allow practitioners to accurately predict who will benefit from AIT before the training is done.

- Be aware that many individuals' initial improvements have faded over time requiring that AIT be repeated.

- Compare different practitioners.

Be aware that there is quite a range of fees, from low to high for AIT treatment. Some community agencies providing AIT have sliding fee scales that are used to charge for the treatment. In a few instances, public schools provide the service at no charge to eligible students.

Irlen Lenses

Irlen lenses were developed several years ago by a psychologist, Dr. Helen Irlen. They were initially used with individuals with dyslexia and learning disabilities. According to

Dr. Irlen, these individuals had a condition called Scotopic Sensitivity Syndrome. This describes a condition in which the eyes react negatively to certain reflections of light. In the past three to four years, that use has extended to individuals with autism. Research has resulted in variable findings depending upon the study quoted. However, there are many anecdotal accounts of positive responses. One of the most famous people to be wearing Irlen Lenses is Donna Williams, author of *Nobody Nowhere* and *Somebody Somewhere*. As with facilitated communication and auditory integration training, there has also been controversy over whether the treatment is proven by research or not.

Personally, I have completed the screener's training and also set up a training workshop for assessment personnel to be Irlen screeners. During that workshop, participants worked with 30 identified students with learning disabilities. Of those 30 identified students, only three were found to have significantly improved reading when a colored transparency was placed over their book. Based on this ten percent figure, a local school district screened their special education population the following year. Since the school serves approximately 900 identified special education students, it was hypothesized that about 90 students would be identified as having Scotopic Sensitivity Syndrome. In actual practice, a much smaller percentage of the identified special education population was identified as having this problem. Dr. Irlen also has indicated that individuals with autism must wear the lenses; they will not benefit from just using colored transparencies as some persons with dyslexia and learning disabilities do. However, my philosophy is that "if it helps just one student, then it is worth trying." If that student was my child, there would be no doubt that I would try it.

Donna Williams reported a very favorable response to the Irlen lenses. As she stated in *The Advocate* (1995), "the effects of Irlen Lenses were shattering." According to her, for the first time she saw a three-dimensional world. The floating facial features of her husband's face suddenly became a whole connected face. In her own words, "I feel more secure in my less fragmented environment and around what are now less fragmented people. I have more time to grasp my thoughts and feelings and my other senses, and since I no longer have to compensate for visual overload, I can also keep up better with processing sound, touch, or body-connectedness."

Like many of the other treatments, the Irlen Lenses don't *cure* autism; they treat one of the symptoms or characteristics. Therefore, if it works for you, great! I would just caution that people need to be aware that nothing works for every person. As said previously, individuals with autism are unique and what works for one person may not work for another.

If the individual shows danger signs during or following sensory integration sessions, abandon the activity and ask a trained therapist for further help. Of course, any signs indicating a medical crisis need to be responded to immediately, following appropriate crisis management strategies.

CAUTION!

Sensory interventions should NEVER be forced. Sensory overload can be damaging. Danger signals include:

- seizure activity,
- overexcitability (the child does not calm down within the 30 minutes following a sensory integration activity),
- increased aggression or increased withdrawal following the activity,
- flush or paled face,
- nausea, or
- loss of consciousness.

A Safe Area

Persons who are hypersensitive to sensory stimuli have a greater tendency to go into sensory overload. It is not uncommon for acting out behaviors such as screaming, aggression, self-abuse or tantrums to accompany such occurrences. When a person is in sensory overload, it will be very difficult for him to regain self-control without removal of some of the incoming stimuli. One strategy that has been highly effective in reducing agitation levels related to sensory overload, is teaching an individual to access an area with reduced amounts of stimulation. Often, reducing any incoming sensory information will help the individual regain control, even when the sensory stimulus that was removed was not the same stimuli that ultimately triggered the behavior.

 Overstimulation can be triggered by:

- environmental or physiological factors (light, noise, temperature, smells, touch, hunger, illness, etc.);

- people (number of people, activity or movement, specific people or specific characteristics such as voice, interaction style, etc.); or

- task demands (number of steps in task, difficulty of task, boredom with task, number of tasks presented simultaneously, abstract nature of task, etc.).

Accessing a safe area is a self-control strategy. The ultiimate goal is for the individual to recognize signs of agitation or overstimulation and access the safe area until agitation or arousal levels decrease to an easily manageable level. In the process of learning this self-control strategy, the person will require prompting from others in order to recognize arousal levels and to access an area of decreased stimulation.

CHAPTER *Four*

Physiological Needs That May Impact Behavior

Individuals with autism can present unique and challenging behaviors. Caretakers searching for answers to the problem behaviors sometimes feel like pirates searching for gold. They know the treasure is there, but they haven't found it yet. As they dig for solutions, new and different behavioral challenges develop. Each new behavior is a mystery to be solved. This is especially experienced when sharing life with nonverbal individuals who do not have an effective way to communicate.

As we attempt to solve these behavior riddles, it is important that we not be distracted by "fool's gold." There is a temptation to rush out and try every new treatment procedure we hear about. Be aware that many of these new ideas and promising approaches do not have scientific research to back them up. The approaches appear to have validity, but not enough research has been completed to be able to predict which individuals will be helped by the new approach. As parents and professionals, we must be able to separate scientific approaches from nonscientific approaches. More importantly, we must be able to recognize strategies that are nonsense.

Some approaches and treatments that have been used for years have a solid research background. These approaches have had "objective observation and measurement of phenomena, systematic arrangements of events, procedures to rule out alternative explanations for what is observed, and repeated demonstrations (called replications) by individuals working independently of one another." (Green, 1996, p. 16). Other approaches may just have anecdotal results or rely on subjective reactions rather than on objective facts. Green (1996) calls these "pseudoscience." They are not backed with true scientific evidence, but the anecdotal accounts appear to report scientific results. Some approaches may have research supporting the use with other populations but not with individuals with autism. Other methods may be fueled by false claims. It is important to realize that *nonscience* is not the same as *nonsense*. Some methods that have not been proven scientifically may still be viable options.

As professionals in the field of autism, we feel each new method or approach should be scientifically investigated. However, new treatment methodologies would never emerge if we rejected every idea and concept that did not initially have a solid background of research to support the approach. Therefore, we believe each new method or treatment introduced should be thoroughly studied. Find out everything possible about each method so that informed decisions can be made. Ask, "How do you know this will make a difference for my child? What kinds of research have been done to validate the efficacy of the treatment?"

Frequently, parents decide to try treatments they know may not work because the anecdotal evidence is promising. As one parent told me, "At least I will know that I have done everything possible to improve the quality of life for my child." Sometimes, we just need to be able to say, "I tried it and it didn't work for my child." However, there's always hope that "my child" will be one of the persons that benefit from the treatment. The best approach that parents and professionals can take is to be as well informed about different methods as possible. Learn about pros and cons. Encourage research to validate promising practices. The more information available, the greater the likelihood that good, informed decisions will be made.

Medical

A good approach to use with all new behaviors is to rule out medical causes first. Does the individual have a sore toe or a stomach ache? Is there a tooth that is hurting? Are there indications that the behavior is related to a seizure disorder? Are there symptoms of allergies? Are there digestive problems? Does the individual have an infection of some kind? Is it possible that the person is reacting to a prescribed medication?

If the individual is exhibiting behaviors as a result of discomfort from a physical cause, no amount of behavior management or preventive structuring will be successful until the basic physical cause is addressed. Therefore, it is necessary to closely observe the individual to determine the cause of the behavior. If there are indications that a particular behavior may be related to a medical cause, contact a medical doctor. If a medically related cause exists, it should be treated by appropriate medical professionals. Appropriate medical treatment usually results in decreases in behaviors associated with the problem. If medical causes have been considered and ruled out, then parents and professionals should start looking at behavioral interventions and other treatments.

Medication Issues

Currently, there is no medical treatment that *cures* autism. Medications that are frequently used with individuals with autism treat *symptoms* — they don't cure the underlying condition. "Most medications used to treat autism were developed primarily to treat some other disorder, and then tried on autistic children or adults because of overlap in certain symptoms." (Siegal, 1996, p. 301). However, there are many reports in medical literature of certain medications that yield positive results in persons with autism.

CAUTION!
Medications that improve behaviors in one person with autism may not work or may cause a worsening of behaviors in another person.

Although everyone would like to find a "miracle cure," this has not happened yet. The best we can do is identify the treatments that benefit the individual. Generally, medications are best when combined with educational interventions and behavioral strategies.

 When deciding to use medications, Siegal (1996, p. 305) lists five criteria for using psychoactive medications. If there is a positive response to at least one of the questions, a trial with medications may be appropriate.

- Is the individual frequently injuring himself or others because of problem behaviors?

- Have behavioral interventions been used with little success?

- Are the behaviors exhibited in all environments?

- Are the behaviors interfering with the individual's ability to learn or work?

- Do the possible benefits outweigh the potential side effects?

Parents and caretakers interested in investigating medication options should consult with appropriate medical professionals. Siegal (1996) also addresses specific medications in Chapter 14 of *The World of the Autistic Child*. Generally, types of medications used by individuals with autism include antidepressant medications that may reduce hyperactivity and anxiety or improve attention span. Other antidepressants tend to reduce the frequency and intensity of compulsions and obsessions, anxiety, and depression.

Stimulant medications, frequently used with hyperactive children, are sometimes used with individuals with autism who exhibit hyperactivity and distractibility. It should be noted, however, that stimulant medications are typically not the treatment of choice for individuals with autism and may produce extremely negative responses in some persons. Neuroleptic medications may be used when trials with other medications have resulted in unsatisfactory results. Although neuroleptics tend to have more side effects, they are sometimes used with individuals who have behavioral outbursts with no clear environmental causes. Some individuals with autism also have seizure disorders and take medications for control of seizures. Other medications from different drug classes are used with individuals with autism because they work for a particular individual.

 **Use of any drug should be under a doctor's supervision with frequent monitoring of the effects of the drug on the individual and its impact on the person's behavior.**

Caretakers should inform doctors about all medications that an individual is taking. Some drugs interact with others and medical personnel cannot effectively and safely treat an individual if they are not completely informed about the individual, their medications, and their behaviors.

Diets and Allergies

Over the years, many diets have been reported to have positive effects for individuals with various disorders including autism. It has been well documented through scientific research that certain syndromes and disorders associated with mental retardation are related to food intake. For example, brain damage results when individuals with phenylketonuria (PKU) eat foods containing phenylalanine, a major ingredient in *NutraSweet*®. Persons with galactosemia develop toxins that cause injury to the brain when foods containing lactose are ingested.

Donna Williams (1996) reports she has found that certain foods cause sensory dysfunctions when she eats them. By removing foods to which she is allergic from her daily diet, her sensory processing of environmental stimuli has been less fragmented. In the book, *Fighting for Tony* (Callahan, 1987), a mother reports her son's autism was triggered by an allergy to milk. When milk was removed from his diet, he began to function more normally. Ingestion of milk caused autistic behaviors to reoccur and last for as long as 24 hours. However, one must question, is this a severe allergy that resulted in positive responses when the allergen was removed, or did the individual truly have autism? From the perspective of the family, it probably didn't matter whether it was a severe allergy or true autism. Regardless, Tony had spent 5 years of his life functioning as an individual with severe autistic behaviors.

Individuals who have allergies can tell you they significantly impact how the person feels, and consequently, the individual's behavior. It does appear that many individuals with autism do have allergies to foods or other substances which may negatively impact their behavior. Although treatment for most won't result in the same type of "cure" as it did for Tony, treatment may improve the quality of their life and may result in improvement in behavior because the person feels better.

Keeping a food diary for a period of time will help determine if any foods are usually accompanied by increased negative behaviors. Trials can be done removing certain foods from the diet and then presenting them again at a later date to confirm relationships between diet and behaviors. If allergies seem to play a part in the behaviors of certain individuals, they may be tested by physicians specializing in allergy treatment.

Vitamin Therapy

Like other treatment approaches, individual responses to vitamin therapy are variable. Some individuals respond positively; others don't respond at all. Most of the parents we work with have tried the vitamin therapy, but few have had significantly positive results. Some still have bottles of vitamins in their cabinets because their children will not take the vitamins.

However, there are experts in the field who recommend a vitamin regimen. Although there are professionals who would disagree with him, Dr. Bernard Rimland (1991), stated that "scientific evidence clearly indicates that treatment with megadose vitamins, particularly vitamin B6 and magnesium, is the biological treatment of choice for autistic children." In an interview for *The Advocate*, Rimland (1994) stated, "B6 and magnesium helps almost 50 percent of autistic children and adults." He also reports that DMG (dimethylglycine) is very often helpful for individuals with autism. The spectrum of autism is so diverse that treatment approaches need to be varied and individualized to meet the unique needs of each person with autism.

CHAPTER Five

Social Skills and Social/Emotional Issues

Social development is one of the most challenging areas faced by persons with autism. Numerous characteristics common to persons with autism contribute to impaired social behavior which may be situationally inappropriate, awkward, or rigid. Social performance can directly impact the emotional state of the individual with autism and those with whom they interact.

 Improving social performance is essential to meeting the individual's needs for:

- acceptance,

- love,

- interaction with others, and

- independence.

How do I help my child's social performance?

A first step when improving a person's social skills is identifying the social behaviors currently used by the individual and behaviors that are interfering with successful social performance.

 The primary focus for change is teaching skills which promote effective social interactions, instead of simply eliminating problem behaviors.

How do I know which behaviors interfere with positive social interactions?

When identifying behaviors that interfere with acceptable social performance, it is important to separate those which are amenable to change from behaviors which are highly resistant to change.

Characteristics

 The following characteristics, frequently manifested in the form of inappropriate social behaviors, are an integral part of having autism:

- sensory overload,

- preference for routine and ritual, and

- motor planning difficulties.

 It is more effective and practical to build upon the strengths of some characteristics, as opposed to directing excessive amounts of effort toward changing behaviors that are merely an expression of the autism.

- Incorporate routine and ritual into the new social skills being taught.

- Teach the person how to recognize and manage sensory overload when in social situations.

- Incorporate strategies for minimizing the impact of motor planning difficulties in a way that allows for maximum independence.

 Remember, the goal is to teach skills which increase successful interactions.

 **CAUTION!**

Avoid the temptation to try to "cure the autism" or mold the person into someone else by eliminating characteristics which define an individual's unique personality.

How do I know which social behaviors to change?

 Practical areas to target for change, include:

- limited repertoire of appropriate social behaviors;

- difficulty initiating social interactions;

- limited imitation;

- limited or no understanding of reciprocal interaction (including turn-taking);

- limited flexibility in choosing appropriate responses;

- difficulty adjusting responses to fit situations;

- difficulty adjusting responses to fit the behavior of others;

- increased anxiety;

- low tolerance of frustration; and

- limited self-help skills, including personal hygiene and grooming

After identifying factors interfering with social success, how do I know what to start teaching?

In order to teach a new skill, the person's current functioning level needs to be assessed. Identify behaviors which are interfering with successful functioning and take baseline data to determine the individual's current functioning level. Refer to Appendix C for a listing of resources for teaching social skills.

 When identifying current social skills levels, focus upon a few main areas. To what extent does the individual:

- understand and follow unwritten social rules,

- direct and sustain attention,

- participate in positive social experiences, and

- maintain an acceptable level of hygiene and grooming?

 Being unaware of various social rules or not adjusting behaviors in response to those rules has a tremendous impact upon social situations.

Persons with autism have difficulties with behaviors associated with social rules such as: those governing personal space, physical contact, dialogue, humor, tact, diplomacy or active involvement, because they are not presented directly or concretely. Although these rules are common and seem simple to us, their abstract, subtle and situational nature can be overwhelming for a person with autism.

 Interaction with others is frequently impaired by limited understanding and use of reciprocity.

When reciprocity is limited, a person has difficulty monitoring and adjusting behaviors when responding to what another person is doing. This is a very important part of interacting effectively because it allows a person to fit actions to the individual needs, interests, and skill level of the other person. Difficulty with reciprocity can appear to others as being insensitive, odd, or offensive. As persons become more socially aware, the desire for social interaction strengthens. This social interest provides a strong motivation for learning the skills involved with social interactions.

 In order to effectively teach social rules:

- directly present the rules in a very clear, concrete manner;
- present rules in a visual manner;
- use a highly structured, systematic approach;
- provide many opportunities for practice;
- build social rules into the person's daily routines and rituals; and
- allow for literal interpretations of language.

Attentional issues can interfere with successful social experiences.

Difficulties attending to relevant aspects of a social interaction along with problems sustaining that attention, cause individuals with autism to miss important verbal and nonverbal information.

 Attending to important social information can be addressed by teaching individuals to:

- attend to relevant social cues;

- attend to a complexity of cues;

- avoid focusing on an extremely limited number of novel cues; and

- sustain attention to those social cues.

 While peers frequently experience more positive social interactions than negative social interactions, persons with autism usually experience a significantly higher number of negative social experiences than positive social experiences.

From a very early age, most children with autism quickly lag behind peers in the development of appropriate social interactions. Behaviors usually associated with expressing affection (for example, attachment and cuddling) are significantly absent or distorted. This gap continues to widen with time. As children grow older, the unusual behaviors lead to numerous unpleasant social experiences. This can be even more pronounced for individuals included in mainstream settings who experience various social situations without having the skills or behaviors required to relate in an acceptable manner. Consequently, without adequate preparation, situations intended to be socially enhancing can actually subject individuals to ridicule, rejection, or harassment from the very persons from whom acceptance and interaction is desired. A high ratio of negative to positive social experiences can contribute to development of negative attitudes and feelings, thus becoming as significant a problem as the lack of social skills. Persons who are higher functioning often experience greater degrees of distress, anxiety, and unhappiness due to lack of friendships.

 To increase the number of positive social experiences:

- teach meaningful, effective social skills; and

- teach behaviors that will increase the ratio of positive over negative social experiences.

 **CAUTION!**

Be careful to avoid unwittingly subjecting an individual to painful, negative social experiences in an effort to increase social interactions.

When designing social experiences, it is important to consider the social skill level of the individual and to access situations which will enhance, not hinder, the person's experience. This does not mean that one must protect an individual from negative social experiences; rather, be aware of the social and emotional impact of those experiences and take steps to balance negative experiences with positive ones so the individual has more positive than negative social experiences.

 **Inadequate personal hygiene and grooming impacts the quality of social interaction, sometimes to the degree that individuals with poor hygiene and grooming behaviors are rejected or ridiculed.**

A person who uses many appropriate communication and social interaction skills will probably continue to have a high rate of negative social experiences if hygiene or grooming skills are offensive. Grandin (Donnelly, Grandin, Bovee, Miller, & McKean,

1996) reports that her first employer had to tell her that she had to "stop being a slob." Teaching appropriate grooming and hygiene skills necessary for social acceptance is an integral part of social skills training. Additionally, the independence experienced by learning adequate self-help skills can enhance a person's emotional well-being and self-esteem.

 Teaching social skills for developmentally young or more severely challenged individuals should focus on:

- imitation;

- turn-taking;

- expressing basic wants and needs;

- cooperating with basic hygiene and grooming tasks;

- increasing attention to tasks and people;

- cooperating with strategies for managing overstimulation; and

- increasing the frequency of positive social experiences.

 For higher functioning individuals, learning skills to improve social performance should focus on more complex social behaviors including:

- improving conversational skills;

- initiating social interactions;

- initiating and refining hygiene and grooming routines;

- increasing flexibility in social situations;

- noticing and responding to the behaviors of others;

- directing attention to numerous cues at the same time;

- sustaining attention to less intense cues which do not provide novelty or excitement;

- recognizing and managing anxiety and other responses to overstimulation; and

- recognizing and managing factors and situations that contribute to negative social experiences.

Social Skills Training

Establish Goals and Priorities

Social skills training covers a vast array of behaviors to teach, approaches to teach those behaviors, and desired outcomes. When designing a plan for teaching social skills to a person with autism, it is important to clearly identify priorities in each of these areas. Desired outcomes or goals need to be very clearly identified **before** starting. When deciding what the goal is, avoid using a short-term approach. Think about the long-term implications and effects the social skill will have on the person's quality of life and emotional status. Whenever possible, involve the individual in the process of setting goals for social skills training.

Ask the following questions when determining which behaviors to teach:

1. <u>Does this behavior significantly interfere with the person's social relationships?</u> If the answer is "yes," the behavior is a priority for change. If "no," then other social behaviors may be of greater importance to address at this time.

2. <u>Can the behavior be changed without making unreasonable demands on the individual, or is the behavior an integral part of autism?</u> If attempts to change the behavior result in excessive stress or trauma for the individual, the target behavior should be approached in another way. If the behavior is a characteristic of autism, use it as a building block for skill development.

CASE EXAMPLE

Terrell has a strong preference for routine and ritual. He becomes upset when scheduled activities are changed. Instead of directing intensive, lengthy efforts toward teaching Terrell not to react emotionally to changes in routine, his teacher implemented a visual schedule of Terrell's activities using pictures combined with words. Whenever a change in the schedule occurs, Terrell replaces the picture of the canceled activity with a picture of the new activity. Terrell no longer becomes upset with changes since he can incorporate these changes into his routine using the ritual the teacher developed.

CAUTION!

Sometimes it is more appropriate to refine a behavior, lessening its negative impact. Total elimination of inappropriate behaviors is not always an option.

CASE EXAMPLE

Jason has a job reshelving items in a local store that specializes in books, videos, and music. He continually rocks back and forth, with the rocking movement worsening when he is anxious. This behavior looks odd and makes others around him uncomfortable. Efforts to eliminate or interrupt this behavior usually result in increased anxiety, thus worsening his rocking. In order to lessen the negative social impact of this behavior, Jason began wearing a walkman with headphones. Now he looks like one of the coolest guys at the store and his rocking back and forth does not make others feel uncomfortable!

3. <u>Will changing this behavior significantly improve the individual's quality of life and emotional health?</u> If the answer is "no," the behavior may not be an appropriate target for change. If the answer is "yes," changing the behavior should be a higher priority. However, avoid the temptation to mold the person into someone else.

Demands that an individual act like "everyone else," and stop acting like a person with autism, are unrealistic because autism is an integral part of the individual.

4. <u>Will newly taught behaviors negatively impact a person's social relationships, quality of life, or emotional health in the years ahead?</u> If the answer is "yes," teach a more appropriate social behavior and proceed with extreme caution. Learned behaviors are difficult to "unlearn."

CASE EXAMPLE

Teaching Henry to hug as a form of greeting was all right when he was five or six. However, now that he is seventeen and runs up and hugs strangers, it is not all right. In fact, the behavior sometimes frightens strangers. Some exhibit very negative reactions toward Henry's behavior. Henry is now learning to shake hands instead. It would have been more appropriate to teach Henry to shake hands or say "hello" when he was five or six than to hug everyone.

Other behaviors can be taught in addition to those learned behaviors, but the first behavior will always be in the person's repertoire of skills and may periodically resurface. It may be wiser to teach a behavior with less potential to cause problems later. If the behavior will not have a negative impact in the future, it remains a viable option.

5. Will the behaviors being taught provide the most independent means for social performance? If "yes," the behavior remains a good choice. If "no," identify a way to teach the social skill using prompts that will enable more independent responses, or teach a different behavior that will promote independent social responses.

CASE EXAMPLE:

Students have learned to sort beans at the food bank. They put a prepared computer label on a ziplock bag, measure two cups of beans, and pour them into the ziplock bag. Because this is not a new task, some instructors assume that visual cues are not needed. When prompting is needed, the person supervising the students provides verbal prompts. However, if visual cues were available, the students performing the task could independently refer to the visual cues and would need no prompting from the instructor.

CAUTION!

Don't assume individuals don't need visual cues because they respond to verbal cues.

How do I do social skills training?

Some strategies for social skills training include:

1. <u>Increase the individual's repertoire of prosocial behaviors.</u> Teach a variety of relevant, meaningful social skills that increase the available choices for response. The more prosocial skills in the person's repertoire, the greater the likelihood that acceptable behaviors will be used in a social situation. If an individual's repertoire of skills is severely limited, then responding with acceptable behaviors will be less likely.

2. <u>Use direct instruction to teach social skills.</u> Social skills, like academic skills, should be taught through direct instruction. Skills should be divided into small, specific steps consisting of concrete, observable behaviors. However, when breaking skills into instructional sequences, be sure to demonstrate what the final behavior should look like.

3. <u>Model the appropriate skill, while pointing out important parts.</u> When modeling is used as a teaching strategy for persons with autism, direct the learner's attention to the critical parts of the behavior. If left to chance, the person may focus attention on a novel detail, missing the relevant factors. This can lead to inaccurate learning.

4. <u>Match skills to situations.</u> Teach social skills that will serve a meaningful, functional purpose for that individual in real situations. Teach the skill in natural environments. This will help to provide meaning and purpose. Motivation is negatively influenced by boring, seemingly purposeless memorization and drill and practice exercises. Skills taught out of context may not be transferred or generalized to real life situations.

5. <u>Practice in real situations that are meaningful and functional with guidance and feedback provided as needed.</u> Once the basic steps of the social skill have been learned, practicing in real situations can increase the probability that the person will be less anxious about using newly acquired skills. The learner will be more likely to use the skill effectively under similar circumstances.

6. <u>Increase opportunities for practice by staging situations in which the individual can practice prosocial skills with guidance and feedback provided as needed.</u> Stage situations that enable the person to practice and gain confidence in using newly acquired skills. Positive, supportive persons can be recruited to help teach new skills. Using skills in controlled situations provides the opportunity to refine skills and allows the person to make adjustments needed for reciprocal interactions under different circumstances.

7. <u>Videotape the appropriate implementation of the skill.</u> Use the student as the model whenever possible. Videotaping can be used to teach prosocial behaviors. An

effective way to develop acceptable visual models is to videotape the person appropriately performing the skill. When using the videotape for modeling, videotape appropriate responses only.

8. <u>Develop books that depict social situations.</u> These stories should reflect real life scenarios and be both meaningful and functional. Supplement these stories with pictures. Utilize the person's visual learning strengths and preference for meaningful, functional information as powerful tools when teaching social skills.

CASE EXAMPLE

Jessica resorts to screaming when she can't reach a desired item on the kitchen shelf. Her in-home trainer wrote a story with pictures that illustrates appropriate alternatives to screaming. Every time Jessica screams when she can't reach an item on the kitchen shelf, her mother calmly walks over to her, says "no scream" and hands the book to Jessica. She prompts Jessica to read the book. She then prompts Jessica to use an acceptable alternative behavior to obtain what she wants. Jessica's mother doesn't give her what she wants until she uses an acceptable behavior such as requesting help or using the stepstool.

 Suggestions for adapting written stories for enhancing social skills development include:

- using a flannelboard to tell the story;

- using objects, pictures, or symbols;

- putting the story on the computer; and

- singing the story.

9. <u>Incorporate cueing procedures that maximize the development of independent functioning by the individual.</u> Use structuring and visual prompting strategies best suited to the individual that are detailed in Chapter Six.

10. <u>Avoid too much reliance on verbal cues or physical prompts from others.</u> Tap into the individual's visual learning strengths and preference for routine and ritual when developing prompting systems.

11. <u>Provide a "social diet" by providing for social interaction on a scheduled basis and upon appropriate request (in addition to unconditional interactions).</u> Incorporate visual prompts to assist with predicting future, planned social interactions and independent requesting. Social interactions should be of the form and intensity preferred by the individual.

12. <u>Factor out social interaction when highly challenging tasks are assigned.</u> Challenging tasks increase anxiety, frustration and stimulation levels. It is advisable to minimize other sources of stimulation during these times. Since social interactions frequently increase stimulation levels, yet are easily removed or minimized, keep stimulation levels from becoming overwhelming by minimizing social interactions during challenging activities. This can be accomplished by relying on more visual prompts than verbal or physical prompts; providing any physical prompts from behind the person (be certain the person knows you are behind him, so as to avoid startling); and minimizing talking or physical contact.

13. <u>Remember, most individuals with autism desire social interaction as a basic human need.</u> Tolerance thresholds and skills for requesting or engaging in interaction may be very different from peers. However, do not confuse this dislike for the type of interaction chosen with a dislike for interaction itself.

14. <u>Be sure to use hand-over-hand guidance from behind when using physical guidance.</u> This increases the likelihood that the individual is focusing on the visual-motor process experienced, as opposed to any perceived social interaction.

But, how do I teach him the steps of the skill he needs to learn?

When teaching the specific steps of the social behavior to be learned, identify the specific steps involved, then use strategies for increasing the desired behavior that are outlined in Chapter Seven.

CASE EXAMPLE

Ben is nonverbal and has few social skills. He frequently hits himself on the side of his head. When he does this, the staff scolds him and physically stops him if he continues hitting himself. Ben's self-abuse continues to occur at a high rate. He is beginning to also hit his head on the floor. His mother asked the teacher to put a helmet on him when he hits his head. Ben wears the helmet at home. Now, he is wearing the helmet more frequently at school.

By working with the school, a plan was developed to decrease Ben's self-abuse. Part of the plan included scheduling social interaction with preferred staff for two minutes every hour. This activity was incorporated into Ben's daily picture schedule. Pictures that he can use to request a firm hug or a tickle are now accessible throughout the day. Ben now uses his pictures to request social interaction and no longer needs his helmet. His mother also uses the system at home and more pictures have been added to increase the types of social interactions he can request.

I need more guidance. Aren't there some guidebooks that I can follow to teach social skills?

There are several good social skills programs available. Although most were not developed for use with students with autism, many are appropriate because most students with special needs require direct instruction in social skills. A specific listing of social skills curriculums is in Appendix C in this book. Most employ similar procedures such as modeling and role playing. Consequently, a certain level of cognitive functioning is required for the student to be able to benefit from most of the social skills curriculums. Younger or more challenged students might benefit from The Alert Program: How Does Your Engine Run? This program is somewhat unique in that it compares the person's body to a car engine. The program teaches young children to begin to recognize when their "motor is getting too revved up" or when it is slowing down to a stop.

Isn't there a program for social skills instruction that was specifically designed for individuals with autism?

Social Stories

Carol Gray (1993) has developed social skills programs for specific use with individuals with autism. The most popular program is *Social Stories*®. She has published two books of social stories, *The Original Social Story Book* and *The New Social Story Book*. Both books include "The Social Story Kit" that provides instructions for developing your own social stories if none of the stories in the two books fit your situation. According to Gray (1994, The Social Story Kit, p. 1), "Social Stories® describe social situations in terms of relevant social cues, and often define appropriate responses." Social Stories® are designed to meet identified needs of persons with autism. They use the visual strengths of these individuals to translate goals into understandable steps. Social Stories® can be used to teach desired behaviors, routines, and academic skills. They may also be used to address undesirable behaviors including aggression, fears, obsessions, and compulsions.

Social Review

Carol Gray (1996) also developed a technique for teaching appropriate behaviors by reviewing the student's behavior in a conference while viewing a videotape of the student exhibiting the undesired behavior. This addresses a characteristic of persons with autism that has been referred to as "Theory of Mind." Many individuals with autism have difficulty understanding or reading social situations because they don't have a perspective of what other people see or feel. Like young children, they tend to view the world as a world revolving around them. For example, when my granddaughter was about two, she had her ears pierced. Later during the day while outside with her Dad, the wind blew her hair back away from her face. She exclaimed, "Look Daddy, the wind is blowing my hair back so people driving by can see my new earrings!" Because her new earrings were important to her, she assumed that they would be important to everyone else.

In a videotape of a young man and Gray (1996) (*Social Stories and Comic Strip Conversations*), she demonstrates how she works through the process of viewing the video to assist the individual in interpreting what is really happening. Eric, the young man, kept interrupting speakers because he thought the speaker was talking directly to him. Even though there were approximately 500 persons in the auditorium, he still maintained that the speaker was only talking to him. Carol and Eric repeatedly viewed the videotape until he understood that he was only one of many persons that the speaker was addressing. Once he understood, he wrote down some simple rules that he took to his classroom to post by his desk. The visual cue enabled him to stop his interrupting behavior when multiple conferences and auditory cues had resulted in no change.

Comic Strip Conversations

Comic Strip Conversations (Gray, 1994), can be used with individuals who enjoy drawing. As the two persons in the conversation interact, they draw their interactions in frames on a sheet of paper. This technique is based upon the belief that the visualization and visual supports may improve the individual's understanding and comprehension of the conversation. As students become skilled at this form of interaction, colors can be added to depict differing emotions. Specific instructions for using this technique may be found in the book, *Comic Strip Conversations* (1994).

What about using books to assist persons with autism to develop more appropriate behaviors?

Books provide an excellent method of helping persons with autism learn more about autism and how it impacts their lives. Of course, books written by persons with autism or their families are wonderful for teenagers or older individuals with autism. They are very beneficial to professionals because these books provide some insight into what it is like to be a person with autism or to have a child with autism as part of the family.

There are also specific books for children about autism. These are good for individuals with autism to read as well as their siblings and peers. If the child cannot read them, they can be read out loud. Other books that are wonderful for use with children and teenagers are books about being different and books about specific behavioral problems. Companies publishing counseling materials also provide a variety of games that are designed to assist in management of behavior. These games allow individuals to practice verbal rehearsal and role playing in nonthreatening situations.

One board game I have used is *The Anger Solution Game* (Childswork/Childsplay). *The Angry Monster Machine* (Childswork/Childsplay) game is also very good for children who have difficulty controlling their anger. Refer to the resources in Appendix C for a list of books and games that can be used to facilitate social skill development in individuals with autism. Books designed for students with learning disabilities are usually well suited for individuals with Asperger's syndrome. Regardless of the method or programs used, most individuals with autism need direct instruction in social skills. This can be a home-made program developed by or for parental use or a program implemented at school or in counseling sessions. Although social skills curriculum books are available, they are not necessary to teach social skills. However, they can be good resources for persons who choose to use them. See Appendix C for social skills resources.

Peer Assisted Interventions

Peers can be used to assist individuals with autism to learn more appropriate social skills. There are several models that have been successful in certain situations. *Circles of Friends* (Perske, 1988) is a national model which has been used in many local areas to facilitate the development of friendships by individuals with special needs. A group of peers is identified as willing to take the responsibility for spending some time with the person. Generally, this group works with a school counselor who provides awareness training and suggestions for group interactions. In some schools, this peer group only participates in activities at school. In other communities, the peer group also makes a point of having at least one person telephone each evening and planning one event for a couple of days a month outside of school.

Peer buddies and peer mentors may also be used to facilitate social interaction. This strategy may be easier to plan and coordinate because activities don't involve a large group of students. However, a single peer may feel different if he or she is the only student interacting with a child with special needs. Peer buddies can be used to coach appropriate behavior in the classroom and on the playground or other school settings. For older individuals, having a peer mentor or helper in the work place or community is desirable.

 Recommendations for peer buddies, mentors, or peer groups are listed below.

- Select peers with care; they should be understanding and compassionate with personalities that will complement the individual with autism.

- Peers should volunteer to be a buddy.

- Peers should receive training from professional staff in disability awareness, appropriate activities, and what to do when they get no response from the individual with autism.

- Schedule regular times for social interactions.

- Instruct individuals with autism in specific skills necessary for certain activities before expecting a peer to interact with the person in a strange situation.

CHAPTER Six

Structuring the Environment for Success

Structuring the environment is a long-term, preventive strategy that facilitates success at home, school, work and community. Behavioral interventions for individuals with autism can usually be classified under two major categories. The first is short-term reactive strategies. These are interventions which are necessary to respond to the behavior of the moment, such as crisis intervention.

Persons attending crisis intervention training sessions frequently ask, "Is crisis management going to be my total behavior management program?" Effective crisis intervention provides the time that both the individual and caretakers need to calm down and start putting other, preventive interventions in place. We must respond to the behavior of the moment.

However, responding to behavioral challenges with short-term interventions is not the goal. Avoid being in a constant state of crisis intervention! Crisis interventions should always be paired with other preplanned behavioral strategies as a part of a total program of behavioral management. Therefore, once the immediate behavior is resolved satisfactorily, it is imperative to look at long-term strategies that will enhance the person's probability of successful functioning in the home, school, and community.

The TEACCH program in North Carolina has developed a method for structuring the environment that has been nationally validated and used in North Carolina classrooms since the early 1970's (Schopler and Mesibov, 1994). *Structured teaching* involves development of routines, schedules, and visual supports. Physical arrangement of the environment is basic to this preventive approach. However, like other behavioral interventions, structuring the environment does not eliminate the need for additional behavioral tools. It decreases the likelihood that other behavioral interventions will need to be used, but does not take the place of other proven strategies.

Physical Environment

Structuring the environment for success builds on the strengths of individuals with autism. Visual cues are used to capitalize on the visual modality strength, and routines are incorporated into the daily schedule that build on the person's need for routines and rituals. In going into a classroom to assist with setting up the environment for students with autism, the first thing to assess is the actual physical arrangement of the room. The following keys include some of the areas to be addressed.

 Is the basic size of the room adequate?

Although physical structure has been established in some very small classrooms, generally, the greater the available space, the easier it is to set up the needed structure.

 **Is the room divided into basic areas which can be labeled with visual cues?**

Are the areas delineated by any type of boundaries such as book cases? If not, can the various areas of the classroom be identified with colored tape or by rearranging the furniture? The purpose of identifying the areas with labels and visual boundaries is to communicate the function for each area. What type of activity is performed? What behaviors are expected when a person is in this area?

Structuring the environment is usually simpler in the home setting because homes are already divided into rooms. If you walk into a kitchen in any house, you generally know that it is a kitchen because it is a separate room with a sink, stove, and refrigerator. You know that the bedroom is a place to sleep because the bed is there. The bathroom is easily identified because it has a lavatory, a bathtub or shower, and a commode for toileting purposes.

 Areas generally set up in a classroom are:

- a group working area with a large table,

- one-to-one work areas,

- individual work areas with a desk or small table,

- a computer area,

- a safe area,

- a snacktime area,

- a leisure area, and

- other areas as needed for a specific classroom (science centers, math centers, reading centers, etc.)

 **What kinds of visual cues and supports are already in place?**

Is the teacher using any visual cues? Are the areas of the room labeled with the name of the area? Are visual cues given to supplement verbal cues?

 **Are daily schedules used?**

If daily schedules are used, where are they located? Are all of the students' schedules grouped together in a common transition area or is each student's schedule near the individual work areas? If schedules have not been used, where should they be displayed?

 What kinds of tasks does the student work with?

Will students be doing simple put-in tasks? Put-in tasks are generally set up so that the student picks up objects on the left and puts them in a container on the right. Some students are unable to do anything more than put-in tasks when they start the program. Other students may be sorting, classifying, or working on academic tasks.

 ## How will the work tasks be physically arranged?

One problem that sometimes occurs is a lack of work space. One solution is three-tiered carts placed next to a desk when limited workspace is a problem. Each bin in the cart is used for one of the tasks and the top leaves a flat surface which can be used for other items. Some classrooms don't have room for each student to have a three-tiered cart so teachers have opted for clear plastic shoe boxes. These are then placed on shelves so that students may access them during work times. There is also a *finish* box on the right side of their desk so that completed activities may be placed in the finish box.

 ## How is the day structured? Does it need to be rearranged?

Teachers have a tendency to schedule academic subjects in the morning leaving the afternoon for less stressful subjects such as physical education and music. A better strategy would be to alternate less stressful activities with more challenging activities. Additionally, it is generally recommended that physical activity be built into the schedule on a daily basis, usually soon after the person arrives at school. Sensory integration activities should precede language activities or tasks requiring more focus and attention because students generally produce more language or work directly after periods of sensory motor activities. Some occupational therapists and speech/language pathologists are pairing therapy sessions to take advantage of sensory integrative activities during the time they are trying to elicit language and communication. This form of therapy is called *conjoint therapy*.

Will all of the students be using schedules or just part of the students?

If only one student is using a schedule, it is fairly easy to set up. If all of the students are using schedules, colors may be assigned so that each individual's program items may be color coded according to the color assigned.

Routines and Rituals

A desire for routines and rituals is a common need for individuals with autism. In structuring the environment, routines and rituals are built into the daily schedule and performed each day. This facilitates transitions because students begin to use the schedule to predict what's next. Therefore, changing activities is not as difficult because the individual is following the routine of the schedule. This makes it easier to transition from one activity to another.

Visual Cues

Most people use visual cues on a daily basis. They write notes or make lists so they don't forget to do certain things. Many people live by a calendar. Most people will generally confirm daily plans by looking at their calendar each morning. If it is misplaced, they are frantic until it is located.

Frequently, teachers ask when to gradually stop using visual cues. The answer is never! Adults don't want to be forced to do without their calendar. Individuals with autism should always have visual cues available. Instead of fading visual cues, look at how visual cues can be built into the environment.

CASE EXAMPLE

Judy won't put trash in the container at Burger King® because it doesn't look like the trash can at home or school. Have Judy practice putting trash in a small white trash bag at school. Take a small white bag into the community when you go to Burger King®. Then, when Judy finishes eating, she puts her trash in the small white bag. This is a routine she already knows. The small white bag containing trash is then thrown into the trash container at Burger King®.

CASE EXAMPLE

Scotty has difficulty going to the restroom. He is obsessed with flushing the commode and squirting the hand soap. He can't use the restroom independently. This is a problem because his teachers are women and he has to use a boy's hallway restroom. Other boys don't like women teachers coming in when they are using the restroom. This problem was solved by preparing a mini-schedule with the steps for using the restroom on it. When Scotty needs to go to the restroom, he takes the mini-schedule with a picture sequence depicting the steps for using the restroom. Now, with the visual cue of the mini-schedule, he is able to independently use the restroom.

Schedules

 Daily schedules should be used to enable the individual to predict the next activity.

If daily schedules are not used, what is the teacher and student's schedule? How do the students know when specific activities will occur? How can the student predict what the next activity will be? If schedules are not in place, how many schedules will need to be made? Schedules will usually facilitate transitions from one activity to another because the student can prepare for the transitions when they know what will be next. The length and type of daily schedule used depends upon the needs of the child. Some individuals can only handle a schedule that provides them with the next activity. Others can handle a half day or full day schedule. It must also be determined whether objects, photographs, picture symbols, or words only will be used for the activities.

If the student orients and attends to pictures, picture symbols are easy to use because they are readily available through companies distributing special education materials (See Appendix C). Objects are more difficult to find because they must have a concrete relationship to the planned activity. Objects that may be used are doll furniture chairs to symbolize work, spoons for eating, a small glass for drink, etc. When parents and school staff use schedules, there should be coordination between home and school to ensure that the same symbols are being used for the same activities.

 Work schedules should be used to tell the student how much work and when work is finished.

Work schedules are different from daily schedules which tell the individual the sequence of the day. Daily schedules enable the person to predict what is coming next. A daily schedule also lets the person predict when favored activities will occur. The work schedule is a mini-schedule that tells the individual what work tasks to complete before they are rewarded. Depending on the needs of the student and the room arrangement, this can take several different forms.

As previously indicated, schedules may be made with objects, photographs, picture symbols, or a written list of tasks. Generally, daily schedules and work schedules are displayed in either a top-to-bottom order or a left-to-right sequence. Daily schedules usually depict time periods during the day such as circle time, work time, reading, math, music, occupational therapy, lunch, recess, etc. An older student's schedule may contain subject areas such as reading or English, math, social studies or history, science, physical education, etc. Work schedules generally have a place for two or three tasks with one additional place indicating what's next. The final activity is generally a reinforcer for completing the work tasks. Initially, some individuals may need a work task, a reinforcer, a work task, a reinforcer, etc. Schedules may have either velcro or paper clips to attach symbols of different activities or tasks. If several students in the classroom are using schedules, then each child should be assigned a different color so that each student's schedule may be immediately identified by looking at the background color. Numbers, letters, color blocks, or picture symbols can be used to identify tasks. As state previously some teachers use three-tier stacked, plastic carts for students. A color block is placed on each bin and a corresponding color block is placed on the student's schedule. A task is placed in each bin. The individual matches the color blocks to identify the tasks to be done. When clear plastic shoe boxes are used for work tasks, they should be identified by symbols in some way so that corresponding cards may be placed on student work schedules. One teacher used colored dots and numbers. All tasks were kept in clear shoe boxes and placed on a shelf with similar tasks. The picture on the left indicates what the shelf looked like. The picture on the right illustrates a sample left-to-right work schedule using color blocks with computer time as the reinforcer.

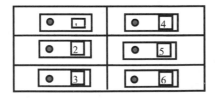 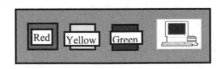

Initially, the individual may need verbal or physical prompts to check the schedule and retrieve the symbolic object or picture. A visual cue to check the schedule might be handing the individual a laminated card with the person's name on it. This color coded card is then taken to the transition area where schedules are located and placed in a pocket beside the person's schedule.

A schedule sequence should occur as follows:

- the individual retrieves the symbolic object or picture from the schedule;

- the object or picture is carried to the area where the activity will take place; and

- the individual places the picture in a card pocket with the same symbol or gives the object to a supervising adult.

In some situations, the object schedule sequences have been modified. For example, one teacher placed a small nerf basketball goal on the wall beside the schedule. The net was tied at the bottom and a plastic bowl was placed inside the net. When the object is removed from the schedule, it is dropped into the basketball goal before moving to the area for the activity. If a scheduled activity such as physical therapy doesn't occur, the object is taken off the schedule and dropped into the basket with an explanation. Some teachers develop an object or picture symbol that can be used for days when the normal routine changes. One teacher calls this an "Oops Day!" A big red card with "OOPS!" printed on it is used to signify a schedule change. This helps students adjust to change because a predictable way for addressing change has been built into their daily routine. Another symbol that can be used is a red, universal symbol for *no*. This can be made on transparency film and placed directly over the original symbol when the activity is not going to occur.

Another important concept to be addressed is, "When am I finished?" Students should always be able to visually see how much work they have to do and when the work is finished. Every activity needs to end with the individual placing the completed task in a "finished" basket or other container. Putting a task in the "finished" basket provides a concrete tactile and visual cue that the activity is over. Placing tasks in the "finished" basket also serves to prompt the person to anticipate the next scheduled activity.

How do I know whether to use objects, photographs, or picture symbols?

Jenson's teacher wanted to develop a schedule for Jenson to follow at school. She was unsure whether to use objects or picture symbols. Jenson does not seem interested in picture books. However, the teacher recalled that Jenson became excited whenever he saw any depiction of the "golden arches", since he loves french fries. She also recalled Jenson's responses to pictures of his favorite purple dinosaur. She decided to use a picture symbol system, since this indicated to her that Jenson is responsive to pictures. If it becomes apparent that a picture symbol system is not working, drop back to objects and implement an object system.

Individuals who are higher functioning, but not ready for written words can use picture symbols in a checklist format. Instead of retrieving pictures to initiate an activity, the person would refer to their checklist schedule and mark off activities as they are completed.

 Include a Sensory Diet in Daily Schedules.

As discussed previously, the sensory diet refers to activities for developing and maintaining optimal functioning levels. Sensory-based activities may be used with hypersensitive individuals to promote calming and prevent sensory overload. Sensory-based activities may also be used with hyposensitive individuals to increase arousal levels. Consequently, it is important to include sensory activities as part of the person's individual daily schedule.

Persons with intense sensory experiences usually have a strong need for long or frequent periods of calmness. Provide planned "quiet" breaks as part of the individual's daily schedules. Furthermore, the individual should have a means for requesting additional quiet breaks as needed. The need for quiet breaks increases as stimulation levels and tasks increase in complexity. It is usually more effective to schedule several small breaks at natural times throughout the day instead of one or two lengthy breaks.

CASE EXAMPLE

David comes into the classroom daily at a high arousal level. To help him calm down, his daily schedule includes either using the exercise bicycle or jumping on the mini-trampoline as soon as he returns from breakfast and the restroom. Because of school scheduling, he had no recess or physical education time until late afternoon. By scheduling early morning time for one of these activities, he was able to calm down and focus on his other tasks after the scheduled activity period. Additional sensory integration activities were scheduled approximately every 90 minutes to two hours during the day. This tended to reduce aggression and stimulated on-task behavior. Periods should also be scheduled for students who need time alone in a safe area with reduced stimulation.

 Integrate sensory-based activities into the daily schedule about every 90 minutes to two hours when possible.

A Safe Place

As discussed in Chapter Three, individuals with autism frequently need a place where they can be alone and calm down. Guidelines for setting up and using a safe area are discussed in Chapter Seven.

CHAPTER Seven

Increasing Desired Behaviors

Persons with autism are frequently challenged by their limited repertoire of appropriate behaviors. Adding acceptable choices to their "pool" of behavioral skills plays a critical role in achieving positive experiences. The more skills available as options, the greater the probability that an acceptable choice will be made.

 Using intervention strategies that will increase desired behaviors are essential to developing positive outcomes.

When planning strategies for increasing desired behaviors, it is important to consider the long-term implications of any proposed changes on the whole person. The primary focus becomes teaching skills that have a positive influence on the quality of life over time. Simply eliminating problem behaviors may provide some temporary relief, but does not guarantee long-term improvements.

How do I decide whether to change my son's behavior by reasoning with him or using some other strategy?

There are numerous schools of thought regarding the most effective ways to change behavior. One way to view behavior change is to picture a triangle. The triangle represents behavior. The sides of the triangle represent thoughts, feelings, and actions. When attempting to change behavior, strategies can be used which change the way a person feels; that change affects the other sides of the triangle—thoughts and actions. Similarly, changes in thought patterns can affect feelings and actions.

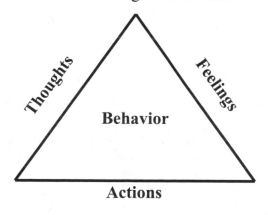

When working with persons whose feelings and thoughts are not readily changed, it is often more practical and timely to focus efforts on changing actions.

 Persons functioning at a higher cognitive level may be candidates for approaches that involve strategies for changing thoughts and feelings, in addition to strategies for changing actions.

Approaches based in applied behavioral theories focus on changing actions. However, it is important to keep in mind the impact of those changes on thoughts and feelings, when planning interventions.

If I want to address a person's behavior problems by changing her actions, what should I do first?

The first step, when using an "action-based" approach, is to complete a functional analysis of the behavior.

Functional Analysis

Functional analysis is the process of gathering information which analyzes the purpose or function that specific behaviors serve for an individual. Behaviors will often *appear* to occur for one reason when they actually serve a different purpose. This information is an important part of understanding specific factors triggering and maintaining behaviors.

When completing a functional analysis, it is essential to find out under what conditions the behavior occurs, what antecedents precede the behavior, and what consequences follow the occurrence of that behavior. The most useful functional analyses include sensory and communication issues identifying conditions, antecedents, and consequences related to the behavior.

A simple way to remember how to complete a functional analysis is to remember "A-B-C"...Antecedent-Behavior-Consequence.

When completing a functional analysis of behavior, ask:

- WHAT happens,

- WHEN it happens,

- WHERE it happens,

- HOW it happens, and with

- WHOM it happens, both before and after the behavior occurs.

Another important part of the functional analysis is to look for **patterns** of conditions, behaviors, or consequences.

When looking for patterns, answer the following questions. Does the behavior occur:

- at a particular time of the day (morning, afternoon, or evening; before or after a meal; etc.)?

- before or after a specific activity or task (physical activities, paper/pencil tasks, social interchange, leisure time, unstructured time, etc.)?

- with certain people (consider categories of persons, hair color, voice quality, interaction style, smells, clothing, number of people, amount of movement or noise, etc.)?

- after a change in routine such as a weekend or holiday (change in activities, location, key people, transportation, other predictable aspects of experiences)?

- with certain materials (consider color, shape, smell, texture, specific letters or numbers, etc.)?

- with certain weather conditions (consider temperature, precipitation, cloudiness, windiness, etc.)?

Once the "A-B-C" has been identified, an intervention plan should be developed. The intervention plan outlines the strategies which will be used to change the behavior.

When making plans to change behavior, interventions may include changing the conditions and cues which *precede* a behavior (antecedents), in an effort to influence the possibility that the behavior will be triggered to occur. Another way to change behavior is to alter the responses (consequences) which *follow* the occurrence of the behavior, in an effort to motivate the individual to increase or decrease the behavior.

Antecedent Control

What is antecedent control?

Antecedent control is the manipulation of cues or conditions in the environment in an effort to trigger a different behavior. Many of the strategies currently in the forefront in the field of autism are actually a form of antecedent control.

 Strategies function as antecedent controls when used as part of the person's <u>scheduled</u> routine or when used <u>before</u> a behavior occurs.

Implementing antecedent control serves to trigger more acceptable responses and helps to minimize inappropriate behaviors. These strategies set the stage for success and can significantly improve the effectiveness of other behavior interventions. Ideally, any behavior intervention plan should include some form of antecedent control.

Using antecedent control may be advantageous when it:

- adds to the effectiveness of the intervention plan;

- shortens time required for successful behavior change;

- increases positive experiences;

- builds upon some of the characteristics of autism such as visual learning style and preference for routine and ritual;

- increases independence; and

- increases autonomy.

 ## CAUTION!

Some disadvantages of antecedent control are that it:

- requires planning and preparation;

- requires the caretaker to be in a position to have control over variables affecting the individual; and

- may require extensive attention to detail when in a group situation where different individuals have conflicting needs.

How can I use antecedent control?

There are many ways to control the triggers which precede a behavior. Deciding which strategies to use depends upon the information obtained from various assessments including patterns determined from the functional analysis (A-B-C), the person's communication and cognitive abilities, long-term goals, and desired behaviors. In planning, it is important to incorporate strategies which address related sensory and communication issues.

 Some strategies that provide effective antecedent control are:

- visually structuring the environment, routines, and tasks;

- clearly communicating behavioral expectations using visual supports;

- physically structuring the environment or materials;

- providing alternative strategies;

- addressing sensory issues;

- controlling stimulation levels; and

- preteaching.

CASE EXAMPLE

Nicky, a 4-year-old, enjoys the feel of hosiery. Every time he sees a woman wearing a dress, he runs and touches her legs, hoping to find some hosiery to rub with his hand. Various positive and negative consequences have not changed this behavior. Finally, his teachers and mother stopped wearing stockings. However, taking Nicky into the community presented a constant problem due to his persistence. At the behavioral consultant's suggestion, Nicky's mother and teachers wore stockings everyday, but placed double-sided tape on the stockings to interrupt the reinforcing sensation. After two weeks, Nicky stopped touching women's hosiery. The feel of the tape prevented him from receiving any sensory gratification from touching stockings. In this situation, antecedent control effectively addressed the sensory issues that were maintaining the inappropriate behavior.

 Preteaching is reminding a person of the task, routine or behavioral expectations immediately <u>prior</u> to the experience occurring.

This may be in the form of verbal, visual, or physical prompts. Visual prompts will most likely promote the greatest level of independence with minimal resistance.

CASE EXAMPLE

Alicia usually squeals and turns her head away when she sees a friend. She is learning to greet people by saying "hi" and waving. Before going into the hallway, Mr. Wilson reminds Alicia by saying "Show me what you do when a friend walks by." He waves his hand and pretends to say "hi." Mr. Wilson is using a preteaching strategy before greeting behaviors occur. This increases the probability that Alicia will use an acceptable behavior.

Self-regulation

A critical part of intervention planning is teaching individuals to monitor and manage their own behavior. The ultimate goal is for persons to be aware of their triggers and early reactions that lead to inappropriate behaviors in order to control the behavior that follows. The response may be to manage the amount of influence from outside triggers, to choose to engage in socially acceptable behaviors or to provide self-imposed consequences.

 **Self-regulation is essential to developing independence.**

 Teaching self-regulation is advantageous when it:

- promotes independence;
- promotes autonomy;
- assists with increasing prosocial behaviors;
- increases self-initiation of behaviors;
- promotes responsibility;
- decreases time demands on caretakers; and
- decreases acting out behaviors, "shutdowns," or "meltdowns."

CAUTION!

When teaching self-regulation, be aware that it:

- requires planning and preparation; and

- may require additional time and expertise for teaching the skills.

When teaching self-regulation, build upon the strengths of visual learning styles and preference for routine and ritual. The various structuring strategies used with antecedent control can promote self-regulation.

 Other strategies which can teach self-regulation include:

- minimizing the impact of stimuli;

- using a safe area;

- deep breathing exercises;

- relaxation training;

- problem-solving; and

- self-monitoring behavioral performance.

Managing Stimulation Levels

Persons who are very sensitive to sensory stimuli have a greater tendency to go into sensory overload. It is not uncommon for acting out behaviors such as screaming, aggression, runaway, self-abuse or tantrums to accompany such occurrences.

Often, reducing incoming sensory information will help the individual regain control. The sensory stimuli that is removed does not need to be the same stimuli that triggers the behavior.

CASE EXAMPLE

Lance is easily overstimulated. He likes to go to school pep rallies. This is very important to him. However, the noise, people, and movement are overstimulating. Lance is able to remain at the pep rally and even chooses to participate when he is able to look away from the activities. He usually looks down at the floor during the loudest and most active times. If too overstimulated, he will start rocking and screaming. This does not happen when he is able to look down at the floor. Lance has learned to manage stimulation levels before problem behaviors occur. He is using a self-regulation technique that involves antecedent control.

One strategy which is highly effective in reducing agitation levels related to sensory overload, is teaching an individual to access a safe area with reduced amounts of stimulation.

Guidelines for setting up and using a "safe" area

To assist with managing overstimulation, set up a safe area. This is an area with significantly lower stimulation levels.

 Select an area which is physically defined, with obvious visual boundaries.

 Some examples of safe areas include a:

- study carrel,
- heavy cardboard or wooden divider or partition,
- plastic "igloo,"
- cloth or sheet draped over a small table,
- rocking chair in quiet area of room,
- private bedroom,

- tent or canopied area,

- private office,

- peaceful outdoor area, or

- desk or table several feet from other activities.

Use your imagination! Remember, there needs to be a significant reduction of sensory stimulation in this area. Reducing visual stimulation can be very helpful since many persons with autism are visually oriented.

 The safe area can be comfortable, calming, and relaxing.

The safe area is **not** a punishment. It is **not** time-out. It is time away from stimulation. It is a self-control strategy. Frequently, time-out, especially isolated time-out, may actually serve as de-stimulation for persons with autism. However, to be consistently effective, a safe area is used differently than time-out.

 The safe area is sometimes referred to as a:

- cool-off place,

- chill-out place,

- de-stim area,

- quiet area, or

- break area.

 The ultimate goal is for persons to recognize when they are becoming agitated and access the safe area until arousal decreases to an easily managed level.

In the process of learning this self-control strategy, persons will require prompting from others in order to recognize arousal levels, manage stimulation levels, and access the safe area. With this goal in mind, label the safe area with appropriate visual prompts. This is particularly important since the safe area will be used when agitation levels are high and thinking skills are minimal.

CASE EXAMPLE

Brandy makes disruptive noises and has problems following directions when she is agitated. Her teacher designates a beanbag chair in the far corner of the classroom as the cool-off area. She has a picture of a penguin posted at eye level next to the beanbag. Brandy also has a small picture of a penguin on her desk. When she repeatedly makes noises, her teacher walks over and points to the penguin on the desktop. Brandy goes to cool-off for a few minutes and stops making noises. The teacher has used a visual prompt to help Brandy calm down.

 **Props may be placed in the safe area which will facilitate relaxation.**

These props need to be tailored to the individual. Find what helps to calm the person who will be accessing this area.

 Some props which can have a calming effect are:

- soft pillows,
- music,
- sensory toys,
- objects used for applying deep pressure,
- weighted clothing,
- books, and
- simple activities requiring slow repetitive movement.

Explore various props to determine what works for the individual. Use the items that are most effective.

Often, objects which the individual seeks out for self-stimulation provide a calming effect. Select props which provide similar sensory input.

CAUTION!

It is important that the props also be accessible outside of the safe area or on request. If these props truly have a calming impact and cannot be accessed in an appropriate manner, the person may resort to agitated behaviors in order to access these props.

Introduce the person to the safe area at a time when the person is calm.

When introducing the area, teach the visual or gestural prompt that signals "use the safe area; go calm down" by pairing the prompt with that area. Allow the person to explore and become familiar with the safe area and the props. If the area or props are totally unfamiliar, then the first few visits during periods of agitation may add even more stress, instead of serving to calm the person.

CAUTION!

Don't panic if the individual accesses the safe area frequently when it is new.

Invite the person to rejoin ongoing activities as soon as agitation is reduced. If this behavior continues, it may become necessary to review the amount and types of positive reinforcement available *outside of the safe area*. In order to prevent overuse of this area, participating in ongoing activities *must* be more reinforcing than the safe area. If the person is totally motivated by low stimulation levels, then use peace and quiet time as a reinforcer for short periods of acceptable behavior.

In some unusual situations that are highly resistant to these strategies, it may become necessary to remove some of the more preferred calming props and use them as reinforcers for participation; however, save this as a last resort strategy. Remember, in using a safe area, the goal is to prevent acting out behaviors resulting from agitation or overstimulation.

 **Cue the person to calm down at the earliest signs of agitation or overstimulation. Refer to Chapter Four for common signs of agitation and overstimulation.**

When early signs of agitation or overstimulation are first noticed, prompt the individual to use an "on-the-spot" anxiety reducer, if appropriate. For example, squeeze a stress ball or look down for a few moments to decrease visual input. If this is not an effective method, prompt the person to access the safe area.

 When anxiety and agitation levels increase, thinking abilities decrease.

Someone who usually responds to auditory cues may be unable to do so as easily when agitated or overstimulated. Decreased rational thinking along with increased anxiety indicate a need for visual cues.

CAUTION!

Be aware that when some individuals are agitated or overstimulated, personal space requirements increase. Physical prompts can result in aggressive responses or total overload because the person might become intolerant of physical closeness.

While in the safe area, the individual can continue to earn reinforcers and work on tasks.

While in the safe area, the individual should focus energy and efforts on calming activities. Some persons may take assigned tasks to this area for completion. Remember, it is not time-out. It simply provides the conditions needed to maintain focus on tasks.

Assistance may be provided to a person in the safe area as needed. Keep any social interactions:

- low key,
- calm,
- nonemotional, and
- gentle.

Once agitation has decreased, it may be necessary to *request* a return to scheduled activities, using visual prompts as needed. A good measure of the person's readiness to return to scheduled activities is completion of a simple manipulative task such as putting pegs in a pegboard. Completion of a manipulative task is a reliable indication that the person is ready to attempt more stimulating activities. If unable to complete a simple manipulative task, the person is not ready to leave the safe area. Check the individual periodically to assess readiness to return to regular activities. If an individual continues to be agitated or becomes more agitated while in the safe area, engaging in an intense physical activity may be an appropriate calming agent.

 Some physical activities that may aid in calming someone who is agitated and unable to calm down in a quiet area include:

- very brisk walking,

- jumping on a mini-trampoline,

- rocking in a rocking chair,

- swinging on a swing or glider,

- running,

- carrying large or heavy objects within the individual's physical capacity,

- pushing and pulling activities that use large muscle groups within the individual's physical capacity,

- pounding and manipulating clay,

- gardening and yardwork, and

- housework such as sweeping, mopping, vacuuming or emptying wastebaskets.

 ## CAUTION!

If the person presents a risk of running away when agitated, be sure to remain in a physically contained area such as a secure room, building, or fenced area.

 Some higher functioning individuals can benefit from learning to recognize their own early stress signals and manage stress levels without removing themselves to another location.

 Additional calming strategies which may be used include:

- using deep breathing exercises;

- using relaxation techniques;

- using small manipulatives, such as stress balls to squeeze;

- closing eyes and counting backwards from ten;

- lacing fingers together and stretching arms and hands out in front of the body;

- looking away or closing eyes momentarily;

- using positive self-talk;

- developing an action plan; and

- obtaining assistance.

 When the individual's anxiety is increasing, techniques to prevent further agitation include:

- using sunglasses to reduce light without bothering others;

- using a walkman to reduce the impact of noise without interfering with others;

- taking periodic breaks;

- engaging in a short motor activity such as walking, bouncing a ball, jumping on a trampoline, etc.; and

- using communication skills to request the removal of particular stressors.

CASE EXAMPLE

Joey becomes overstimulated by artificial lights, but his classmate Tyrone needs high light levels in order to focus his attention. Joey is prompted to wear dark glasses or to take his task to an area which has dimmer lighting when the lights become overstimulating. Joey is learning self-regulation by managing stimulation levels.

How do deep breathing techniques and relaxation training help with self-regulation?

Deep breathing exercises can assist with self-regulation by interrupting the irritating stimulus and providing a focus for attention. This has a physically calming impact. These exercises may also help persons learn to monitor arousal levels.

Relaxation training can help individuals monitor and manage muscle tension. With training, the learner develops an awareness of muscle tension and can respond to anxiety or stress at an early stage by practicing relaxation exercises, muscle stretching, or other calming strategies.

Using Consequences To Change Behaviors

The consequences which follow a behavior can be manipulated in order to increase or decrease the occurrence of that behavior. Altering consequences can be more effective when used in combination with antecedent control strategies and self-regulation strategies. When consequences are used alone in an effort to change behavior, the individual may require more time and experience associating behaviors with consequences before behavior change occurs.

Consequences which **increase** the occurrence of a behavior are called **reinforcement**.

Consequences which **decrease** the occurrence of a behavior are **punishment**.

When deciding whether a behavior has increased or decreased, be sure to examine not only *how often* the behavior occurs, but *how long* it lasts, and *how intense* it is. Changes in behavior may be deceiving.

CASE EXAMPLE
Before interventions, Sheila had tantrums lasted 2 hours. She continues to have 10 tantrums every day, but her tantrums last only 1 minute. This indicates a decrease in the duration of Sheila's tantrum behavior.

Reinforcement

What can I do to teach my son to use acceptable behaviors more often?

To increase a preferred behavior, provide a reinforcer following that behavior.

Reinforcement is defined as any action or object which follows a behavior and increases that behavior.

Reinforcement usually makes people think of various types of rewards; however, it is important to remember that *rewards are not always reinforcing*. Sometimes a great reward can follow a behavior, but the behavior does not increase. In this case, the reward is *not* a reinforcer. To be a reinforcer, the behavior it follows *must* increase.

CAUTION!
Avoid assuming something is a reinforcer simply because it is something most people like. It may not be reinforcing for that particular learner or the specific behavior being taught.

To find out if something is a reinforcer, ask the following questions:

- Did the reinforcer occur after the behavior was exhibited?

- Did the behavior happen more often, for a longer period of time or at a more intense level?

If the answer to both questions is "yes," then the object or action is a reinforcer. If either answer is no, the reinforcing quality is still undetermined.

Reinforcer assessments

How do I find out what reinforcers to try at first?

People commonly experience some amount of uncertainty when attempting to identify what is reinforcing for persons with autism. Reinforcer assessments can assist in developing a selection of reinforcers. A reinforcer assessment which may provide guidance is included in Appendix B. It is very helpful to have numerous reinforcers that can be used when needed.

 Consider the individual's preferences when identifying potential reinforcers to use.

 Individuals who are developmentally younger or more severely challenged may prefer sensory-based reinforcers.

 Persons who are higher functioning may also find pleasure in sensory-based reinforcers, but may enjoy a larger variety of other reinforcers.

Tap into individual obsessions and interests when developing reinforcers to use. Sometimes the behaviors which are constantly being interrupted or corrected are potential reinforcers.

CASE EXAMPLE

Jared's mom frequently stops Jared from staring at light beams. Playing with a flashlight or sparkly object for 2-5 minutes is a potential reinforcer for Jared.

CAUTION!

It is not unusual for persons with autism to have a preference for novelty. This can significantly impact the effectiveness of reinforcers that you use over time. Varying reinforcers used or offering choices can increase their long-range effectiveness.

Positive Reinforcement

Reinforcers come in two general categories: positive and negative.

 Positive reinforcement is any object or action which is applied following a behavior that increases the behavior.

 Positive reinforcers may involve some form of:

- sensory experience;
- social interaction;
- activity; or
- access to a tangible item.

Avoid allowing free, unlimited access to reinforcers which are being used to increase desired behaviors. If the learner can freely access these reinforcers without demonstrating the desired behavior, then the reinforcing value will be greatly diminished.

Sensory Reinforcers

Sensory-based reinforcers follow a behavior and provide pleasurable sensations of sound, taste, smell, sight, movement or touch. Sensory-based reinforcement is a powerful tool for increasing appropriate behaviors in persons with autism.

 Some examples of sensory-based reinforcers include:

- preferred music,
- water play,
- a flashlight,
- colorful, liquid timers,
- objects that glitter,
- bubbles,
- sensory toys: spinning tops, water toys, talking toys, etc.,
- lotions and powder,
- rocking in a chair,
- peace and quiet time,
- vibrating objects,
- body pillows,
- deep pressure, and
- "double rubby"—place one hand firmly on chest and rub the back in a firm circular motion with other hand.

Be creative! Build upon the individual's sensory preferences.

Social reinforcers

Access to social interaction should not be controlled in the same way as access to foods or toys. Social acceptance and support should always be freely available throughout the day. However, recognize that some individuals exhibit misbehavior to engage your attention.

 Manage social interactions by providing positive attention for desired behaviors and avoiding social interaction in response to inappropriate behaviors.

CASE EXAMPLE

Jerry frequently refuses to attempt a task. His teacher continues to verbally cue him to do his work. The longer Jerry refuses, the more the teacher interacts with him by sitting next to him and helping him with each step of the task. Even when Jerry can do the work, he will not try without her assistance. In this case, the teacher's attention may be reinforcing Jerry's refusal to work. Visual cues might be developed to provide Jerry with more independent prompts, so that verbal or physical prompts are not needed. His teacher points to visual cues as needed, with minimal talking. He must complete a certain number of task steps before she will sit or interact with him. In this way, the teacher is controlling her social attention so that it positively reinforces desired behaviors instead of reinforcing inappropriate behaviors. She has also used antecedent control to help reduce the number of social interactions required to prompt Jerry to do his work.

CASE EXAMPLE

While at preschool, Lee frequently darts around the classroom. When he does this, the aide moves within arms reach and begins talking to him, following him around the room and eventually resorting to holding him in her lap. He wiggles and wrestles with her. The teacher realizes that Lee is using this to obtain the aide's attention. She instructs the aide to stay close to Lee and interact with him only when he is showing acceptable behaviors. Visual prompts are presented every minute to cue him to return to task when he starts darting around the room. When these cues are presented, the paraprofessional avoids touching or any extra talking. Lee begins staying in his assigned area with the aide. Lee's teachers are using social attention to reinforce desired behaviors. They are also using antecedent control by presenting visual prompts, to increase the probability that desired behaviors will occur.

CAUTION!

When an individual tends to resist usual social interactions of touch, conversation, and eye contact, misconceptions may be formed by caretakers.

This resistance does *not* indicate an aversion to social interaction, it simply indicates discomfort with those *particular forms of social interaction*. Carefully identify the types and intensity of social interaction preferred. Social reinforcers need to be part of any positive reinforcement strategies. They may be used alone or in conjunction with other forms of positive reinforcement.

CASE EXAMPLE

Larry earned a plastic chip for every task he completed. His teacher knew the importance of pairing social reinforcement with other types of reinforcement. Therefore, everytime she gave Larry a chip, she made a positive social comment or gesture. Eventually, Larry learned to work for social reinforcers only. Pairing social reinforcers with tokens eventually helped fade-out the use of tokens.

Activity reinforcers

Another type of positive reinforcement is activity-based reinforcement.

 An activity-based reinforcer may include:

• participating in a preferred activity;

• using preferred objects, toys or materials;

• earning a preferred job responsibility; or

• increasing independence following a desired behavior.

Anticipation of participating in desired activities will be most effective when represented visually. For example, a daily work schedule may have a picture of a computer after the work tasks to visually represent computer time. With developmentally younger or more severely challenged individuals, activity reinforcers need to be sensory-based and applied immediately following a desired behavior. With higher functioning persons, access to earned reinforcers can be delayed, but visual representation of earned reinforcers need to be present.

When using activity-based reinforcers that do not have a discrete beginning or end, use a kitchen timer, digital timer, or sand timer to indicate when the activity is finished. For example, if the activity is a puzzle, the activity is finished when the puzzle is complete. There is a discrete beginning and end to using a puzzle appropriately. If the activity is bouncing a ball, it needs to be timed to indicate the beginning and end of the activity.

 **CAUTION**

When time is not presented concretely as an indicator that an activity is finished, some individuals will erroneously conclude the activity ended due to some action on their part. Consequently, they may attempt to change appropriate behaviors based on this inaccurate conclusion.

CASE EXAMPLE

Joey worked for playtime with a truck. He recently learned to play with the truck appropriately. He rolled the truck on the floor a few times when his Dad said "Truck time is over". He removed the truck and directed Joey to another activity. This happened on repeated occasions. Joey incorrectly paired removal of the truck with rolling the truck on the floor. He eventually stopped rolling the truck on the floor. Joey's Dad learned to prevent this problem by setting a kitchen timer for five or 10 minutes when Joey began playing with the truck. The sound of the timer indicated truck time was over. Joey accurately learned to pair the sound of the timer with the end of truck time.

Tangible reinforcers

Tangible reinforcers are objects that are given to an individual following a desired behavior. Tangible reinforcers are the most artificial form of positive reinforcement.

 Tangible reinforcers are appropriate for use with persons who are developmentally young or severly challenged.

When providing tangible items such as food or drink for reinforcement, it is important to limit the amount of the item provided. Instead of providing a can of soda, present one swallow of soda poured into a small cup. Similarly, instead of providing and entire bag of chips, present one chip or even a piece of a chip. This allows more learning experiences to occur without the person becoming satiated with the reinforcer.

CAUTION

Avoid breaking food reinforcers into pieces if the person is bothered by the shape of food being altered.

Occasional use of tangible reinforcers with higher functioning individuals can be effective when teaching a new behavior or when working with a behavior which is very difficult for the person to perform.

CAUTION!

Avoid relying solely on tangible reinforcers for higher functioning individuals. Instead, link the tangible reinforcement with a closely related preferred activity.

CASE EXAMPLE

George earns a cookie for participating in a regular Math class at school. The teacher does not want to continue with such an artificial reinforcer, but George really likes working for cookies. The teacher changes George's reinforcer to an activity by having George work for a leisure activity. A choice for leisure time is a five minute break with cookies or snacks available. George's teacher has changed a tangible reinforcer into an activity choice.

Like activities, tangible reinforcers can be delayed for higher functioning individuals when they are visually evident. Visual supports indicating when the earned reinforcer can be accessed may be necessary if the person continues to direct excessive attention to the earned reinforcers.

CASE EXAMPLE

Benji earned some popcorn. His teacher placed a picture of popcorn in Benji's work area to indicate that he earned the popcorn and would collect it later. Benji kept looking at the picture and talking about popcorn, which interfered with completion of other tasks. His teacher placed the picture of the popcorn beside the snack symbol on Benji's schedule so he knew when it was time to collect his popcorn.

What are token systems?

Token systems are systems of reinforcement in which an object or visual symbol is provided following a desired behavior. This object or symbol is not inherently reinforcing, but is used to trade for a positive reinforcer. Point systems and level systems are highly abstract and more complex versions of token systems. Token systems delay receipt of the desired item or activity.

Persons who are developmentally young or more severely challenged usually are not the best candidates for token systems. Candidates for token systems need to be able to understand visual symbols and be able to delay gratification.

CASE EXAMPLE

Molly responded to cues by whining, complaining, or using various delay tactics. It usually took five cues before she was compliant with a request. Her in-home trainer developed a token system in which she earned tokens for complying without delay. At the end of each day, Molly traded her tokens for preferred activity time. Molly began complying more readily. She seldom whined and complained anymore. A token system was used to improve Molly's compliance.

Token systems may take the form of written behavioral charts. These charts track behavioral performance for set periods of time. The recordings on the chart serve as visual evidence of behavioral success which is traded for reinforcers at a later time.

 Written token systems can be more appealing to a person who is higher functioning since the consequences are:

- more natural;

- logically related to the behavior;

- visually evident;

- predictable; and

- based on routines and rituals.

CASE EXAMPLE

Chuck's teacher used a behavior chart on which she recorded Chuck's behavioral performance at the end of each class by circling "yes" or "no" to indicate if Chuck used his cool-off strategies and completed his assignments. At the end of each day, Chuck colored one block on his bar graph for each "yes" earned. When he reached the happy face on his bar graph, he collected a reinforcer. Chuck's teacher used a modified written token system to improve and monitor his behavioral performance. Samples of a behavior chart and bar graph are included in Appendix B.

CAUTION!

Avoid using token systems with individuals who do not readily respond to delayed reinforcement.

Negative reinforcement

Isn't negative reinforcement the same as punishment?

Negative reinforcement is a widely misunderstood concept. It is very important that anyone working with a person with autism understand negative reinforcement. It is frequently overlooked or misinterpreted when planning how to increase desired behaviors. Yet, negative reinforcement is often at work in the world of a person who uses behaviors to end uncomfortable situations.

Negative reinforcement is not punishment. It is not used to decrease behaviors. Negative reinforcement is used to *increase* preferred behaviors. First, it is important to consider the presence of the word "reinforcement" in "negative reinforcement." That means when it follows a desired behavior, the *behavior increases*. Next, consider the word "negative." This indicates that *something is taken away*. With positive reinforcement something is added to increase a behavior.

Table 7.1 Reinforcement versus Punishment

	Positive (+) Reinforcement	Negative (-) Reinforcement	Punishment
Action	Give Learner desired object	Remove or end a disliked experience	Remove desired object or impose a disliked experience
Purpose	Increase desired behavior	Increase desired behavior	Decrease unwanted behavior

Table 7.1 is a visual representation of the concept of reinforcement versus punishment. It was designed to illustrate the differences between positive reinforcement, negative reinforcement, and punishment. Punishment results when you remove a desired object or when you impose an undesired experience to a situation. For example, you take away computer time (desired activity) or you add minutes in time-out (a disliked experience). Both situations are examples of punishment if the person desires computer time and dislikes time-out.

The same illustration can be used to explain the difference between positive and negative reinforcement. If I add (+) a desired activity, such as computer time (reinforcer), it increases the likelihood the preferred behavior will be repeated. It is *positive* (+) because something is *added*. If I take away or remove (-) a disliked experience, it is a reinforcer because it *increases* the probability that the behavior will be repeated ("You did so well on your work, you don't have to do homework tonight."). It is *negative* (-) reinforcement because something (homework) is *taken away*.

 Negative reinforcement is the removal or ending of something that is disliked or uncomfortable, in order to increase a desired behavior.

CASE EXAMPLE

Jack was not working on his assigned task. The teacher walked over to Jack and stood within 3 feet of his desk. Jack was uncomfortable with the teacher standing so close. He began working on his assignment and the teacher moved away from Jack. Jack stopped working and the teacher moved close again. Jack began working again. In this situation, the negative reinforcer was the teacher moving away from Jack. Jack was uncomfortable with her being so close. The teacher ending the close proximity followed the desired behavior of Jack doing his work. Consequently, Jack increased work behavior to end the teacher being close to him. Jack was negatively reinforced by the close proximity of the teacher being removed.

Table 7.2 Removal of Close Proximity as a Negative Reinforcer

	Punishment	Negative Reinforcement
Close Proximity for Jack	Teacher's close proximity	Removal of close proximity
Target for behavior	Reduce off-task behavior	Increase on-task behavior
Teacher's perspective	Walk toward Jack	Walk away from Jack

CASE EXAMPLE

Susie was sensitive to sounds. She fussed when she heard the radio. Susie's mother did not turn the radio off when Susie fussed. Instead, she taught Susie to turn the radio off when the sounds bothered her. Ending the sound of the radio was the negative reinforcer for the behavior of turning off the radio.

Table 7.3 Removal of Radio Sounds as a Negative Reinforcer

	Punishment	Negative Reinforcement
Radio sounds for Susie	Sounds from radio	Ending of radio sounds
Target for behavior		Teach control of radio

Be careful to avoid confusing negative reinforcers with punishment. Although both involve aversives, negative reinforcement is used in a way that *increases* a desired behavior. Unlike punishment, with negative reinforcement, a mild aversive is *taken away* to increase the likelihood of the *desired* behavior. With punishment, an aversive is *added* following a misbehavior in an effort to decrease that behavior.

Since persons with autism find many situations and experiences aversive or uncomfortable, problem behaviors are frequently learned as the result of negative reinforcement. It is critical that caretakers recognize this, so they do not unintentionally reinforce unwanted behaviors through negative reinforcement.

CASE EXAMPLE

Ginger is often overwhelmed by too many people or too much activity. She is watching TV at home when her brother Mitch enters the room with several friends. When Ginger asks Mitch to leave the room, he refuses. Ginger begins screaming and tantruming. Mitch and his friends leave the room. What behavior was negatively reinforced? Screaming and tanruming was negatively reinforced. What will Ginger be more likely to do the next time she wants someone to leave the room? Requesting with words did not end the aversive situation of Mitch and his friends. Thus, a verbal request was not reinforced. It is less likely that Ginger will use oral language to make a request in a similar situation in the future. There is an increased likelihood that Ginger will scream and tantrum in the future under similar circumstances. In this situation, Mitch and his friends leaving the room is the negative reinforcer that increases Ginger's screaming and tantruming behavior.

Table 7.4 Removal of Mitch and Friends as Negative Reinforcement

	Punishment	Negative Reinforcement
Ginger and too many people	Presence of Mitch & friends	Mitch & friends leave room
Target for behavior		Screaming & yelling
Mitch's perspective	Ginger's screaming	Leaving the room (Ended the screaming behvior)

When teaching a person to manage overwhelming stimulation levels, high anxiety, or other uncomfortable conditions, focus on the desired behaviors needed to end such situations. Failure to teach sensitive people appropriate ways to manage uncomfortable situations can lead to seriously inappropriate behaviors being learned through negative reinforcement experiences. The individual will resort to whatever action is necessary to decrease discomfort. If appropriate responses are limited or have failed to decrease discomfort in the past, the individual may resort to inappropriate behaviors to obtain the goal of being more comfortable.

 Increase appropriate behaviors as responses to discomfort by:

- planning and structuring for uncomfortable situations;
- teaching and practicing management of uncomfortable situations;
- applying negative reinforcement following desired behaviors; and
- incorporating self-regulation and antecedent control strategies.

When do I use reinforcement strategies?

Reinforcement strategies *only* work to increase a behavior when the desired behavior is already in the person's repertoire. Adding reinforcement cannot make individuals perform behaviors that they cannot do.

> ## CASE EXAMPLE
> Keisha does not talk. She has never uttered any words and seldom makes any vocalizations, just occasional squeals and screams. She is highly motivated by music. However, using music as a reinforcer will not make Keisha talk. That behavior is not in her repertoire of skills.

CAUTION!

Attaching reinforcement to behaviors that a person is unable to do may:

- increase anxiety,

- increase stress,

- increase negative behaviors,

- create mistrust,

- damage rapport, and

- create anger and frustration.

If a person is unable to do a skill correctly, *first teach the skill*. Once the person has learned the skill, then provide effective cues to prompt use of the skill. Finally, reinforcers may be used to increase use of the learned skill. Reinforcers may also be used when motivating the person to use smaller steps of the skill. It is also appropriate to reinforce the person's efforts that approximate the skill.

Developing New Behaviors

Developing new behaviors is an ongoing process with individuals who have limited repertoires of effective skills. Developing new behaviors is critical to success.

Use the following teaching techniques when teaching new behaviors to persons with autism.

- Present the behavioral expectations using visual prompts.

- Provide a functional, meaningful perspective when presenting behavioral expectations.

- Avoid presenting expectations in a fragmented manner.

- Show the learner how the expected behavior is supposed to look.

- Provide prompts to direct the focus of the person's attention on the relevant details.

- Use reinforcement to motivate the learner to use the newly acquired skills.

- If necessary, reinforce smaller steps toward the new behavior.

- Reinforce attempts to perform the new skills in order to encourage improved behaviors.

Task analysis and chaining

Task analysis is the process by which a skill is broken down into smaller steps. Mastery of each step is learned before adding new steps. Chaining is sequencing the steps together to make a complete skill.

 New or complex behaviors can be taught more readily if broken into smaller steps.

When teaching persons to exhibit new behaviors, teach successive steps that lead to the final behavior. As each new step is added, link it to the previous one by presenting the separate steps as a chained sequence. This approach is important because individuals with autism may not be able to link steps in a chained sequence when step is taught as an isolated skill.

 **CAUTION!**
When using task analysis with persons with autism, **always** present the successive steps as part of **a whole sequence**. Avoid presenting the steps in isolation as if each step were a separate skill.

CASE EXAMPLE

Jackson is learning to ask a friend to join him in a game. He has practiced the various steps involved. His father taught him the first step of approaching a friend. Once he learned the first step, his father added the second step of looking at the friend. Then he added the next step of speaking to the friend. When he introduced speaking, he had Jackson first approach a friend, then look at the person, then speak. He avoided having Jackson practice any step by itself. By chaining the steps together in sequence as each step was learned, Jackson can readily perform the behavior correctly.

CASE EXAMPLE

Billy's father taught him to ask a friend to join in a game by having Billy practice each step in isolation. First, he practiced approaching friends. Next, he practiced making eye contact. Then he practiced speaking to friends. After Billy learned each step separately, his father began teaching him to do the steps in a sequence. Sometimes, Billy did the sequence correctly. Frequently, he demonstrated each behavior separately. He would approach someone, then leave. He would make eye contact or speak without approaching the friend first. Teaching the steps separately resulted in Billy learning several isolated behaviors that were ineffective when he was unable to sequence the steps together.

Backward Chaining

Another type of task analysis strategy involves using backward chaining. Skills are broken into smaller steps that are taught in a sequence, starting with the *last* step in the sequence. The steps are learned in succession, moving from the last step to the first step.

How do I know when to use backward chaining?

Backward chaining is most commonly used to teach self-help skills such as dressing. It is most appropriate for use when the learner can be reinforced by a sense of accomplishment.

CASE EXAMPLE

Jimmy is learning to put on his pants. His mother pulls his pants up until they are one inch from his waist. She then prompts Jimmy to finish pulling up his pants. Once he masters this step, his mother only pulls his pants up to his hips. She prompts Jimmy to finish pulling up his pants. Jimmy is reinforced by the sense of mastery he feels when the lessons always end with his finishing this task independently. The backward chaining of small steps in the task eventually leads to Jimmy pulling up his pants without any assistance.

CASE EXAMPLE

Skip's mother is also teaching him to put on his pants. She is using small sequenced steps, but is not using backward chaining. She prompts Skip to pull his pants over his ankles, then she finishes pulling up his pants. Once Skip masters this step, his mother has him pull his pants up to his knees before she finishes helping. Skip becomes frustrated with these lessons. No matter how hard he tries, he is always left feeling dependent on his mother for help. The lesson always ends with his mother finishing the task. He does not receive the reinforcement from a sense of mastery. With frequent encouragement and praise from his mother, Skip eventually learns to pull up his pants unassisted. The small sequenced steps help Skip learn this skill, but he requires more social reinforcement since he is not receiving reinforcement from the sense of mastery.

 Teach a new or complex behavior using the following steps:

- break the behavior into smaller, easier steps;

- use positive reinforcement to teach those smaller steps, adding one step at a time;

- always present the successive steps as part of a whole sequence;

- avoid teaching each step as an isolated event;

- always incorporate each new step into the current sequence;

- continue to add one more step onto the sequence of successive steps; and

- if the step can only be taught in isolation, then use visual prompts to symbolize the steps. This will facilitate incorporating the isolated step into the whole sequence.

Successive approximation

What is successive approximation?

Often, learners are unable to produce the exact response expected when attempting a new behavior. In such instances, it is highly appropriate to provide reinforcement for efforts that are *close t*o the expected behavior. As the learner improves performance, provide reinforcement only for closer approximations.

 To motivate continued improvement, provide learners with reinforcement for performance that approximates the desired behavior.

CASE EXAMPLE

Lon is beginning to learn how to use a picture swap system to request food. He reaches in the general direction of the picture for "chips." His teacher asks "Lon, want chips?" and gives him a piece of a chip. Later, the teacher waits until Lon places his hand within one inch of the picture before giving him a chip. Then, she waits until he touches the picture before providing the chip. Eventually, Lon learns to pick up the picture to exchange it for chips. Lon's teacher is gradually requiring responses that more closely approximate the desired behavior. She is using successive approximation.

Compliance Training

What is compliance training?

Compliance training is used to increase the amount of instructional control over an individual. The ability to follow another person's directions is critical not only for safety reasons, but for successful experiences in school, at work, at home and in the community. Compliance also plays a critical role in the learning process for persons who need to actually experience an activity in order to learn.

 **Noncompliance occurs in many different forms; however, it is still noncompliance.**

It is sometimes difficult to recognize noncompliance. It can take on the appearance of other behaviors and go undetected. An important point to realize is that failure to follow an instruction is noncompliance, no matter what the reason for the noncompliance. Recognizing the different forms of noncompliance can help you plan effective strategies for managing behaviors.

 Some of the more common forms of noncompliance are:

- **Passive noncompliance**: The person simply acts as if unaware the directive has been presented.

- **Simple refusal**: The person is obviously aware a directive has been given, but does not attempt to comply.

- **Inaccuracy**: The person attempts to comply, but does so incorrectly.

- **Direct defiance**: The person overtly challenges authority when refusing to comply.

- **Negotiating/bargaining/arguing**: The person attempts to change the conditions of the directive given.

- **Distracting**: The person attempts to direct attention away from the expected response; often orally agreeing to comply (for example says "OK"), then changes the focus rather than actually complying.

How can I teach my son to be compliant, if I can't distinguish when he is defiant or manipulative from the times he does not understand what I want him to do?

Trying to distinguish between deliberate refusal, manipulation and not understanding cues can be an overwhelming task. It is important to recognize when a behavior is actually some form of noncompliance. However, determining the type of noncompliance is not necessary, when part of the intervention includes effective cueing procedures.

 Consistently presenting **effective** cues eliminates the need to identify the intent behind the noncompliance.

 The way in which a cue is presented can impact the amount of compliance that follows.

Cueing procedures play a critical role in the amount of compliance exhibited by individuals with communication-based disabilities. In order to be followed accurately, a cue must be presented so that it is clearly understood and the expected response must be a behavior that the individual is able to perform under the circumstances.

 An effective cue is:

- clear and concise;
- logical;
- meaningful;
- communicated in a manner which is readily understood and processed by the recipient;

- used to prompt a behavior which the individual can perform;

- presented without excess emotion;

- presented in close proximity to the person being cued; and

- presented after obtaining the person's attention.

Table 7.5. Comparison of Effective Versus Ineffective Cues

Examples of effective cues:	Examples of inaffective cues:
"Stop and sit."	"Come back!"
"Go to the TV room."	"Go find something to do."
"Run and break the bubbles."	"Run around the gym three times."
"Put the flatware in the correct compartments."	"Sort these nuts and bolts, then put them all back in this box."
Presenting a picture with a verbal cue.	Presenting the same verbal cue in a louder tone, without additional information.
Calmly saying "Use a tissue."	Excitedly saying "Stop picking your nose!"
Presenting a written list of the day's schedule change.	Repeatedly saying the schedule changes for the day.
Walking over to the person and pointing to the symbol for "cool-off".	Loudly saying across the room "Go to cool-off!"
Walking up to the person and saying "Brian, look," then giving the directive.	Walking up to the person and giving a cue, then saying "Pay attention! Look at me!"

Three-step Prompting

An easy way to remember how to provide effective cues is to learn a three-step prompting procedure. This method provides cues without having to decide if noncompliance is due to deliberate refusal or lack of understanding.

How is Three-step Prompting done?

 Three-step Prompting consists of three basic steps:

- provide a verbal prompt,

- supplement with a visual prompt (picture, gesture, sign, etc.), and

- provide a physical prompt (facilitative touch or hand-over-hand physical guidance from behind).

Complete only the parts of this prompting sequence necessary for compliance.

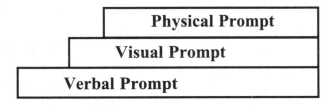

CASE EXAMPLE

Ms. Jones wanted Shawn to put the blocks in a container. She said "Shawn, put blocks in can." Shawn did not comply. Ms. Jones repeated this cue while demonstrating placing some of the blocks in the can. Shawn did not comply. Ms. Jones repeated this cue as she stood <u>behind</u> Shawn and guided his hand in placing the blocks in the can. She guided his hand by placing her hand over the top of Shawn's hand. When Shawn began to comply, she faded out the physical guidance. She also provided social reinforcement. Ms. Jones used Three-step Prompting and reinforcement to increase compliance.

How can I get my son to follow a direction without arguing, bargaining or distracting me from what I asked him to do?

This form of noncompliance can be very frustrating. Suddenly caretakers may realize that the person has once again managed to evade complying with a directive. This becomes even more challenging when the evasive tactic involves arguing, bargaining, or whining and complaining. It is important to avoid being drawn into the argument. Avoid bargaining or responding to complaints.

 When providing directives to a person who tends to use arguing or other distracting tactics to avoid compliance, use the Speak and Spin strategy.

How do I use Speak and Spin?

 To use Speak and Spin:

- Provide the directive, using effective cueing procedures.

- Immediately turn and walk away.

- With persons who are developmentally younger or more severely challenged, it may be more appropriate to turn attention to another task, instead of walking away.

- Periodically return to the person and cue again or reinforce for compliance.

- Repeat this procedure as often as needed.

 **CAUTION!**
When using Speak and Spin, avoid changing the way in which cues are repeated. If cues are presented using different words or inflection, the novelty of changing the caretaker's behavior may be reinforcing to the person being cued.

CASE EXAMPLE

Rhett's mother cues him to clear the table. He whines and complains. She immediately turns and goes to the kitchen. One minute later, she returns, repeats the cue, and goes back to the kitchen. Again, she returns and repeats the cue. Rhett tries to argue. His mother has already returned to the kitchen. Rhett begins to bring a few items into the kitchen. His mother reinforces him and cues him to finish. He finishes clearing the table. Rhett's mother uses <u>Speak and Spin</u>. Not lingering to hear his complaints or arguing helps her avoid being drawn into these delay tactics.

CASE EXAMPLE

Garrett's mother cues him to clear the table. He whines and complains. She tries to reason with him. This becomes an argument. The arguing worsens until Garrett is sent to his room. Once again, Garrett has successfully managed to avoid clearing the table. His mother is easily drawn into his evasive maneuvers. Garrett does not consciously plan to avoid compliance. He does not say, "I have to start an argument to get out of clearing the table." It simply works out that way without any deliberate manipulation. Garrett is a good candidate for <u>Speak and Spin</u>.

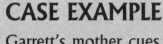

CAUTION!

It is very easy to be drawn into arguments or other delay tactics. When caretakers realize they are participating in an argument or other delay tactic, they should stop responding and begin using <u>Speak and Spin</u>.

I give my daughter clear cues to do a task I know she can do, but she still only does it if she wants to do it. How can I get her to comply with requests?

Another critical part of compliance training is the use of reinforcement. Compliance will occur more frequently when a reinforcer follows compliant responses.

 Compliance with effective cues will increase when followed by a reinforcer.

In the early stages of intervention, when compliance seldom occurs, a reinforcer needs to be provided every time the person is compliant. As the individual follows directives more frequently or more rapidly, begin fading the reinforcement to every three to five times compliance occurs. Over time, the reinforcement can be faded out even more so that it is provided when the person is compliant for an entire activity or time frame.

 Frequent experiences pairing compliance with reinforcement increases the likelihood that the individual will follow such directives in the future.

One approach to teaching compliance involves planned practice sessions in which various simple cues are given. The learner's response is followed with consistent, preplanned consequences. This is sometimes referred to as discrete trial training or compliance training. The goal of these practice sessions is to increase the amount of instructional control over an individual's behavior.

 Some advantages of compliance training include:

- decreased safety risks;

- decreased frustration levels of caretakers;

- increased frequency of positive interactions;

- scheduled, predictable social interactions; and

- increased repertoire of learned skills.

 CAUTION!
Compliance training may:

- teach "odd-looking" sequences of behaviors;

- teach situationally inappropriate behaviors;

- increase dependence on others;

- require extensive time and effort from caretakers; and

- interfere with development of self-awareness and responsibility.

Lovaas Program and Other Compliance Training Programs

One of the most widely recognized behavioral treatment programs that utilizes compliance training procedures is a program developed by Dr. O. Ivar Lovaas. Dr. Lovaas' treatment program contains several unique features which are described in *Teaching Developmentally Disabled Children, The Me Book* (1981). Dr. Lovaas emphasizes the importance of intensive one-to-one teaching at an early age, based in the principles of operant conditioning. Compliance training and operant conditioning are basically the same. Both involve presentation of a specific cue followed by a preplanned consequence in an effort to increase an individual's compliance.

There are numerous published programs that provide compliance training based on operant conditioning principles. *The Sure I Will* program by Dr. William Jenson (Rhodes, Jenson, & Reavis, 1993) is another example of a published compliance training format.

It is important to note that compliance training can be provided as part of behavioral intervention programs in schools or at home. Educators or caregivers trained in the implementation of intensive behavioral intervention can provide the strategies needed by each individual. The greatest difference between this type of approach and the intensive intervention provided through the Lovaas program is the amount of time and resources dedicated to individual treatment. Lovaas' treatment strongly suggests that intervention encompass most of the child's waking hours, about forty hours per week. This can involve a significant commitment of time and financial resources. Options involving the use of compliance training at a less intense level do not present as significant a demand on resources. Ultimately, decisions regarding the appropriateness of compliance training and the type and intensity of the training provided depends on the unique needs and circumstances of each individual.

 The options for compliance training can range from:

- no compliance training;

- compliance training as an integral part of daily programming;

- compliance training presented in a scheduled, discrete-trial format;

- intensive, frequently scheduled compliance training; to

- intensive, one-to-one training using the Lovaas method.

Compliance training is a critical part of learning for individuals who have limited awareness of safety risks and who display very limited self-regulation. As the individual becomes more socially aware and displays greater skills in self-management, direct compliance training should be replaced by the development of visual cueing systems that allow for greater independence and responsibility.

 **CAUTION!**

- Avoid devoting so much time and effort toward compliance training that other areas of need, such as communication, social interaction, and other social skills, are ignored.

- Avoid "overtraining" compliance to the degree that an individual will not attempt to spontaneously initiate a response without a specific cue.

- Avoid settling for teaching the easiness of simple obedience, instead of focusing on the importance of teaching independence and responsibility.

- Avoid coercing or harassing the individual into compliance.

CHAPTER

Eight

Decreasing Unwanted Behaviors

Punishment vs. Negative Consequences

Strategies used to decrease inappropriate behaviors are called "punishers". By definition, punishment must *decrease* the behavior it follows.

 An experience that follows a behavior is a punishment if the behavior it follows happens:

- less often,

- for shorter periods of time, or

- with less intensity.

 Punishment is designed so that it follows an unwanted behavior and causes enough discomfort that the person, in an effort to avoid discomfort, avoids engaging in the behavior.

 What seems punishing to most people may be reinforcing to others.

CASE EXAMPLE

Belinda had numerous sensory issues which interfered with learning. She enjoyed deep pressure and firm touch. She did not like loud noises. Belinda bit her peers. Everytime she bit someone, she was punished with a spanking. Belinda's biting behavior was increasing. Was the spanking a punishment for Belinda's biting? Were there other ways to reduce the biting? In this situation, the spanking (although it seems painful) was functioning as a reinforcer, NOT a punishment. Biting increased with the use of spanking as a punisher.

The family's parent trainer taught the parents to use a punisher which did not satisfy Belinda's need for deep pressure and touch. The family was taught to respond to Belinda's biting by clapping hands together loudly and saying "NO BITE!!!" The words were said loudly and firmly, without emotion or yelling. This was achieved by dropping the voice two octaves. After consistently experiencing this for two weeks, Belinda seldom bit others.

CAUTION!

Don't assume something is a punisher because most people find it uncomfortable. It may not be punishing for that particular person or effective for the specific behavior being addressed.

 To determine if a consequence is a punisher, ask the following questions:

- Did the consequence follow the behavior?

- Did the behavior happen less often, for a shorter period of time, or at a less intense level?

If the answer to both questions is "yes", then the consequence is a punisher. If either answer is "no", then the punishing quality is still undetermined.

How do I know what punishers to use?

When using punishment, always select the strategy that decreases unwanted behaviors and is the least intrusive. It is important to realize that punishment carries a risk of psychological and sometimes physical harm due to the element of discomfort involved. Select consequences that carry the smallest risk of physical or psychological harm.

 Punishment may involve some form of:

- social discomfort;

- emotional discomfort; or

- physical discomfort.

CASE EXAMPLE

Terry kept bothering his sister while she was doing her homework. Terry's father warned him to stop bothering her, but Terry continued. Finally, after two warnings, Terry's father sent him to his room for 10 minutes. Terry's father used sending him to his room as a punishment.

CASE EXAMPLE

Billy did not want to take his medication. He looked at his mother while slowly and deliberately pouring the glass of water she provided, onto the kitchen floor. She calmly gave Billy another glass of water and prompted him to take his pill. She then made Billy wipe up the spill and mop the kitchen floor. His mother used cleaning the kitchen floor as a punishment.

 Punishment that entails social or emotional discomfort usually addresses thoughts or feelings associated with the misbehavior.

 Socially-based punishers may include:

- being unable to earn reinforcers;
- removing social attention;
- correcting a behavior;
- losing an object or activity that is valued; or
- requiring participation in a specified activity.

CASE EXAMPLE

Marty enjoyed visiting. Sometimes he made offensive comments. When Marty made an offensive comment, his co-workers stopped conversing with him. Marty decreased the frequency of offensive comments. His co-workers used socially-based punishment as a consequence to decrease this behavior.

CAUTION!

Some examples of socially-based punishers which carry a high risk of harm and should be avoided for persons with autism, include:

- long periods of time-out ("Go to your room for the rest of the day!");

- sarcasm ("You can't even do that?");

- humiliating remarks ("You are so slow.");

- threats ("If you touch that, I'll beat you!");

- rejection ("I can't stand the sight of you. Just get away from me.");

- lengthy punishments ("You're grounded for the next month!"); or

- severe or harsh punishments ("You have to scrub the entire kitchen floor with a toothbrush.").

 Punishers that involve physical discomfort are usually sensory-based.

Sensory-based punishments may tend to be more effective with individuals who are more severely challenged and do not respond to socially-based strategies.

 Sensory-based punishment can be dangerous and should only be considered when:

- other strategies are ineffective;

- the misbehavior is seriously harmful; and

- the person is unresponsive to other forms of punishment.

Sensory-based punishment involves following an unwanted behavior with consequences that use sounds, tastes, smells, looks, or touch to cause discomfort.

 **When using sensory-based aversives, always pair the aversive with a simple social correction.**

Pairing a sensory-based aversive with simple correction teaches the learner to respond to a socially-based strategy which is less intrusive. This helps fade-out the use of the more intrusive strategy.

 Sensory-based aversives may include:

- loud or irritating noises;

- foul tasting substances;

- unpleasant visual stimuli; and

- uncomfortable forms of touch, tactile sensations or movement.

 CASE EXAMPLE

Cruz, a fourteen year old, frequently bit others. Once he visually selected a victim, he chased the person until he bit that person. The staff at Cruz's school spent the majority of each day physically stopping Cruz from biting staff and students. Cruz was nonverbal, noncompliant and had minimal prosocial skills with no academic skills. He did not like to be touched.

Part of Cruz's behavioral intervention involved touching him with a small vibrator and firmly saying "No bite!" everytime he began to pursue a potential victim. Cruz's teacher and paraprofessionals began carrying small vibrators attached to wristbands or waistbands for immediate access. Within one week, Cruz stopped pursuing victims as soon as he heard the sound of the vibrator. Within three weeks, he stopped pursuing a victim as soon as he heard "No bite." The staff no longer needed to carry the vibrators. Within six weeks, Cruz stopped biting people at school.

DOUBLE CAUTION!

Using punishment can be very dangerous!

- Avoid using any aversives which carry a risk of physical or psychological harm.

- Avoid imposing tissue damage in any way.

- Be aware of any allergies, medical conditions or other physical or psychological sensitivities before resorting to using aversives.

- Consult with a behavior management expert who is familiar with autism before using strategies which carry any risk of physical or psychological harm.

- CORPORAL PUNISHMENT SHOULD NOT BE USED.

It can be very tempting to use these strategies without considering the risks, since most of the strategies are relatively easy to apply. Although most sensory-based strategies are readily available and easy to use, it is *CRITICAL* that the benefits outweigh the risks involved. If at all possible, *use less intrusive strategies*.

 Punishment used without reinforcing acceptable behaviors can lead to even more negative behaviors due to:

- increased anxiety levels, confusion, fear, anger and difficulty learning, all of which can fuel problem behaviors;

- increased avoidance behaviors including running away, self-stimulation and noncompliance, since the person's efforts are focused on avoiding discomfort; and

- increased focusing on stopping the misbehavior, instead of teaching the preferred behaviors.

 **CAUTION!**
Avoid using punishment alone to change behaviors.

- Punishment does NOT teach acceptable behaviors.

- Persons exposed to excessive amounts of punishment or overstimulation, may become desensitized to the discomfort of punishment.

- *Always* include strategies for increasing preferred behaviors when using punishment to change behavior.

If punishment is harmful and should not be used, how can bad behaviors be stopped without using punishment?

Punishment is commonly thought of as something very negative, uncomfortable, or painful. A more effective way to address unwanted behaviors may be to distinguish between simple punishment, as it is commonly perceived, and "negative consequences" which address inappropriate behaviors as "teachable moments." If difficulty in academic learning is viewed as a problem to be remediated, then inappropriate behaviors should be viewed as behavioral problems to be remediated. The *Boys Town Social Skills Model* (Dowd, & Tierney, 1992) does this in its response sequence for inappropriate behaviors. All staff are taught to include reteaching and practicing of an appropriate response for each inappropriate behavior that warrants a consequence.

 Negative consequences are actions which follow a behavior and serve to decrease that behavior while including a teaching component.

Negative consequences may or may not cause some discomfort, but most importantly, unlike simple punishment, negative consequences increase the probability that the person will choose an appropriate response in the future by pairing punishment with cues for appropriate responses.

 Many commonly used punishments can be refined into negative consequences by:

- providing a teaching component;

- being logically or naturally related to the behavior;

- increasing the possibility that a more appropriate behavior will be used in the future under similar circumstances; and

- not appearing unfair or illogical to the recipient.

The following negative consequences that are frequently effective for persons with autism meet the above criteria by including an instructional component, by being logically related to the behavior, or by increasing the possibility of more appropriate behaviors occurring in the future:

- ignoring inappropriate behavior while directing the person to a more acceptable behavior;

- correcting misbehavior, while directing the person to a more acceptable behavior;

- managing stimulation levels;

- adjusting prompts;

- imposing various forms of short time-out;

- losing time from a preferred activity;

- participating in social skills assignments;

- failing to earn reinforcers;

- losing reinforcers already earned;

- imposing restitution; and

- practicing correct responses.

When selecting a specific strategy to use as a negative consequence, be sure it is naturally or logically related to the misbehavior.

CASE EXAMPLE

Robbie hit Ms. Smith with his toy. Ms. Smith firmly said "No hit. Time-out." She took the toy away for 10 seconds. After 10 seconds, she returned the toy to Robbie. Ms. Smith used a negative consequence that was logically related to Robbie's misbehavior. Using <u>short</u> time frames allowed for frequent opportunities to pair the consequence with the misbehavior.

CASE EXAMPLE

Kathy was mad at her sister Gina. She ran into Gina's room and broke her computer monitor. Kathy's parents considered spanking her and grounding her for two weeks. They realized this might result in an excessive amount of anger, resentment, and behavior problems during the time she was grounded. Additionally, grounding did not teach an acceptable behavior. Instead, they had Kathy write an apology to Gina, make a plan for responding appropriately the next time she was mad at someone, and loan Gina the monitor from her own computer. Kathy's parents devised a plan for Kathy to earn money for a new monitor for Gina by demonstrating acceptable behavior during the next several weeks. After a week of acceptable behavior, Kathy was allowed to borrow Gina's computer for very short periods of time if she asked appropriately. Instead of using simple punishment, Kathy's parents used several negative consequences logically related to her misbehavior. These consequences increased the probability that Kathy would respond in a more acceptable way when she was mad.

CASE EXAMPLE

During storytime at school, Barry continually touched his peers. After one warning, the paraprofessional had Barry quietly sit in a chair two feet away from the group for the remainder of the story. Barry could still see and hear the story, but could not touch anyone. A negative consequence logically related to Barry's behavior was being used. This strategy taught acceptable responses since Barry could still watch his peers model acceptable behaviors, and he could still benefit from the activity.

Ignoring misbehavior

My daughter loves attention and engages in bad behaviors to demand my attention. How can I get her to choose more acceptable behaviors without giving attention to the bad behavior?

Individuals with limited social skills often learn to use negative behaviors to obtain attention. The key to increasing preferred behaviors is to provide reinforcement *ONLY* following desired behaviors. If attention is reinforcing, then *ONLY* provide social attention when the desired behavior has occurred. This strategy is called *planned ignoring*, since ignoring the misbehavior is usually planned in advance.

CASE EXAMPLE

Macy had been taught how to greet people. However, he frequently attempted to obtain attention by putting his face two inches from another person's face and staring at the person. So long as he was looked at or spoken to, he continued with this behavior. Ms. Jones was visiting Macy's class. When she arrived, Macy immediately put his face within two inches of her face. She ignored this behavior by not looking at him and not speaking to him. Within one minute, Macy moved out of her personal space. Ms. Jones immediately looked at Macy and greeted him. Ms. Jones used planned ignoring in response to Macy's misbehavior.

Simply ignoring a misbehavior can result in the person doing the behavior more often, more intensely, or for longer periods of time. This is highly probable when the experience of the behavior itself provides some amount of pleasure. Be prepared to deal with an increase in the misbehavior when using this as a strategy. Some behaviors will eventually decrease or stop when consistently ignored long enough.

CASE EXAMPLE

When Gary self-stimulates by flapping his hands in front of his face, his mother uses planned ignoring by not telling Gary to stop flapping. She simply acts as though Gary is not flapping. Gary's flapping continues to occur and some days happens more often.

CAUTION!

Be very careful when using ignoring strategies with persons with autism. Some behaviors will worsen to the point that they can no longer be ignored.

If less severe forms of the behavior are ignored and the behavior worsens to the point that it demands attention, there is a strong possibility that the more severe behavior will be used again to obtain attention. This also occurs with behaviors that eventually lead to obtaining a desired object or action.

CASE EXAMPLE

Joey quickly and very lightly bumped his head on the floor or wall when bored or frustrated. His mother decided to ignore this behavior. Joey began hitting his head harder and for longer periods of time. His mother worried that he might hurt himself, so she held him. The next time Joey wanted his mother's attention, he hit his head on the floor very hard until she held him.

When working with persons who engage in behaviors due to a limited repertoire of appropriate skills, ignoring **MUST** be accompanied by cues which prompt the individual to an appropriate behavior.

CASE EXAMPLE

To continue with the previous example of Gary, when he flapped his hands, his mother ignored the flapping and directed him to a more appropriate activity. She responded by dropping her voice two octaves and quietly saying, "Gary, play with your water toy." She supplemented this cue with a visual prompt by either pointing to the water toy or handing the toy to Gary. This form of responding to Gary's behavior was especially effective, since Gary's mother cued him to an activity which he enjoyed and which provided similar sensory input as the misbehavior. The activity which she selected was also incompatible with the misbehavior; that is, he could not flap his hands and play with the water toy at the same time.

CASE EXAMPLE

Maggie, an adult, worked as a stocker at a community bookstore. Maggie became anxious and flapped her hands when too many people were near. Sometimes Maggie became anxious while stocking shelves when the bookstore was more crowded than usual. At these times, she stopped shelving books and flapped her hands. In an effort to regulate this behavior, a shiny charm bracelet was given to Maggie to wear when she worked at the bookstore. This bracelet, her "work jewelry," made noise if moved excessively. When she began handflapping, the shininess and sound of the bracelet caught her attention, and cued her to begin working again. This example used self-regulation techniques that consisted of pairing planned ignoring with redirection to an appropriate task.

Differential reinforcement

Replacing inappropriate behaviors with more acceptable responses increases desired behaviors without giving misbehavior too much attention.

Differential reinforcement uses positive reinforcement for acceptable behavior while ignoring misbehaviors.

Differential reinforcement can be used to increase:

- acceptable responses that are alternatives to the misbehavior (DRA);
- acceptable responses that are incompatible with the misbehavior (DRI); or
- any other acceptable behaviors (DRO).

CASE EXAMPLE

To continue with the previous example of Joey, his mother realized that he was learning to bang his head so she held him. She also realized that headbanging might increase to the point of being dangerous. She decided to teach Joey a more acceptable way to request being held. Everytime Joey started banging his head, she walked over to him and prompted him to hold out his arms. When he held out his arms, she picked him up. She also prompted him to request being picked up when he was not banging his head. In this way, he wouldn't conclude that headbanging is part of the sequence of requesting to be held. Joey's mother used differential reinforcement of an alternative behavior (DRA). Holding out his arms to request being held is an acceptable alternative to headbanging.

CASE EXAMPLE

When Trina sat in someone's lap, she usually pulled the person's hair. Trina's grandfather encouraged her to play "Pattycake" and other games using her hands, whenever she sat in his lap. He reinforced Trina with attention when she played these games. When Trina pulled his hair, he simply directed her to use her hands to play a game. Trina's grandfather used differential reinforcement of incompatible behaviors (DRI). Trina could not use her hands to play games and pull hair at the same time.

CASE EXAMPLE

Leslie learned to gag to obtain attention. Whenever Leslie made herself gag, her mother withheld social attention. Her mother made sure that Leslie was physically safe anytime she started to gag, but did not provide social attention as part of keeping her safe. Anytime Leslie was not gagging, her mother gave her social attention. Leslie's mother was using differential reinforcement of other behaviors (DRO).

Behavioral momentum

Another way to use differential reinforcement is through the use of an approach known as behavioral momentum. To use behavioral momentum, ignore and redirect the misbehavior by guiding the misbehavior into a more appropriate response. Initially follow along with the problem behavior, then guide that behavior into one that is more acceptable. The unique aspect of this approach is that, instead of interrupting or stopping a behavior, the caretaker uses the force that is driving that behavior, to direct the person's energy and efforts toward a more appropriate response.

CASE EXAMPLE

Cody was preparing to go to bed. He heard the TV and walked toward the den where the TV was located. Cody's mom knew that he would resist her efforts to send him back to his room once he had focused his attention on the TV. Instead of trying to interrupt or stop this behavior, she cued him to go and turn off the TV for bedtime. Cody turned off the TV and went to bed. His mom used behavioral momentum by refraining from interrupting his behavior. Instead, she used the driving force behind his behavior to guide him into the desired response.

CASE EXAMPLE

Behavioral momentum strategies can be used to help young children overcome difficulties falling asleep. When a child was restless at naptime, his aide laid on the floor next to him and began audibly breathing in unison with his breathing. Then, she gradually slowed her breathing rate and his breathing rate continued in unison with hers. The slowed breathing rate calmed the child, who quickly fell asleep. This approach has helped several children overcome difficulties falling asleep.

CAUTION!

When ignoring a behavior, be sure to only ignore the behavior, <u>not</u> the person.

CAUTION!

When ignoring a behavior, commitment to consistently ignore the behavior is critical or more severe forms of the behavior may accidentally be learned.

There are some behaviors that have the potential to become so severe as to be harmful. If ignoring a behavior is not resulting in improvement, then redirect to a task or a more appropriate behavior, along with ignoring the misbehavior.

CAUTION!

Planned ignoring will <u>not</u> work if the individual is able to receive reinforcement from other sources.

In a class of boys with behavior disorders, ignoring cursing and vulgar language did not work. Other interventions had to be used. Although the teacher was ignoring the language, the other boys in the class were not. The speaker was getting reinforcement from the laughing and giggling of the others in the classroom which the teacher could not control. For some individuals with autism, the reinforcement of certain sensory behaviors may be so great that planned ignoring will not work because the source of the reinforcement cannot be removed.

 For ignoring to be most effective, ignore the misbehavior consistently AND:

- prompt to the desired task;
- prompt to another task;
- prompt to a more appropriate behavior;
- prompt to a more appropriate activity; or
- prompt to an activity which is incompatible with the misbehavior.

  Remember to incorporate visual prompts!

CAUTION!
When using planned ignoring, avoid:

- failing to redirect the person to a more appropriate behavior or activity; and

- redirecting persons to behaviors or activities which can be done while they continue to engage in the misbehavior.

Time-out

Time-out is defined as a period of time in which a person cannot access reinforcers. There are numerous forms of time-out. When planning time-out as an intervention, be sure to keep in mind the definition of time-out (no reinforcers). It is not unusual for some forms of time-out to actually function as time away from stimulation. When this happens, time-out can be highly reinforcing for some persons with autism. Therefore, careful planning is essential for effective use of time-out.

 When time-out is used correctly:

- beginning and ending the time-out is controlled by an adult;

- no reinforcers are provided during time-out;

- social interaction does not occur; and

- **talking is only for providing prompts.**

Time-Out-On-The-Spot (TOOTS)

Most people think of time-out as a person being removed from a situation. However, there are other forms of time-out which do not involve sending a person to an isolated corner or room. TOOTS is a time-out strategy which involves minimal action, yet can be very effective, especially with persons who are developmentally young or more severely challenged.

 <u>TOOTS</u> consists of a short, mild time-out which is performed without moving the person to another area.

One form of *TOOTS* is to have individuals place their heads down on the table, desk or in their lap while the adult calmly counts out loud to 10.

> ### CASE EXAMPLE
> When Josh screamed, Ms. Jones firmly said "Josh, no scream. Time-out. Head down. 1-2-3-4-5-6-7-8-9-10." Then Josh was cued to sit up and the activity continued with no further discussion of the behavior or the time-out. Ms. Jones was using <u>TOOTS</u> in response to Josh's screaming.

Another similar form of *TOOTS* consists of removing materials to a count of 10.

> ### CASE EXAMPLE
> When Jenson threw a puzzle piece, his mom said "Jenson, no throw. Time-out (she removed the puzzle). 1-2-3-4-5-6-7-8-9-10." Then she replaced the puzzle and the activity continued with no further discussion of the behavior or the time-out. His Mom used <u>TOOTS</u> in response to his object throwing.

A different version of *TOOTS* involves the caretaker shutting down to a count of 10.

CASE EXAMPLE

When Robbie whined, grabbed and pulled on his sister one evening, she firmly said "Robbie, no grab. Time out." She then turned her head away from Robbie and counted to 10 out loud. Then she returned her attention to Robbie with no further discussion of the behavior or the time-out. Robbie's sister was using <u>TOOTS</u> in response to inappropriate attention-seeking.

TOOTS is most effective when used in conjunction with positive reinforcement strategies aimed at increasing desired behaviors.

Contingent Observation

Contingent observation is a form of time-out that requires minimal action and does not totally exclude the individual from ongoing activities.

Contingent observation involves moving the person 1-3 feet away from the activity or people for a short period of time. The person still faces the ongoing activity and may be included in a limited manner with minimal reinforcement. Keep time frames short, preferably two minutes or less for younger, more involved individuals and ten minutes or less for persons who are higher functioning.

CASE EXAMPLE

Nathan had been bothering his peers during circle time. He did not respond to prompts and continued to bother those around him. The teacher calmly walked over to Nathan and said "Nathan, no bothering others. Time-out." She moved Nathan's chair two feet outside of the circle. Nathan was still facing the other children and could see and hear the story. After Nathan had sat appropriately for one minute, he returned to the circle. There was no further discussion regarding his behavior. This procedure was repeated whenever Nathan bothered others. Nathan's teacher used contingent observation.

Isolated time-out

Isolated time-out, a more restrictive form of time-out, involves sending the person to an isolated spot, removed from peers and activities, but still in the same room or general area.

CASE EXAMPLE

Marshall hit his sister while they were watching television. Marshall's father had him sit in a chair in the corner for five minutes. He used isolated time-out.

Exclusionary time-out

The most restrictive form of time-out is exclusionary time-out. This procedure consists of removing persons to an area where they are totally excluded from peers and ongoing activities.

CAUTION!

When using time-out procedures, especially isolated or exclusionary time-out, be aware that they may actually be functioning as time away from stimulation.

If this is suspected, then refine behavior interventions to include early use of de-stimulation procedures. Use de-stimulation strategies *before* misbehavior occurs. Save actual time-out procedures as a negative consequence for *after* misbehavior occurs.

CAUTION!

When misbehavior occurs, it may be necessary for the person to use de-stimulation strategies to calm down, before imposing negative consequences.

However, negative consequences still need to follow the misbehavior. If there is a significant delay, be sure to use visual strategies to depict the negative consequences owed. Failure to do this can result in the person not making a connection between the misbehavior and the negative consequences.

CASE EXAMPLE

Lena was argumentative and defiant at the dinner table. She screamed and refused to eat. She began hitting at her brother for no apparent reason. Her father sent her to the spare bedroom for 15 minutes. After 15 minutes of no screaming, he told Lena she could rejoin the family. Lena's father used exclusionary time-out. He also allowed Lena to calm down before beginning the actual 15 minute time-out.

Delayed Time Loss

There are situations in which usual time-out procedures are not feasible. In these situations, it is possible to delay the time loss incurred. This approach is effective with persons who are higher functioning and who are able to benefit from delayed reinforcement strategies. To be effective, visual cues must be used as a reminder of the time loss owed. Delayed time loss needs to occur in the same day it was imposed.

CASE EXAMPLE

Dean and his family were returning from a shopping trip. Dean spit on his sister. His mother said "No spit! Time-out at home." She showed Dean the symbol depicting time-out at home. She had learned to carry a few basic picture symbols on family outings. When the family arrived home, she showed the symbol to Dean and had him sit in time-out. She used a visual cue to delay time loss imposed for a misbehavior.

CAUTION!

Imposing delayed time loss without using visual cues may result in:

- confusion,

- anger,

- resentment,

- misunderstanding, and

- inaccurate conclusions regarding behavior and resultant consequences.

Response Cost

Response cost describes a variety of negative consequences that involves imposing a loss of a preferred object or activity, or participation in a required task as a result of misbehavior. Response cost can be an effective strategy for use with persons who are higher functioning. Uses for this approach are very limited for persons who are developmentally younger or more severely challenged.

 Some forms of response cost are:

- simple correction;

- overcorrection;

- positive practice;

- loss of a valued object or activity; and

- loss of earned reinforcers.

 **Simple correction consists of requiring a person to restore the environment to its original condition, following misbehavior.**

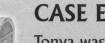

CASE EXAMPLE

Tonya was toilet trained using a schedule. Sometimes, when engaged in a task, she refused to comply with cues to use the toilet. Usually when this happenned, she wet herself. When she wet herself, her mother required Tonya to clean herself and change clothes. Tonya's mother is using simple correction.

Overcorrection goes a step beyond simple correction by requiring the person to also do a related task, in addition to the simple correction.

CASE EXAMPLE

Andre did not like certain foods. At the dinner table, he scooped the foods he found offensive onto the table and mashed them until they were unrecognizable. This was very offensive to his roommates. The staff reminded him of the table rules. After dinner they required Andre to clean up the mess he made. They also required Andre to clean and disinfect the table, chairs and the floor. The staff used overcorrection by requiring Andre to complete other tasks related to the misbehavior.

Positive practice requires the person to practice a behavior that is an appropriate alternative to the misbehavior.

CASE EXAMPLE

Lamont was learning to greet people by waving instead of hitting. On the way to the playground, Lamont hit a friend as they passed in the hallway. Ms. Wilson required him to stand still and wave to greet the next five people who passed by. Ms. Wilson used positive practice as a negative consequence.

CAUTION!

When using techniques such as overcorrection or positive practice, be sure the required actions are logically or naturally related to the misbehavior.

If not, the teaching component is missing. Without the teaching component, the procedure is merely a punishment and can result in resentment or anger, instead of improved behavior.

 Response cost can also entail loss of a valued object or activity.

 **CASE EXAMPLE**
Ricky refused to get ready for bed. He continued to play video games, despite repeated prompts by his mother. She removed the game and did not allow Ricky to play with it the next day. Ricky's mother used a form of response cost.

CAUTION!
When taking away a valued object or activity, be sure to clarify how long the loss will last.

Keep the time relatively short (preferably one day or less). It is also effective to attach a behavioral requirement instead of a time frame. For example, Ricky's mother may have said the game would be returned after Ricky complied with getting ready for bed on two different occasions. This encourages the person to be compliant, thus avoiding angry defiance. Remember to use visual cues.

 A highly intrusive form of response cost is loss of reinforcers that have already been earned.

Use this strategy sparingly! This is an appropriate negative consequence for use with very serious misbehavior only. Ideally, it should only be used following physical aggression to self or others, or property destruction. Other less serious misbehaviors should be consequated with *failure to earn* a reinforcer, not loss of a previously earned reinforcer.

CASE EXAMPLE

Jared used a token system. When he was compliant, he earned tokens. When he was disruptive, he did not earn a token. When he was in time-out, he could not earn tokens. If he hit or bit, he lost three tokens. Jared's program used response cost for aggression.

CASE EXAMPLE

Lenora worked hard all day and earned three cookies for snacktime. While walking to the snack table, she used loud profanity. Miss Jackson placed her in time-out. Lenora missed snacktime. Miss Jackson put the cookies in a clear bag and placed them on Lenora's picture schedule for the next day, above the symbol for snacktime. The next day she ate the cookies at snacktime. Lenora still kept the cookies she earned, but collected them at a time when her behavior was appropriate. Miss Jackson knew that losing an earned reinforcer should be reserved for very serious misbehaviors, so she selected a different negative consequence. She also knew that Lenora needed visual cues to remind her that she did not lose the cookies, but collecting them was delayed.

CAUTION!

Overusing loss of earned reinforcers can result in:

- anger,
- resentment,
- loss of interest in working for reinforcers, and
- failure to improve behavioral performance.

CAUTION!

When responding to inappropriate behaviors using punishment or negative consequences, it is critical to include positive reinforcement for acceptable behaviors as part of the intervention plan. Punishment or negative consequences alone will not improve behaviors.

CAUTION!

When planning behavioral interventions, be sure to consider the long-term impact of the strategies and the behaviors being learned. If the strategies or behaviors might contribute to problems in the future, select a different strategy or behavior that will have a lifelong, positive impact.

Consider the case example of Belinda on page 159. A complete behavioral program was needed to address her problems. The plan for Belinda should include a functional analysis of the biting along with a reinforcer assessment and information regarding Belinda's sensory issues, communication abilities and cognitive functioning levels. The results of the functional analysis will provide guidance in developing:

1. sensory strategies to address the sensory needs currently being met through spanking;

2. communication strategies to enhance acceptable behaviors to use instead of biting;

3. antecedent control strategies to increase success experiences and decrease agitation;

4. self-regulation strategies;

5. positive reinforcement for using appropriate behaviors, and

6. negative consequences for biting.

If negative consequences for biting are the only strategy used, there is a greater likelihood that an extensive amount of time and numerous biting episodes will need to occur before any progress is noted. Also, if appropriate behaviors, including communication and sensory-related responses are not taught, the likelihood is greater that the biting will merely be replaced by another inappropriate behavior.

Negative consequences can play an important role in behavior intervention plans. However, just as in the example of Belinda, the behavior intervention also needs to include positive strategies for teaching acceptable behaviors and addressing other needs. It is not unusual for positive strategies to make negative consequences unnecessary.

CHAPTER

Nine

Crisis Management and Other Special Problems

When sharing life with persons with autism, one of the most frustrating and stressful challenges is management of crisis situations. With some individuals, crises occur several times daily. With others, crisis situations are rare. The keys to successful management of crisis situations are to plan ahead and be prepared to respond calmly.

 Recognize the potential for possible crisis and plan strategies for managing the situation calmly and safely.

 Minimize the negative impacts of crisis by preparing response plans in advance. Plans need to include:

- identification of the potential crisis behaviors;

- early warning signs that crisis is likely;

- what to do;

- what to say; and

- when and how to obtain assistance.

 CAUTION!

The early warning signs of a possible crisis include:

- increased agitation;

- decreased performance;

- increased attempts to withdraw;

- decreased problem-solving skills;

- increased demands;

- decreased compliance;

- marked change in impulsivity;

- more abrupt body movement; or

- increased muscle tension.

As soon as early warning signs are recognized, intervene using preplanned strategies.

 # CAUTION!

Failure to recognize or respond to the early warning signs of crisis can result in being challenged by more frequent crisis situations.

 In the early warning stages, when a crisis is possible, use the following interventions.

- Reinforce acceptable behaviors and redirect inappropriate behaviors.

- Decrease stimulation.

- Change the environment or the task.

- Use problem-solving strategies.

- Set limits that are reasonable and can be enforced.

- Give choices.

- Do not threaten.

- Increase the use of visual cues.

- Help the person focus attention.

- Recall the crisis plan steps.

- Formulate a plan for obtaining assistance.

- Maintain a nonemotional tone of voice.

- Maintain nonthreatening body language.

CASE EXAMPLE

Mrs. Smith took her two children to a local discount store. During their shopping trip, Denise began to fuss and whine. She stopped following Mrs. Smith's directions and began grabbing items off the shelves. Mrs. Smith knew Denise's behavior could escalate into running away and property destruction. She stopped walking and obtained Denise's attention. She calmly told Denise that she can either follow directions and walk beside Mrs. Smith, or they can leave and go home. Denise agreed to act appropriately. Mrs. Smith assigned her a task on which to focus (pushing the cart, while Mrs. Smith guided it). Mrs. Smith planned how to leave the store with the two children if Denise's misbehavior worsened. Mrs. Smith intervened early to prevent a crisis. However, she still made a plan for managing the situation if a crisis occurred.

CAUTION!

Failure to plan for a possible crisis can result in more difficulties, along with increased risk, when a crisis occurs.

What can I do if responding to the early warning signs does not work?

Sometimes, responding to those early signs does not prevent a crisis from occurring. In the midst of a crisis, the main goals are to maintain everyone's safety and interrupt or diffuse the crisis.

 Use the following interventions during a crisis.

- Be alert, intervene as early as possible.

- Remain calm to aid in clear thinking and to help other persons involved stay calm.

- Assess the element of risk.

- Use the least restrictive means necessary to provide for safety.

- Control the person who is in crisis until that person regains self-control.

- Maintain low stimulation levels.

- Obtain help if needed.

- Only one person should be talking or providing cues to the individual.

- Minimize talking.

- Use visual cues.

- Allow for increased personal space.

- If possible, remove the individual from the situation.

- If possible, minimize the audience.

- Once the individual starts to calm, focus the person's attention.

Occasionally, crisis behaviors may escalate to the point of being physically dangerous. When behaviors present an immediate threat of harm and non-physical management strategies are ineffective, it may become necessary to impose physical intervention.

 Progressive physical interventions include:

- guided walk or other physical activity;

- physical redirection;

- physically blocking the aggression;

- protective gear, such as a helmet (for the individual, not the caretaker!);

- hands held to side;

- chair restraint;

- "bear hug" restraint;

- full four-point restraint; or

- mechanical restraint.

CAUTION!

- Anyone using manual restraint in crisis situations needs to be trained in the correct application of restraint procedures.

- Physical restraint carries a very high risk of physical and psychological harm to all persons involved.

- Avoid using physical restraint as a punishment for inappropriate behaviors. It should only be used to protect from immediate harm, when no other means of intervention can be used effectively.

- Persons who have a need for deep pressure, touch or excitement may actually find physical restraint reinforcing. In such cases, individuals may engage in serious misbehavior, in order to be restrained. If this is suspected, provide acceptable ways for the person to have these needs met, without resorting to serious misbehavior.

- If the behavior that leads to a restraint increases, find another crisis intervention technique or put behavior change strategies in place to decrease the occurrence of that behavior.

CAUTION!

- It is often very easy to physically manage the behaviors of persons who are younger or smaller. Avoid the temptation to do this!

- Physically managing behavior, when not part of a planned systematic cueing strategy, can lead to physical resistance and aggression as the person grows larger and stronger.

CAUTION!

- Crisis management is *not* a strategy for teaching acceptable behaviors.

- Crisis management procedures may tend to serve as reinforcers for the misbehavior.

- Following a crisis, behaviors that may have led to the crisis need to be addressed, using behavior change strategies.

- Crisis situations will continue to occur, if crisis responses are the only behavior interventions used.

- Caretakers who ignore behaviors until crisis situations occur, are at high risk for stress and eventual burnout.

- Caretakers who ignore behavioral issues until crisis situations demand intervention, add to the increased risk for injury or tragedy as the individual becomes larger, stronger or more independent.

Managing meltdowns or catastrophic reactions

 Meltdowns or catastrophic reactions occur when a person is overwhelmed by stimulation from the environment, people, tasks, sensory input or emotions.

Meltdowns or catastrophic reactions may include out-of-control screaming, aggression, runaway, panic attacks, severe withdrawal, or tantrums.

 When managing meltdowns or catastrophic reactions, use the following interventions.

- Intervene early, before behavior worsens.
- Decrease stimulation levels.
- Remain very calm.

- Increase visual cues.

- Be reassuring, positive and supportive.

- Allow for increased personal space.

- Physically intervene only if safety is immediately jeopardized and no other options are available.

- Assist the individual in retreating to a "safe" area, if needed.

The main goal in this type of crisis is to help the person regain self-control by reducing stimulation levels.

CASE EXAMPLE

Elliot was on a field trip to the mall. He was waiting in line to visit Santa, and he was becoming overstimulated. Elliot started screaming. Ms. Anderson calmly reassured him and pointed to a small bench away from most of the other children. He did not respond to her attempts to cue him to cool off and screamed louder and harder. She put her right arm around Elliot's shoulders and, firmly but gently, held his left wrist with her left hand. Then she quickly walked Elliot over to the bench, to sit until he was calm. Ms. Anderson used crisis management techniques to respond to Elliot's meltdown.

Aggression

Aggression can be verbal or physical. When managing aggression, it is very important to realize that the normal human tendency is to respond to aggression with more aggression. Caretakers who share life with a person who displays aggressive behaviors need to learn to suppress those tendencies and calmly use planned strategies to interrupt the aggression and maintain safety. Remember the powerful impact of visual information on persons with autism, when managing crises involving aggression.

What can I do when my one of students is verbally aggressive to another student?

Verbal aggression occurs when someone directs name calling, profanity or threats toward another person. Simply using profanity or other offensive language does not create verbal aggression. To be considered as verbal aggression, the language must be directed at someone in a threatening manner.

 Interrupting verbal aggression is an important step toward averting further aggression or crisis.

 Do not ignore verbal aggression thinking it will go away. Instead, respond by using some of the following procedures.

- Calmly, but firmly move between the persons involved (caretakers should avoid endangering themselves).

- Redirect the aggressor or the intended victim so they cannot readily see one another.

- Redirect the focus onto another activity.

  Carefully monitor any further interactions between the parties.

- Impose appropriate negative consequences per the aggressor's behavior intervention plan.

The main goal during this crisis is to break the visual contact and provide a new focus.

CASE EXAMPLE

Jason was playing a portable video game when Mark walked over and tried to take it from him. Mark verbally threatened to hit Jason. Mr. Johnson calmly, but quickly, walked over and stepped in between Mark and Jason. He took the video game out of Jason's hand and held the game aside while he directed Mark to go sit at the table on the other side of the room. He directed Jason to sit at a particular desk, far away from Mark. He then returned the video game to Jason and praised him for responding to Mark in an acceptable manner. Mr. Johnson assigned a task to Mark. He also imposed a negative consequence for the misbehavior, once Mark was calm. Mr. Johnson interrupted the verbal aggression before it escalated. He broke the visual contact and provided a new focus. He waited until Mark was calm before imposing a negative consequence.

What is physical aggression?

Physical aggression consists of any physical action applied to a person or object with the potential to inflict harm or damage.

 Physical aggression includes:

- kicking,
- hitting,
- spitting,
- pinching,
- biting,
- poking,
- grabbing, pulling or pushing,
- fighting,
- property damage,
- throwing objects at a person or property, or
- self-injury.

Intervening in physically aggressive acts is very important to prevent further harm from occurring.

 ## CAUTION!

Sometimes caretakers erroneously think it might be a "good lesson" for an aggressor to simply suffer aggression returned by the victim as a natural consequence.

This can be a very dangerous way to manage physical aggression. This does not ensure safety or interrupt the crisis behavior. It also does not teach acceptable behaviors.

How do I stop physical aggression once it is occurring?

 When physical aggression occurs use the following procedures that apply to the specific situation.

- Be alert.

- Intervene early.

- Identify the aggressive person(s).

- Remember, the caretaker must remain safe to be able to intervene effectively and keep everyone else safe.

- Remain calm and confident.

- Cue the victim to go to a safe area.

- Redirect the aggressor's focus.

- Use the progressive physical interventions as needed.

- Use restraint only for the protection of person or property—never as a punishment for misbehavior.

- Use restraint only for assaultive behaviors, not for physical displays that are not assaultive.

- Do not attempt physical restraint unless it can be done safely and effectively.

- Obtain assistance.

CASE EXAMPLE

Damon began running around the lunch table, trying to steal food from his peers. He began biting at them if they tried to protect their food. Miss Evans placed her arm between Damon and a potential victim just as Damon was biting. He bit her forearm and did not let go. Miss Evans knew that if she pulled away, serious tissue damage could occur. She calmly pushed her arm against Damon's mouth, with her other hand steadying the back of his head. He released his grip. Miss Evans firmly told Damon "No bite. Time out." and escorted him to an isolated area until he was calm for 10 minutes. She also sought first aid for her arm. Miss Evans managed this crisis by remaining calm and using the progressive interventions needed. She sustained only a minor bruise on her arm, for which she obtained assistance. If she had panicked and pulled away, more serious tissue damage might have resulted and Damon might have attacked another victim.

CASE EXAMPLE

Lorenzo was returning from a mainstream PE class. He suddenly tried to attack the aide who was with him, grabbing and hitting at her. Lorenzo was much larger and stronger than the aide, but could not move as quickly. She walked rapidly towards his classroom, remaining alert to his location, while avoiding his personal space. She periodically said, "If you are mad at me, use your words." She supplemented these cues with visual prompts. Upon arriving at his classroom, she remained out of his sight until he was focused on a task. When he was calm, negative consequences were imposed per his behavior intervention plan. The aide realized that Lorenzo might continue to be agitated by being able to see her. She used this to motivate Lorenzo to walk briskly back to a more controlled environment. The aide managed this crisis successfully by remaining calm and alert, providing brisk physical activity, returning to an area where assistance could be readily obtained, using visual cues, and directing Lorenzo's focus to a task.

CASE EXAMPLE

Rodney was upset. He ran over to the living room windows and started beating his fists on the glass. His mother was several feet away, next to the table. She hit the table, making a very loud noise and loudly said "No hit! Sit down!" She gestured by pointing to the floor. Rodney stopped momentarily as he watched his mother's response. In a few seconds, she was beside him and physically directed him to another task, away from any windows. She had Rodney sit down to do this task. Rodney's mother used loud noises to interrupt the dangerous behavior and redirect his focus until she could physically intervene. Rodney was no longer hitting the window, so physical restraint was not necessary for maintaining safety. She redirected Rodney to a different focus in an area where such behavior was less likely to be repeated.

Self-injurious Behavior

Self-injurious behavior (SIB) is a type of physical aggression in which individuals direct aggression toward themselves. SIB is very challenging to manage since the motivations involved are often complex. However, it is still important to intervene when threat of tissue damage is highly probable.

 Some of the more common forms of self-injurious behavior include:

- headbanging;
- hitting self;
- biting self;
- pulling out own hair;
- pinching or scratching self;
- picking at skin or nails; and
- eye gouging.

Protective gear, such as helmets, mittens or arm splints, is frequently used with persons who engage in SIB. Protective gear is appropriate for use in crisis situations, to shield the individual from immediate harm. However, it is important to remember that such devices do not teach acceptable behaviors. Using protective gear does not decrease the *motivation* to engage in SIB; it merely decreases the *opportunities* to do so.

 Any intervention using protective gear needs to be supplemented with interventions for decreasing the tendency to engage in SIB, using appropriate behavior change strategies.

When planning behavior change strategies for SIB, be sure to analyze the role of sensory issues, communication efforts, boredom, frustration, and inappropriate attention-seeking. Redirection to activities that are incompatible with the SIB is a critical part of planning.

CASE EXAMPLE

Nina frequently hit herself on the side of her head with her fist. When she hit herself, her mother calmly and firmly said "Nina, no hit" and directed Nina to an activity that required the use of her hands. If Nina continued hitting herself, her mother repeated the cue and put a helmet on Nina, until she showed no SIB for 15 minutes. During this time, she directed Nina to an activity that required the use of her hands. Then she removed the helmet. She also used positive reinforcement for no SIB. This was repeated as often as necessary. Nina's mother managed the SIB using a calm approach with firm limits and redirecting Nina's focus to an activity that was incompatible with hitting herself. She used protective gear only when needed, instead of continuously.

Temper Tantrums

Temper tantrums can be alarming, highly disruptive and embarrassing. It is very easy to accidentally reward tantrum behaviors in an effort to minimize their negative impact on others.

 The most important goals during a tantrum are to:

- insure safety;

- minimize the audience;

- stay calm, but firm;

- avoid promising rewards once a tantrum has started;

- reduce stimulation levels;

- use visual prompts;

- avoid giving in to the tantrum demands;

- wait out minor tantrums;

- interrupt major tantrums in the early stages;

- if necessary and able to be done safely, escort the person to a quieter place;

- help the person focus attention on something else; and

- after the crisis is over, develop an intervention plan to address tantrums, using behavior change strategies.

Although plenty of tantrums occur at home and school, the risk of tantrums is often greater in the community. This is due to increased stimulation levels, changes in routines and the power of having an audience. Make a plan for preventing and managing tantrum behaviors *before* one is needed. This will prevent accidentally reinforcing tantrum behaviors by giving in to demands or offering rewards.

CASE EXAMPLE

Maggie enjoyed going to the zoo. However, she became overstimulated and tired after the first hour. When it was time to leave, she began to tantrum, demanding to stay at the zoo. Several people were staring and whispering. Some of them tried to calm Maggie. Her mother politely told them that an audience made Maggie more upset. She then directed her attention to Maggie, who ignored her mother's cues to sit on a nearby bench. Her mother escorted her to the bench, away from others. She calmly, but firmly, told Maggie that it was time to go home to begin cooking dinner. She cued Maggie to choose between three items for dinner. They planned dinner as they walked to the car. Maggie's mother managed this crisis by reducing the audience effects and stimulation levels. She directed Maggie's focus. She avoided the temptation to offer Maggie a reward to stop the tantrum. However, when she plans for their next outing, she will shorten the trip and offer Maggie a reinforcer for "using good manners" during their outing.

Self-stimulatory Behaviors

Many persons with autism engage in some ftype of self-stimulation. Self-stimulation comes in a variety of forms, including verbal and motor stereotyped behaviors. An individual may engage in self-stimulation, regardless of the social context or situational appropriateness.

 Verbal stimulation may include:

- repetition of words or phrases, regardless of meaning;

- repeating jingles or songs excessively; or

- repeating data information such as historical dates, weather reports, and phone numbers excessively.

Physical self-stimulation may include:

- arm-flapping;

- jumping excessively;

- repeatedly grimacing;

- rocking;

- hand-flapping;

- finger-flicking;

- twirling;

- blinking;

- headbanging;

- repetitive, complex body movements;

- preoccupation with parts of objects, such as spinning wheels of toy cars;

- repetitive feeling of textures of objects; or

- attachment to unusual objects, such as carrying a rubberband or string.

Self-stimulation increases in boring or nonstimulating environments. With some individuals, it also increases during times of overstimulation. The individual may use the stereotyped behaviors to block out environmental stimulation. Most people engage in some forms of self-stimulation, such as wiggling feet, pulling hair and tapping fingers. However, persons with autism often engage in self-stimulation to the point that it interferes with learning and social situations. When persons are intensely focused on self-stimulating behaviors, they miss important cues and learning opportunities.

 **In learning and social situations, interrupting self-stimulation provides increased opportunities for learning and social interaction.**

In nonlearning environments, self-stimulation should be allowed. One approach that is effective is to reinforce task completion with short periods of time for self-stimming behaviors.

 Use the following strategies when managing self-stimulation behavior.

- Interrupt self-stimming only when in a learning environment.

- Interrupt self-stimming by redirecting the person to another activity.

- Direct the person to an activity that is highly interesting.

- Direct the person to an activity that is incompatible with the self-stimming behavior.

CASE EXAMPLE

Zach was walking around, rocking and flapping his hands. Ms. Lowry did not address the self-stimming behavior directly. Instead she directed Zach to his work area and cued him to complete his assigned tasks. When Zach finished his sequence of tasks, he collected a reinforcer. His reinforcer was spending five minutes alone. Sometimes when he was alone he self-stimmed. If he self-stimmed during reward time, Ms. Lowry did not interrupt or redirect him. Ms. Lowry managed the self-stimulation by using planned ignoring while interrupting the behavior. She directed him to activities that were interesting, rewarding and incompatible with the self-stimming behavior. She used self-stimming behavior as a reinforcer for work completion.

 **CAUTION!**

Avoid interrupting self-stimulation without directing the person to a more acceptable behavior.

Running Away

There are different forms of runaway behavior, each requiring different responses. Runaway behavior can be very frightening for caretakers. It can be frightening or fun and exciting for the person who runs.

 When managing runaway behavior, it is important to distinguish the type of runaway that is occurring.

 Some different categories of runaway behaviors include:

- wandering;

- premeditated, sneaky escapes;

- impulsive darting; and

- dramatic exits.

 Wandering behavior usually involves aimlessly walking away.

 Use the following strategies for managing wandering behavior.

- Maintain visual supervision.

- Direct the person to a more appropriate area.

- Use visual and physical prompts, if needed.

- Once in an appropriate area, direct the person's focus to an interesting task.

- Plan for preventing future wandering.

Respond to premeditated, sneaky escapes using the same strategies for managing wandering. However, once the person has returned to an appropriate area and is able to focus attention, impose a mild negative consequence. Develop a behavior change plan to increase "remaining in assigned areas".

 ## CAUTION!

- Avoid obviously chasing a person who has wandered away or is escaping in a planned manner.

- Always maintain visual supervision.

- When actually chasing the person, do so in a way that is discrete and does not lend excitement or emotional reactions.

- Obtain assistance when needed.

CASE EXAMPLE

Paul was on a shopping trip. He wandered away from the group and found numerous items of interest. Mr. Myers noticed Paul was missing and began looking for him. He stopped a security guard and provided a description of Paul. When Paul was located, Mr. Myers calmly cued him to rejoin the group. He resisted the temptation to fuss at Paul at that time, but firmly reminded him to stay with his friends. During the next outing, Mr. Myers assigned Paul's best friend as his shopping partner. Mr. Myers remained calm and obtained assistance. He used a strategy to help prevent this behavior during the next outing. If this behavior occurs again, a behavior intervention plan should be developed in order to increase "remaining in the assigned area".

A type of runaway behavior that might pose a greater immediate risk is impulsive darting. This type of runaway can be highly dangerous, since the person is usually oblivious to safety.

 Impulsive runaways carry a significant element of danger and should not be ignored.

Impulsive runaways are often a result of overstimulation, agitation, or impulsive reactions to novel cues (usually visual) outside of the assigned area. Some persons have learned to run to create excitement, or they like being chased.

 Use the following strategies when impulsive runaway occurs.

- Be alert and maintain visual supervision.

- Assess risk factors.

- Use unusual noises or movements to interrupt the runaway and obtain the person's attention.

- Firmly cue the person to come to you or to stop and sit.

- Supplement with visual and physical prompts as needed.

- Prompt the person to a physically contained area (for example, inside a fenced area) as quickly as possible.

- Use progressive physical interventions, if required for safety.

- Develop a plan to prevent future runaways.

- Develop a behavior intervention plan to increase remaining in assigned areas.

- Provide compliance training, to increase the likelihood of immediate compliance with demands such as "Come to me" or "Stop and sit." This will increase safety controls if runaways occur in the future.

CASE EXAMPLE

Devon was fascinated with doors. Everytime he saw a door, it served as a visual cue to "open and run". He was oblivious to safety and would dart in front of cars or run down the highway. There was a very busy highway in front of the school, where the roadway was at the top of a steep hill. Drivers could not see what was in the road, on top of the hill, until it was too late to stop. Devon's teachers used many preventive strategies, including visual symbols depicting "no run," posted on classroom and school entry doors at his eye level. They also implemented a behavior management plan using reinforcers and negative consequences, which successfully decreased running away. They also made sure that one adult was always between Devon and the door while activities were going on. However, occasionally, Devon would impulsively dart out of the class. Once he was out, he was near the highway in less than one minute. In response to this occasional but dangerous situation, the school staff worked together as a team to create a coordinated crisis plan. The office secretary kept a walkie-talkie on her desk and served as the communication center during a crisis. The maintenance man, an aide and a bus driver who work at campus during the school day, carried walkie talkies. Anytime Devon left the room unsupervised, the teacher called a "Code blue" to the office, over the intercom. One of the classroom staff was already out of the room, in calm pursuit of Devon. The secretary calmly relayed the "Code blue" over the walkie talkies. The support staff with walkie-talkies went to previously assigned posts. One person went to the road at the bottom of the hill, while another went to the other side of the hill. Their job was to stop traffic, in case Devon reached the road. The third person's job was to pursue Devon and interrupt his running without creating too much excitement or fun. Within a few weeks, Devon's behavior intervention plan eliminated runaway behavior. In the meantime, his safety was ensured without excessive rewards for running away. This served as an example of planning ahead to obtain assistance in a crisis. Such an elaborate plan is difficult to plan and carry out. It should only be used as a back-up plan to ensure safety under unusual circumstances. Always have intensive behavior intervention plans in place to supplement safety plans that place great demands on resources.

CASE EXAMPLE

Another challenging situation involving a boy who was fascinated with doors, was managed using a different approach. Cedric also responded to every door he saw by opening the door and running. He also disliked loud noises. The classrooms and building where he attended school had at least two entry doors per room. Loud alarms were placed on doors leading outside the building. This did not prevent Cedric from going out, but he consistently stopped to cover his ears when the alarm sounded. This gave the staff enough time to physically prevent his opening the door completely and running. The sound of the alarm was paired with an adult firmly saying "No door!" Inside slide locks (approved by the Fire Marshal) were installed on the other doors to prevent Cedric from being reinforced by the natural action of opening the door. These safety features decreased the opportunities for Cedric to open doors successfully, but plans needed to also include strategies for decreasing Cedric's motivation to open doors. A behavior management plan was developed that included compliance training in natural settings to teach door opening only when prompted or given permission. Visual or verbal prompts were used. Using reinforcers and negative consequences, Cedric was taught a routine for door opening that involved checking for prompts, or checking with the nearest adult prior to opening a door. In this situation, management of runaway behavior included crisis strategies that used protective devices and a behavior intervention plan to increase acceptable behaviors.

Dramatic exits

Another type of runaway that can be highly reinforcing for the runner is the dramatic exit. This type of runaway behavior usually follows overstimulation, high levels of anxiety or extreme emotional states. In the dramatic exit, emotions, anxiety or stimulation levels build until the person runs to escape the stressful overload.

 As with other situations involving overstimulation, during dramatic exits, the individual cannot regain self-control until stimulation levels are reduced.

When responding to dramatic exits, incorporate the strategies used for managing meltdowns. The main goal in this type of crisis is to help dramatic runners regain self-control by reducing stimulation levels and directing the runner to a safe place. Once safety is assured, assist the person in using strategies to aid in reducing stimulation levels (refer to Chapter 8).

CASE EXAMPLE

Randy was working on an assignment. He suddenly jumped up, knocked the papers to the floor, and ran out of the room. Ms. Jones followed him, maintaining visual supervision. She quickly assessed the risk level and realized he was heading for a door that led to a fenced area. She decided that physically stopping Randy was unnecessary. She approached him, remaining alert and not violating his increased personal space. Once she was within three feet of Randy, she started walking with him, maintaining his pace. Once she had his attention, she prompted him to walk with her at a brisk pace. Once she noticed that he was beginning to calm down, she prompted him to go to the safe area in the room and gave him a manipulative activity to focus his attention. She posted two pictures on the door of the room, at Randy's eye level. One picture symbolized <u>not running out the door</u>. The second picture was a visual reminder to use the safe place in the room. Ms. Jones managed Randy's dramatic exits by using the least intrusive strategies required to maintain safety. Ms. Jones lessened the risk of increasing Randy's agitation levels, by not violating his personal space. She physically intervened by turning his behavior into a guided walk (she incorporated behavioral momentum). As he calmed and regained a focus, she cued Randy to a safer area and refocused his attention to an activity.

Safety Issues

Some persons with autism are oblivious to safety. They do not realize or understand the potential for harm when engaging in certain behaviors.

Some of the more commonly experienced crisis behaviors related to being unaware of or uninhibited by safety risks include:

• wielding common objects as weapons;

• pica behaviors; and

• climbing.

Weapons

Being oblivious to safety can lead to impulsively wielding common objects as weapons. Often, the person is not aware of the object's potential for harm to self or others. However, lack of safety awareness paired with impulsivity can lead to dangerous situations.

 If a person has a tendency to use objects as weapons, then common household, workplace, or classroom objects that can readily be wielded as weapons should be locked away, out of sight and out of reach.

The imitation behaviors often exhibited in the form of echolalia, can also occur in the form of actions. In today's world, people are frequently exposed to visual images of persons wielding weapons. Easy access to objects that can be used as weapons, can easily turn imitation into crisis.

 Some common objects that can be impulsively used as weapons, include:

• kitchen or pocket knives;

• letter openers;

• lighters or matches;

• kitchen utensils;

- pointed scissors;

- pens and pencils;

- lids from tin cans; or

- tools.

 Besides keeping potential weapons locked away, use the following strategies to prevent harm from other common objects.

- Keep electrical outlets covered.

- Keep all household and cleaning chemicals, cosmetics, all medications, vitamins, and other potentially harmful substances that can be ingested, locked away.

- Keep tools, appliances and other objects which may visually cue imitation attempts, inaccessible.

Managing crisis situations involving dangerous use of an object should be responded to with urgency. Ignoring such behaviors can result in serious tragedy. When intervening with these behaviors, use antecedent control in order to prevent the occurrence of this type of crisis situation. Don't wait until a crisis occurs!

 Use the following strategies when managing crisis situations involving dangerouse use of objects.

- Remain alert but calm.

- Interrupt the behavior as quickly as possible.

- Be extremely cautious when selecting strategies to interrupt the behavior.

- Avoid jeopardizing your own safety or the individual's safety.

- Calmly and firmly prompt the person to place the object in a specific location within immediate reach.

- Supplement with visual prompts.

- Obtain assistance if needed.

- Once no longer in possession of the object, direct the person's attention to another activity or focus.

- As quickly as possible, remove the object so that it is out of sight and inaccessible.

- Develop a plan to prevent this from happening again.

CAUTION!

If the situation does not allow time, due to immediate serious risk to safety, use physical intervention to remove the object. Do this with the least amount of safety risk to the individual or yourself. Use strategies that are the least intrusive, while still maintaining safety.

CASE EXAMPLE

While exploring in the garage, Jeremy found a hammer. He had watched his dad use a hammer. Jeremy went into the house and began hammering on various objects. His mom scolded Jeremy and asked him to give her the hammer. At this point, Jeremy became agitated and began swinging the hammer wildly at his mom. Since Jeremy was a large, strong adolescent, his mom realized that she could not take the hammer away. No one else was at home to help. She moved out of reach and prompted Jeremy to use the hammer on a small nail she noticed on the cabinets. He complied. She then told him hammering was finished and prompted him to put the hammer down and help her with another task. She supplemented these firm prompts with visual cues. As soon as he complied, she took possession of the hammer. Once his attention was focused on a new task, she locked up the hammer. His mom managed this situation using behavioral momentum, by going along with his behavior, then guiding it into more appropriate actions. After assessing the risk, she realized physical intervention was too risky. If safety issues are greater, physical intervention may be appropriate. If Jeremy had the hammer poised above his sister's head, physical intervention would have been appropriate.

Pica

Pica behavior involves eating non-food substances such as dirt, plastic, feces, cigarettes, paint chips or small objects, such as toys. Pica behavior may create dangerous situations due to poisoning, intestinal blockage, parasitic infection, or other physically harmful effects. Theories regarding pica explore causes such as nutritional deficiencies, boredom, and lack of sensory stimulation or appropriate oral activities.

 Use the following strategies for managing pica behaviors.

• Control access to substances being ingested.

• Offer more appropriate oral activities that provide similar sensory stimulation.

• Increase supervision during times and situations where risk for pica is higher.

• Develop a behavior intervention plan that includes antecedent control, positive reinforcement for appropriate behaviors and negative consequences such as short time-outs or overcorrection.

 CASE EXAMPLE

Tiffany was outside playing. Her teacher provided her with interesting activities that she enjoyed. After thirty minutes, Tiffany sat down and began eating dirt. Her teacher interrupted this behavior by firmly saying "no dirt in mouth!" She had Tiffany rinse her mouth and brush her teeth. She then planned to shorten time spent playing outside, in the future. She also decided to have high interest activities at the end of outside time. The teacher was managing Tiffany's pica behaviors by using antecedent control. She also planned to consult with the Occupational Therapist to identify some appropriate oral activities to satisfy Tiffany's sensory needs. Tiffany's teacher shortened playtime and provided interesting activities, especially at the end of playtime, in order to minimize boredom. She used overcorrection as a negative consequence for pica behaviors and included reinforcement for appropriate behaviors in the behavior intervention plan.

Climbing

Some persons with autism will engage in climbing behavior that places them in dangerous situations. Sometimes the climbing is on furniture or shelving. Occasionally, an individual may climb to the top of a building or other tall structure, such as a TV tower. Climbing behavior is usually accompanied by apparent disregard for safety and an absence of fear of falling.

 Climbing behavior has the potential to be very dangerous and should be interrupted.

Early intervention is critical to maintaining safety when climbing occurs. If climbing has the potential to reach dangerous heights, interrupt it early, before the person is so far out of reach that physical intervention would be too risky. This is one of the few crisis situations that warrants early physical intervention. If the person is moving rapidly, it may be more appropriate to immediately intervene physically in order to stop the person from climbing higher.

 Use the following strategies to intervene with climbing behavior.

- Remain alert but calm.
- Interrupt the climbing so the person stops climbing higher.
- Be extremely cautious when selecting strategies to stop the climbing.
- Prevent further climbing, once the person has stopped climbing any higher.
- Calmly but firmly prompt the person to return to the ground.
- Supplement with visual prompts.
- Remind the person of an upcoming event.
- Obtain assistance if possible.

- Avoid using physical guidance when climbing down, unless it can be used safely.

- Plan prevention strategies for future use.

- Develop a behavior change plan including compliance training; managing stimulation levels; along with antecedent control, reinforcers and negative consequences that target "remaining in assigned areas".

Remember:

- *Stop* the climbing;

- *Prevent* from climbing higher; then,

- *Return* to the ground.

 **CAUTION!**

- Avoid trying to physically return the person to the ground as they are climbing. This places both persons in danger of falling. Remember the first goal is to stop the person from climbing up any further.

- Avoid using startling prompts (for example, a loud noise) that may cause the climber to redirect attention and fall. This type of strategy can be used before the person actually begins climbing, in order to interrupt the initiation of climbing.

Other Special Problems

Some individuals may develop special problems that do not pose a threat of physical harm, but are still highly disruptive. Such problems can significantly impact a person's quality of life and social acceptance. These problems may include feeding issues, stripping and disrobing, masturbation, toilet training, sleep problems, legal problems, obsessions and compulsions, and fixations.

Other Feeding Issues

It is not unusual for some individuals with autism to develop behavior problems related to foods and eating. In planning for feeding interventions, you should begin by keeping a record of the foods that the individual eats each day. This record should be kept for at least a week, but it would be better to keep the food diary for one month. Then, several questions should be asked.

Is the feeding problem related to a physical disorder?

 Some of the possible problems which might be related to physical disorders include:

- allergies,
- dental problems,
- sores or injuries in the mouth,
- oral-motor problems, and
- sensory preferences.

When did the feeding problems begin?

Has your child always exhibited this problem? If not, when did the problem begin? Could it be associated with any illness or other event in his life? Did the problem begin when he saw someone else exhibit the same type of behavior? Record the answers to these questions in the food diary for the doctor.

My child will not eat vegetables or meat; what can I do to encourage better eating habits?

1. <u>Organize and structure the environment to facilitate better habits</u>. Look at the location and the eating schedule. Does the family follow a routine related to

mealtimes? Does the child need smaller, more frequent meals instead of three large meals per day?

2. <u>Don't force feed and don't talk about the problem in front of the child.</u>
   Force feeding is an unpleasant experience and may result in very negative feelings which could result in even greater desires to be alone. Talking about the problem with the individual present reinforces the person, which could result in prolonged resistance to change.

3. <u>Implement routines and rules.</u>
   Most individuals with autism like a structured approach. If dinner is built into the routine and schedule, the meal becomes another routine occurrence that individuals do because it is on their schedule.

4. <u>Begin with foods similar to those the person likes.</u>

5. <u>Involve the individual in the purchase and preparation of the food.</u>

6. <u>Prepare a symbol for the foods and place it with other food symbols.</u>

7. <u>Role model eating the food.</u>

8. <u>Use social stories about eating different foods.</u>

9. <u>Put the daily menu on the calendar using objects, photographs, magazine pictures, product labels, or picture symbols.</u>

10. <u>If the person continues having problems, request an occupational therapy evaluation for oral-motor sensitivities.</u>

11. <u>If oral-motor defensiveness exists, use oral-motor stimulation activities recommended by an occupational therapist to address the issues.</u>

Stripping and Disrobing

Undressing or stripping behavior can range from a person removing one article of clothing such as shoes, to completely removing all clothing at the wrong time and place. This behavior can be extremely embarrassing to others. It can also create situations that place the person in danger of being exploited, socially rejected, or subjected to criminal consequences. Consequently, it is important for undressing behaviors to be controlled. Individuals must be taught that different forms of dressing are appropriate to different places and situations. Impulsive undressing should be interrupted and directed into a more appropriate behavior for the situation.

Stripping and disrobing usually occur as a result of discomfort, overstimulation, or agitation. The least disruptive form of this undressing consists of the removal of one or two articles of clothing in a manner that is not offensive, but not totally acceptable.

 Stripping and disrobing behaviors can be addressed by:

- interrupting the undressing;

- reducing discomfort; be sure that clothing sizes are appropriate - not too tight or too loose, with irritating labels removed;

- leaving the piece of clothing off for a short time period, then putting it back on;

- redirecting the person's focus to another task; and

- using positive reinforcement for staying dressed or for other behaviors incompatible with undressing.

 ## CASE EXAMPLE

When Kevin was overstimulated or agitated, he removed his shoes and socks and walked on his toes. His teacher preferred that he wear his shoes and socks so he was prepared for transitions or other trips outside of the classroom. Once he became comfortable being barefoot, it was difficult to get him to put his shoes and socks on again. His teacher developed a program that reinforced him for "clothes on at school." When Kevin became upset and started to remove his shoes, she cued him to his quiet area and redirected Kevin to a simple manipulative task. One day Kevin quickly removed his shoes before his teacher interrupted and cued him to the quiet area. She used picture prompts and said "Shoes off, 1 minute." She set a kitchen timer. When the timer sounded, she said "Shoes on now" using the picture prompts. Kevin tolerated having to put his shoes on without resistance. The teacher addressed his "shoes off" behavior by allowing him one minute for shoes off and then cueing him to put them back on.

The types of undressing behavior that involve one or two articles of clothing can often be prevented by:

- recognizing and providing the types of clothing the person prefers;

- avoiding clothing that is uncomfortable or irritating;

- paying special attention to areas of pressure, such as wristbands, textures, weight, warmth, colors, length, looseness, or irritation from tags or seams;

- keeping a change of clothes to replace irritating outfits;

- providing ways for the person to communicate the desire to change clothes; and

- using removal of the article of clothing such as shoes, as a reinforcer for short time periods or as a scheduled activity to anticipate.

 ## CAUTION!

Avoid allowing a person to impulsively shed clothes. This can lead to regular undressing in response to agitation.

A more alarming form of undressing behavior consists of removing several or all articles of clothing at the wrong time or place. This behavior should be interrupted with a nonemotional response. Ignoring this behavior will not result in improvement if sensory rewards are experienced following the stripping behavior. If freedom from the discomfort of binding or irritating clothes feels good, stripping behaviors will continue or increase.

 Respond to stripping behavior by immediately and calmly using the following strategies.

- Interrupt the behavior as soon as possible.

- Avoid an emotional reaction.

- Reduce discomfort;. Reduce stimulation levels.

- Redirect the person's focus to another activity.

- Teach and reinforce acceptable behavior.

- Plan to prevent future stripping by managing stimulation levels and using a behavioral intervention plan that includes reinforcement for remaining clothed, and, if needed, a mild negative consequence for stripping.

CASE EXAMPLE

Brandon was in a self-contained special education class on a regular high school campus. He wanted to be around other teens, but became very excited and stripped when around his peers in the hallways. This caused quite a disruption since he can completely strip in less than one minute. The paraprofessional who assists Brandon was unable to stop him from stripping. An intervention plan was developed to address this behavior. Initially, transitions were limited to times when most students were in class. Brandon was taught how to greet others by shaking hands and saying "hi." His schedule included set times to go into the hallways to practice this social skill with anyone he met. He also wore a walkman that played his favorite music whenever he was in the hallway. As soon as he touched his clothes as if to start stripping, the aide unplugged the walkman and cued Brandon to sit and relax. As soon as he moved his hands away from his clothes, the walkman was plugged in again. As his greeting skills improved, his agitation levels decreased, as did his stripping. He gradually began using the hallways with larger numbers of people until he was able to greet people during class changes. He no longer stripped and several students looked forward to their daily encounters with Brandon.

Masturbation

Masturbation is an issue that can present behavior problems at all ages. However, it can be a very challenging behavior to address with persons with autism. It often evokes strong emotional reactions from caretakers due to the sexual and moral implications.

Use the following strategies to intervene when children masturbate.

- Interrupt the behavior without any emotional reaction.

- Redirect the individual to an activity that is incompatible with masturbation.

- Redirect the person into an activity that provides repetitive sensory stimulation that is socially acceptable.

- Use antecedent control as a prevention measure by involving the individual to an activity that requires the use of both hands.

- Use antecedent control to reduce high anxiety and stimulation levels that may trigger this behavior in the future.

- Be sure the person wears clothes that are comfortable and not too tight, too loose, or twisted in order avoid directing the person's attention to the genital area.

CASE EXAMPLE

Jordan was seven-years-old. He masturbated at school when he was at his desk. His teacher placed a felt square on his desk. She walked by his desk and cued him to rub the felt square whenever she noticed he was masturbating. He eventually initiated rubbing the felt whenever he was anxious instead of masturbating or requiring a teacher prompt.

Adult masturbation

Adult masturbation presents a different problem. Public masturbation by an adult can result in exploitation, social rejection, or criminal consequences. It is also very difficult to find any reinforcement or replacement behavior that feels as gratifying to the individual. Substitution of other sensory activities is generally not a viable option because the other activities don't provide the same satisfaction level. It is usually impractical to demand total stoppage of masturbation in adults. A more viable option is to teach the person the appropriate time and place for this activity.

Use the following strategies to intervene when adults masturbate in public.

- Interrupt the behavior.

- Remind the person of the appropriate time and place for the behavior.

- Redirect the person to another activity or to an activity that requires the use of both hands.

- Redirect the person to an activity that involves intense focus or high amounts of physical movement.

- Redirect the person to an appropriate place to have privacy, such as a bathroom, shower, or private bedroom.

- Reinforce staying in assigned areas and taking breaks as scheduled, to decrease the likelihood that excessive breaks or trips to the bathroom will occur.

- Provide visual evidence of scheduled breaks or private leisure time, so the person can anticipate and plan for personal needs.

CASE EXAMPLE

Leo occasionally masturbates at work. His job coach interrupts this behavior by walking over to Leo and privately reminding him that masturbating is not acceptable at work. He reminds Leo that the place for such behavior is in the bathroom, during leisure times. He redirects Leo back to his work assignment. Sometimes Leo continues to masturbate. His job coach cues him to take a timed five-minute bathroom break. On the days Leo takes his breaks only as scheduled, he gets to leave ten minutes early. On the days Leo takes extra breaks, he stays for an additional period of time equal to the extra break time taken. During this time, he finishes the work assignments he missed during those extra break times.

CASE EXAMPLE

Having reached puberty, Max was masturbating frequently in public places. Many people kept saying, "You just have to get Max to stop the masturbation." As we all know, that is a difficult task. Realistically, Max was not going to stop this activity. However, it was important for him to learn appropriate times and places for the activity to occur. An even greater problem was getting some of the staff to contain their reactions to the problem. The paraprofessionals riding the bus were "freaked out" by this behavior. As was stated earlier, an unemotional response should be used. The overreactions just further reinforced the undesired behavior. Several visits were made to Max's home to talk to his mother about teaching Max appropriate times and places for this type of activity. Finally, everyone knew progress was being made when the school principal stopped Max on the school sidewalk and told him, "Max, you're in public." Max responded with, "Can I go to the bathroom and do it?" He had learned the bathroom was a more appropriate place than a public setting.

Toilet Training

Toilet training is a problem that many families of children with autism struggle with for years. Some families have teenagers that are not independent in toileting skills. Siegal (1996, p. 291) states, "Children with mental ages below two-to two-and-a-half years (in terms of performance IQ) are usually not fully ready for toilet training, irrespective of their chronological age." Condon (1992), however, says that "readiness for bladder training occurs when the child remains dry during naps and regularly stays dry for one-and-a-half to two hours. He suggests a toilet training readiness age between 18 and 30 months. Some important concepts to remember about toileting are discussed below.

 Toilet training a child with autism is different than toilet training most children.

Bowel training should not begin until there is regularity in bowel movements and there are no accidents while the individual is sleeping. (Condon, 1992).

 When toilet training, individuals must wear clothing that allows them to feel wetness. Diapers or plastic protectors may be worn outside of clothing that allows the wetness to touch the skin, but should not be worn alone.

 All children may experience setbacks or regression when:

- they are ill,

- they have major changes in their daily routines,

- they start to school or change schools, and

- a new sibling becomes part of the family.

 Basic procedures involved in toilet training are:

- Conduct a baseline for a week. Check the child every fifteen minutes. Record whether the diaper is wet or dry. This information will be used to determine when to schedule toilet time.

- Analyze the data. Are there specific times that the child usually urinates or has a bowel movement?

- Set up a schedule training the child to follow verbal or visual cues.

- Some tricks that might help include running water, pouring lukewarm water on the child's penis, squirting a water gun in the toilet to show the child what is expected, having other children model the procedure, using a mini-schedule, or even showing the child a picture of feces in the toilet to show "this is where 'poop' goes."

- Increasing fluid intake during toilet training may help.

- If constipation is a problem, using stool softeners may help.

- Be sure that the child is well-positioned on the toilet seat and feels comfortable and secure. If the child feels unstable, this can result in tension which causes physical changes that interfere with elimination.

- Try to schedule regular meals and toileting times during the training period.

- Teach a functional sequence of steps for toileting. A mini-schedule visually depicting the steps works well.

What if my child refuses to go into the bathroom or refuses to sit on the commode?

Begin by letting the child get used to the bathroom. Make going into the bathroom a positive experience.

What if my child doesn't go to the bathroom very often?

Increase fluid intake and exercise to increase the probability that the child will need to eliminate. If the child appears to be withholding elimination because it is painful, consult your physician about using a stool softener.

What if nothing has worked?

There are some in-depth resources on toileting and programs specifically designed for students with developmental disabilities. Obtain one of these programs and implement that training procedure.

 Use verbal praise and powerful reinforcements when toilet training a child.

Sleep Problems

Many children with autism need fewer hours of sleep than their parents. This is a problem since parents are totally exhausted trying to stay up with them. Safety is an issue if parents go to sleep while the child is roaming the house.

 Set up a highly structured bedtime routine including bedtime stories, music or some other well-liked activity.

 If necessary, stay with the young child until he falls asleep. But put a limit on the length of time that you will stay in the room. Have a visual timer to indicate the length of time. When the timer is through, leave the room.

My child goes to his room, but he doesn't go to sleep. After I go to sleep, he gets back up and wanders around. I'm afraid he will get out of the house.

For safety purposes, it may be necessary to put a gate over the door or a lock to keep the child from wandering around. Many are perfectly content to play in their room while the rest of the family sleeps. Some families have installed alarm systems to wake them if the child should try to leave the home.

CASE EXAMPLE

Sammy loves to roam around and get away from everyone. One night while everyone was asleep, he got out of the house and took a four wheeler to a neighbor's house about a mile away. He was able to get into the home; the neighbors contacted the police and parents. Thankfully, he was not mistaken for a burglar. The family has since installed an alarm system which rings if Sammy leaves his room at night.

Legal Problems

In this discussion of special problems, there are several instances that could have led to police involvement if certain behaviors persisted in public places. Individuals should know what to say and do if approached by authority figures or police. Therefore, it is imperative that teenagers with developmental disabilities receive direct instruction in the Miranda rights. Persons should know what their rights are should they be arrested. They may not understand what an officer reads to them, particularly since it would already be a stressful situation.

 **It is very important for adolescents and adults with autism to know their personal rights, including the Miranda rights.**

If it appears the individual would not be able to function in that type of situation, prepare a card that says, "I have autism. I want a lawyer." Teach them to hand that card to the police officer and say nothing else whenever the situation warrants it.

Obsessions, and Compulsions

Obsessive-Compulsive (O-C) behaviors commonly occur in persons with autism. O-C behaviors are frequently internally driven and the person is either unaware of doing them or cannot stop doing them. Since some of the most successful interventions have been through the use of prescribed medications, notify the individual's physician or psychiatrist of any suspected or observed O-C behaviors.

In addition, some behavioral interventions may include:

- using a checklist or other visual evidence to indicate the behavior was completed;

- redirecting the person to another activity;

- reducing anxiety and high stimulation levels that can trigger the O-C behaviors;

- incorporating the O-C behavior into a routine that has a distinct end; and provide strategies that cue the person to recognize and stop O-C behaviors.

CASE EXAMPLE:

Whenever Becky was under stress, she exhibited the O-C behavior of handwashing. Sometimes Becky would wash her hands so many times that they became raw and bled. There were times when there was no apparent stress or other trigger to set off the handwashing. Becky's mom redirected her to another activity involving repetitive movement when Becky began the handwashing, such as washing dishes. She also created a routine to revolve around the handwashing which was depicted by visual cues posted by every sink. This routine included using hand lotion and making a checkmark on a chart beside the sink to visually note that handwashing was complete. There was only one box on the chart for each two hour period of the day. Becky could wash her hands if the box was not checked. Otherwise, she had to wait until the next time period. There was a picture cue to prompt her to another activity. This decreased handwashing.

CASE EXAMPLE

Robert will sometimes go through the house straightening pictures, knickknacks, and even the fringe on the rugs. He does not like it when he does this, but cannot stop himself. He becomes so obsessed with straightening everything repeatedly, that he must be interrupted in order to stop. When someone tells him to stop, he becomes agitated. The increased agitation results in his straightening objects even more than if he is left alone.

A simple way was devised by the home trainer for Robert to independently interrupt this behavior. He wears a rubber band on his wrist. The rubber band is loose fitting. He is allowed to straighten things in the house only two times per day. Once he uses up those two times, he firmly snaps the rubber band on his wrist, anytime he straightens a picture, knickknack, or rug fringe. He keeps a simple chart to track when he uses his two allowed straightenings and when he snaps his wrist with the rubberband. His family provides an activity reinforcer for any day that has fewer straightenings than the previous day. Robert has visual reminders that help interrupt his O-C behaviors. He also has motivation from the routine of charting his behaviors, seeing visual evidence of his performance, and receiving a preferred activity for self-improvement. His agitation levels have decreased since others are no longer correcting him frequently. Finally, he has a mild sensory-based negative consequence to decrease the O-C behaviors.

Fixations

Rather than trying to eliminate fixations, Dr. Temple Grandin (Grandin, 1996, Grandin & Scariano, 1986) suggests directing fixations into constructive channels. Her childhood fixation on cattle chutes became a career. If an individual has interests in specific subject areas, the best course of action may be to support those interests. If these fixations are interfering with normal functioning and they cannot be used to build new skills, they can generally be remediated through the use of medication and behavior strategies which were previously discussed.

CHAPTER
Ten

Discipline Procedures and Behavior Intervention Plans

How do I know that my child needs a Behavior Intervention Plan?

Some states require that a behavior management or intervention plan be written for students with autism. In other states such as Texas, it is left to the decision of the IEP Committee to determine whether there is a need for a behavior intervention plan. The question then becomes, "What indicates the need for a behavior intervention plan?"

 Behavior intervention plans should be developed when:

- the results of the assessment team or the IEP committee identify behavior problems that are interfering with the student's ability to learn;

- students exhibit unacceptable behavior in the school or home environment; and

- a student's misconduct results in repeated removals from classes which may deny the student an equal opportunity to participate in and benefit from the school's educational programs. This would be a direct violation of Section 504 and IDEA regulations.

What about the 1997 Amendments to the Individuals with Disabilities Education Act (IDEA)?

As a result of these amendments, more students will probably have behavior management plans written for them. The new amendments have several provisions related to the discipline of students with disabilities.

 Provisions of the 1997 Amendments to IDEA related to discipline of students with disabilities include:

- School personnel may change the placement of a student with a disability to an appropriate interim alternative education setting, another setting, or suspend the student for not more than 10 days.

- Before placement, or before the 10 days is up, the IEP Committee must convene to develop an assessment plan to address the problem behavior (s).

- A child carrying a weapon to school may be placed in an alternate setting for up to 45 days or the same amount that a child without a disability would receive provided it does not exceed 45 days.

- A hearing officer may order the change of placement of a child to an interim alternative setting for no more than 45 days if the school established that the child is a danger to himself and others.

- A manifestation determination which examines the relationship between the disability and the behavior must be completed by a knowledgeable committee.

Manifestation Determination

 In the area of manifestation determination, the IEP team must meet to determine that the behavior was not a result of the student's disability. In order to make this determination, the IEP team must determine that:

- The child's IEP and program placement were appropriate and all supplementary aids and services specified in the IEP were provided.

- The student's disability did not impair the ability of the child to understand the effect and consequences of his behavior.

- The student's disability did not impair the child's ability to control the behavior. It is possible that a student could understand the effect and consequences of a behavior, but still not have the behavioral control to refrain from exhibiting the behavior.

If any of these three items cannot be affirmed, then the IEP committee must determine that there is a behavior link between the behavior and the disability.

If there is no behavior link, the new amendments would allow relevant disciplinary procedures applicable to children without disabilities to be applied to a child with a disability, in the same manner that the procedures are applied to other students. However, students with disabilities must still continue to receive a free, appropriate public education.

Weapons at School

If a child carries a weapon to school or a school function, the student with a disability may be placed in an interim alternative education setting for no more than 45 days.

What is an Interim Alternative Educational Setting (IAES)?

An IAES is a different setting, usually away from the school campus. Students participating in an IAES should continue to participate in the general school curriculum and should continue to receive services and modifications as specified in their IEPs. These IEPS should include services and modification designed to address the problem behaviors for which they were sent to IAES.

What about parent appeal procedures? I don't want my child in an IAES.

As a result of the new amendments, parents who disagree with the manifestation committee may request an expedited hearing.

My child who is not currently enrolled in special education, has violated a school rule in the school's code of conduct. Is there anything that I can do?

If the local school district had knowledge that your child had a disability before the behavior occurred, you may assert all of the protections of IDEA, including the ability to request a due process hearing.

My child with autism exhibits behaviors that interfere with his learning. Does that mean he should have a behavior intervention plan?

Probably. According to the *1997 Amendments to IDEA*, anytime that disciplinary actions occur placing a child in an alternative setting, an IEP meeting must be convened before, or not later than 10 days after to develop an assessment plan that addresses the problem behaviors.

What about functional assessments?

If the school district has not conducted a functional assessment and implemented a behavioral intervention plan before the behavior occurrs, the IEP team must do so at this time. If your child has a discipline management plan, the IEP committee must review the behavior intervention plan and make necessary modifications for addressing the problem behavior. The need for additional functional assessment information may be indicated if a behavior intervention plan is not effective.

Why is a functional assessment of behavior needed? I know what he does and I know he can't control his reactions.

 A functional analysis or assessment of behavior enables parents and educators to:

- clarify a problem behavior;

- determine the effect of different factors in the environment;

- construct effective interventions that take relevant factors into consideration and address the effects they have on behavior; and

- address the communicative and functional intent of the target behavior.

What else should we know about a behavior intervention plan?

1. Present levels of performance, sometimes referred to as learning competencies (educational strengths and weaknesses), should include behavioral and educational performance areas.

2. Specific descriptive statements about behavior should be included and limited to behaviors to be targeted as objectives in the IEP.

3. Specific goals and objectives calculated to enable the student with behavioral problems to progress in behavioral and social skills areas should be included in the behavior intervention plan.

   Example of an objective: The student will sit in his seat without talking for 5 minutes.

4. A detailed description of interventions designed to increase prosocial behaviors and interventions designed to decrease negative behaviors should be addressed and included.

5. Appropriate consequences for prosocial and/or inappropriate behaviors should be delineated.

6. Methods of evaluation should be specific so that measurement of progress may be completed on a regular basis.

7. A schedule for review of behavioral interventions should be determined.

 **You should be able to link present competencies and behavioral goals and objectives to the behavior intervention plan.**

 Some examples of present levels of competencies for John Doe are:

- John can sit quietly for 2 minutes without talking.

- John can sit and listen to a story for 1 minute.

- John can attend to a work task for 2 minutes.

- John can sit and listen to preferred music for 15 minutes.

- John can eat with his fingers, but not utensils.

- Although John can pick up food and chew it, he frequently spits it out at the beginning of the meal. Some have interpreted this to mean he doesn't want to eat. However, it may be related to oral defensiveness.

- John can follow simple one-step commands when the activity is desired.

    NOTE: John should be evaluated for oral-defensiveness so that his IEP committee knows if he is exhibiting a behavior related to his disability (oral defensiveness) or if he has developed a behavioral response to attention that he receives when he misbehaves.

 Examples of present levels of competencies for an academic student are:

- Jerry can read the seventh grade level vocabulary list.

- Jerry can do multiple digit addition, subtraction, and multiplication.

- Jerry can scan the text to find answers to questions but does not always understand the questions or answers.

- Jerry can respond to questions asked of him, but will not initiate communication with others.

What is the difference between a discipline plan and a behavioral plan?

A discipline plan is usually a list of consequences for student misbehaviors. The behavioral management plan includes the *methodology* by which the behavioral goals and objectives will be implemented. It is the *how* and goals and objectives are the *what*. A behavior management plan must include positive intervention strategies to increase appropriate behaviors.

How should behavioral goals and objectives be written?

1. Goals and objectives should be based on collected assessment data.

2. Objectives should be written for each target behavior.

3. Objectives should be observable and written in measurable terms.

4. Objectives should be clearly stated, specific, and functional.

5. Goals and objectives should focus on achievable levels of performance.

6. Goals and objectives should be written to develop behaviors that will improve student's chances for success in the least restrictive environment.

How high should goals be set?

 In order to set a fair goal for student achievement, the IEP committee should consider:

- baseline information that describes present levels of competency;

- goals that are reasonably calculated and achievable; and

- what the student can be expected to do by the end of the IEP year.

Example: Janice completes her math assignments 45% of the time.

Example: The student can sit in his seat without talking for 2 minutes.

Chapter Eleven of this book discusses data collection procedures which can be used to establish baselines for each behavioral goal and objective.

How are goals prioritized?

Identify the behavioral areas which are deemed most critical by those working with the student. *Aggression, active resistance*, and *non-compliance to demands*, and/or *excessive noise or activity* are generally given the highest priority for elimination. As these high priority behaviors begin to decrease, other behaviors such as *passive non-compliance* and *inattention to task* should be addressed.

Student progress can be measured using the following methods:

- classroom observation and data collection;

- completion of a behavioral contract;

- reports from teachers, parents, and student;

- self-concept scales;

- behavior rating scales; and

- number of discipline referrals.

 Schedules for checking the student's progress should be stated in the IEP (daily, weekly, monthly, yearly, or at the end of a specific study or skill unit.)

Forms for collecting data and reporting the information home are included in Appendix B.

In what kind of classroom setting should a student with autism be placed ?

Placement must be determined on an individual basis by the IEP team. The determination is a team decision and cannot be made by one person. Challenging behaviors may impact the decision, particularly if the behaviors are disruptive to others. An inclusion setting may be perfect for one student, but not right for another. Some students will need lots of support in a general education classroom and others may need little support.

What mistakes do school districts commonly make related to behavior intervention plans?

1. Discipline procedures are substituted for a behavior intervention program. (*St. Mary's School District* [Pennsylvania], 20 IDELR 46 1993]).

2. Repeated removal of a student from the classroom and failure to formalize a plan for addressing the student's misconduct. (*School Admin. Unit No.* 38 [New Hampshire], 19 IDELR 186 [OCR 1992]).

3. Failure to consult the student's IEP before imposing discipline. Consultation with the special education staff is also strongly recommended.

4. Failure to determine if there is a link between the behavior and the disability (the manifestation determination).

5. Developing a behavior management plan with inadequate information (i.e., insufficient assessment data).

6. Accumulating numerous discipline referral slips without evaluating the appropriateness of the student's program. A stack of student discipline slips does not mean that the school staff is on top of the student's program. They are really an indication that the current program is not working well and needs to be revised and modified.

7. Using handcuffs, ropes, chains, blunt instruments, and sharp objects. School employees can be held personally liable in cases where students suffer bodily injuries due to excessive or negligent discipline.

8. Using emergency removals when there is no emergency.

9. Expelling a student with disabilities without making provisions for a continuation of services during the expulsion.

10. Trying to do the right thing. Proposing a behavior intervention plan without adequate assessment information OR not including a behavior intervention plan because parents object to it.

11. Failure to offer a ten day recess when parents and school personnel have disagreements.

 If the behavior management plan isn't working:

- call an iep meeting to review and modify the plan when it isn't working;

- review the consistency with which it has been implemented by all school personnel working with the student;

- arrange for a qualified psychologist or behavior specialist to perform a full day of classroom observation where significant ongoing problems are experienced.

- consider the need for updated assessment information; and

- consider an increase in related services (i.e., counseling, occupational therapy for calming techniques, etc.).

What about seclusion, time-out and physical restraint?

1. Courts have scrutinized these procedures as to

    a. the necessity of the method,

    b. the reasonableness of force employed, and

    c. the effectiveness of the intervention in the specific situation in which it is being used.

2. If these procedures are to be used, they should be stated as consequences in the behavior management plan.

3. Complete documentation of the event should be made by all persons involved.

4. Frequent use of the technique should trigger an IEP review of other alternatives.

What kinds of consequences should we use for inappropriate behaviors?

Chapter Seven and Chapter Eight described numerous consequences which can be incorporated into behavior intervention plans for increasing desired behaviors and decreasing negative behaviors.

What about corporal punishment?

 CORPORAL PUNISHMENT SHOULD NOT BE USED WITH STUDENTS WITH AUTISM.

 Consequences should be determined based upon the functioning level of the student and the types of behaviors exhibited.

How do I know which consequences to use?

The IEP committee should specify the consequences in the behavior intervention plan. Some plans include a hierarchy of consequences (a sequence of responses) which should be used to intervene with a specific person.

 A sample hierarchy of consequences includes the following sequenced steps:

- reminder of rules/restatement of instructions;
- redirection to appropriate behavior;
- warning (state verbal limits and options);
- time-out at desk/table (no longer than 1 minute per year of age) or withdrawal of teacher attention;
- response cost-withhold privilege or reward;
- restitution or practice of appropriate behavior;
- teacher/student conference;

- time-out in chair away from other students (1 min. per year of age); and

- call parent to discuss concerns if misbehavior continues to be inappropriate.

What about Level Systems?

Level systems tend to be used more frequently with students with serious emotional disturbances than with students with autism. However, if a student with autism is placed in a class for students with behavior disorders, the person with autism may be expected to conform to the rules of the level system being used.

A level system is set up for a specific program or child with certain consequences available at each level. When a level system is established as part of a specific classwide program, each student must progress through the system in the same way. Generally there are four or five different levels. Students begin at the lowest level and must earn their way to higher levels. Frequently, there are no privileges at the lower level. In some schools, students at the lower level have no interaction with other students and are required to eat in the room. After demonstrating appropriate behavior for so many days, the student moves to the next level. Some programs require students to stay at the first level for six weeks. With each progressive level, students gain more freedom and more privileges. The highest level usually involves inclusion in some or a majority of general education classes and activities. While these systems may be appropriate for students with emotional disturbance, level systems may not be appropriate for students with autism.

Level systems have been criticized by the courts in special education due process hearings because they were not individualized. Since IDEA requires an individualized educational program, a programmatic level system with no allowances for individualization doesn't meet the requirements of an appropriate education. Another concern related to students with autism is that there is no consideration of their sensory needs.

Appendix A includes sample copies of behavioral intervention plans.

CAUTION!

If a level system is to be used with a student with autism, the following cautions should be observed.

- Make sure the system is individualized for every student.

- Evaluate how the system is designed. Does the student have to stay at each level for a specific number of days?

- Does the level system consider the special sensory needs of the student with autism?

- What does the student have to do to reach higher levels?

- Are the requirements realistic and attainable for the student?

CASE EXAMPLE

Mandy, a high school student with poor impulse control and hyperactivity, got into a physical fight with another girl. She was sent to the Alternative Program for five days. During these five days, she was expected to refrain from talking to anyone. She was expected to stay in her chair at her desk all day with a restroom break in the morning and one in the afternoon. Lunch was brought to the alternative classroom. Each time Mandy violated a rule, she was assigned another day in this discipline setting. By the end of five days, her original time had been extended to 15 days because of rule violations. When the IEP Committee met during the second week, her days had been extended to 35. It was obvious that the rules were not realistic or attainable for Mandy. At the rate she was accumulating days, her original five days could have resulted in a "life sentence." The IEP Committee intervened and placed this student in a more appropriate setting where she could function successfully.

CHAPTER *Eleven*

Putting It All Together

In order to address behavior problems successfully, observations and numerous decisions based on those observations, need to occur as part of an ongoing process. Understanding behaviors targeted for change, and planning appropriate intervention involves several steps: (1) determine that a problem exists; (2) ask questions to analyze the specific nature of the problem; (3) select the behavior to target for change; (4) determine the goal of the intervention; (5) decide which intervention approaches will best accomplish the goal; (6) evaluate the effectiveness of the intervention program using observational techniques; (7) change or refine the interventions when necessary; and (8) communicate information regarding observations and interventions to persons who need to know.

Observations

Effective observation plays a critical role in successful behavior change programs. When making observations, describe exactly what individuals *do* or *say*, instead of using abstract terms. Describe behavior in words stating what can actually be seen, heard or otherwise perceived through the senses. This provides a way to measure the effectiveness of interventions. Some examples of changing abstract descriptions into behaviors that can be observed and measured, are illustrated in the following table.

Table 11.1 Behavior Descriptions

Abstract	Observable
He is hyperactive.	He sits in a chair for thirty seconds.
She is noncompliant.	She follows directions three out of ten times.
He is anxiety-ridden.	He has a panic attack three times per week; or He has episodes of fast and shallow breathing, while covering his face with his hands, and complaining of being afraid. This happens three times per week.
He has a short attention span.	He attends to a task for one minute.
She has a bad temper.	She tantrums four times per week; or she has episodes of throwing herself on the floor while screaming, four times per week.

Once behavior is stated in observable and measurable terms, the effectiveness of strategies can be determined. This provides a foundation for making successful decisions regarding behavior interventions.

Measuring progress

The amount or type of progress made needs to be considered when making program decisions. Sometimes interventions may result in progress, but the progress is minimal. Measuring progress in this situation may guide the caretaker toward a more effective intervention that will result in greater progress.

Sometimes progress can be hidden. To the caretaker interacting with the individual on a regular basis, it may appear that the person is not making progress. However, examining the *types* of changes in behavior may indicate significant progress.

> ## CASE EXAMPLE
>
> Josh was having severe temper tantrums that lasted for two hours. These tantrums occurred three times per day. During these tantrums, Josh screamed, destroyed property, ran around the room wildly and hit or kicked anyone who tried to intervene. A behavior intervention plan was developed to decrease Josh's temper tantrums. Two weeks later, the family insisted the plan was ineffective. Josh was still having tantrums three times per day. However, upon closer examination, it was found that Josh's tantrums lasted for only fifteen minutes. During tantrums, he still screamed and ran around the room, but he no longer destroyed property or attacked people. The intervention was effective and needed to be continued. However his family, who dealt with these tantrums everyday, were so frustrated they were unable to recognize Josh's progress. Once observable behaviors were measured and compared, they realized he was making progress. After this realization, they felt satisfied with their efforts and continued the intervention. Josh's tantrums eventually stopped.

People often measure behavior in terms of frequency. *Frequency* is how often the behavior occurs. However, behavior can also be measured by examining the intensity and duration of that behavior. *Intensity* refers to how extreme or severe the behavior becomes. For example, hitting behavior may be so intense as to cause tissue damage or it may be so mild that it does not even result in the recipient saying "ouch." *Duration* is how long the behavior lasts. In the case example of Josh, his temper tantrums decreased in duration, from two hours to fifteen minutes.

When measuring behavior consider the frequency, intensity and duration of that behavior.

Various forms that document behavior are helpful when measuring progress or change. Some forms are appropriate for use with tracking expected behaviors across the day. Others are appropriate for use with tracking behaviors that occur very frequently. Sometimes it is more appropriate to use a custom-made form to track a particular behavior. However, no matter which form of documentation is used, behaviors targeted for change need to be tracked in order to measure progress and make intervention decisions. Narratives that describe behaviors may be helpful when first analyzing a behavior to be changed; however, they are time-consuming and do not facilitate measurement of observable behaviors. Samples of behavior tracking charts for data collection are included in Appendix B.

Reporting information to persons who need to know

When other persons or agencies are involved in the treatment of an individual, effective communication between all parties involved needs to be ongoing. Accurately communicating the information needed by other parties can impact the success of interventions. The effects of time and frustration on caretakers can lead to inaccurate reporting of behavior changes.

 The most common situations warranting ongoing communication are:
- communication with a prescribing physician;
- communication between home and school; and
- communication with the individual's employer.

Accurate and effective communication with an individual's prescribing physician is a critical element in successful medication treatment. Providing the physician with a summary of the individual's behavior changes, stated in observable and measurable terms, can facilitate sound treatment decisions. The physician relies on caretakers to provide information regarding behavioral patterns and changes. Incomplete, outdated, dramatic, or vague reporting can result in the physician receiving inaccurate messages regarding the effects of medications or treatments.

 When providing behavioral information to an individual's physician:

- Keep a log documenting behavioral changes, physical changes, medication issues, changes in alertness or arousal levels, and other related matters.

- If related to the behavior or medication, document the individual's sleep patterns, eating habits, behavioral performance, and school or job performance.

- Note the times of day any changes occur, including changes in behavior patterns and alertness or arousal levels.

Communication between home and school plays an important role when working cooperatively in the student's best interest. However, due to numerous time constraints, consistent daily communication is often sacrificed. Teachers and families can maintain this extremely valuable communication when time constraints are great. Daily log books that keep narrative accounts of relevant information may be replaced with daily communication checklists addressing the same areas of information. A sample checklist is included in Appendix B.

 Communications between home and school need to address:

- changes or problems that may impact performance at home or school;

- disturbances in sleep patterns, eating, physical functions, medication regime, performance levels, alertness and arousal levels, or behavior patterns;

- significant accomplishments;

- important or relevant experiences; and

- significant future events.

Timely communication between an individual's employer and caretakers who are authorized to intervene in that individual's job situation, can prevent minor difficulties from escalating into job loss. With employment situations, the caretaker needs to initiate communication so that an employer knows what to do and who to contact when behavioral difficulties impact job performance. Periodically initiating follow-up contacts may keep small concerns at the job site from becoming unmanageable. Do not expect the individual's supervisor to initiate contact when minor difficulties arise. It is not unusual for caretakers to be unaware of a long-standing problem at work, until the person is fired. Avoid this dilemma by periodically contacting the individual's supervisor and addressing any concerns related to the person's behavior at work.

CAUTION!

Only caretakers, including family members, with legal permission to intervene in an individual's job situation can discuss the person's job performance or behavior at the worksite. Avoid engaging in such communications if you do not have the authority to do so.

Deciding when to make program changes

Decisions are an integral part of developing and maintaining effective programs for behavior change. Measures of behavioral performance provide guidance in the decision-making process. If measures show satisfactory progress, it may be appropriate to continue the current intervention. If progress is unsatisfactory, examine the intervention strategies, changing and refining them as needed.

Appendix B includes the information from the following two pages in a checklist format to use when progress is unsatisfactory. Answering each question can guide caretakers toward effective intervention change.

When progress is unsatisfactory, answer the following questions:

- Is the behavior stated in specific, observable, and measurable terms? If no, restate the behavior using these terms.

- Does the behavior need to be measured differently? If yes, consider measuring frequency, intensity, and duration.

- Is the intervention plan being implemented consistently? If no, remove the barriers that interfere with consistent implementation, or develop strategies that can be implemented effectively.

- Is the individual still engaging in misbehavior that gives sensory stimulation? If yes, examine and address the individual's sensory needs.

- Is the individual communicating effectively? If no, provide communication strategies which the individual can access and use in all settings.

- Are cues and conditions in the environment structured in a way that triggers desired behaviors? If no, include antecedent control strategies in the intervention plan.

- Are reinforcers used consistently, and do they actually increase the behaviors they follow? If no, develop an effective menu of reinforcers and use them consistently.

- If negative consequences are used, do they actually decrease the behaviors they follow? If no, identify negative consequences that are reasonable and naturally or logically related to the misbehavior.

- Has the plan been implemented long enough for the person to consistently connect with consequences on numerous occasions? If no, allow more time for the person to experience consequences.

- Is the individual showing signs of increased agitation or anxiety, since the implementation of the intervention? If yes, re-examine the demands being placed on the individual, making sure expectations are clear, and not too high or too low. Make sure the demands are logical and meaningful to the person. Re-examine the negative consequences being used, making sure they are not too harsh, lengthy, severe, unpredictable, or illogical.

- As goals are reached, another decision to consider is when to end the intervention. Behavior interventions are not truly complete until the individual shows the behavior changes across a variety of situations, without the constant use of reinforcement or negative consequences. Once this is achieved, then the decision to end the intervention is appropriate.

Generalization training

Generalization training is critical to successful behavioral change. Generalization training is the process of teaching a person to perform behaviors across a variety of conditions. Some persons with autism exhibit a certain behavior *only* when the same conditions exist as when they first learned that behavior. In such instances, the intervention plan needs to include strategies for teaching the individual to perform the desired behavior in a variety of situations, with different people, at different times, and using a variety of materials. During generalization training, the same intervention strategies for teaching the behavior need to be used. The only parts that vary are the conditions under which the behavior occurs.

CASE EXAMPLE

Jacob learned to communicate at school using a picture swap system. Although he had the same pictures at home, he did not use them to communicate. Jacob needed to be directly taught to use the picture swap system at home. He had not generalized what he learned at school to other settings. Once Jacob was taught to use his picture swap system in other settings with various people, generalization training had occurred and interventions could be faded to more natural, less obvious supports.

Fading intervention

Once the individual has learned to generalize behavior changes to new situations, the next decision is *how* and *when* to begin fading out *which* intervention strategies. When ending the use of intervention strategies, always gradually fade out these strategies. Avoid abruptly ending the use of an effective intervention strategy.

When fading out the use of antecedents, use the following guidelines:

- Fade verbal and physical prompts into visual prompts so the person can function more independently and with increased autonomy.

- Gradually fade visual prompts so they become smaller, more age appropriate, easily accessed independently by the individual, and less obvious.

- Gradually fade sensory-based antecedents so they are a natural part of the individual's routine and can be accessed independently.

- Gradually fade communication supports so they are more portable, are easily understood by most people, and can be used independently.

 Use the following steps when fading out the use of reinforcement and negative consequences.

- Gradually shift from reinforcing *every* desired response to reinforcing every three to five times the person shows desired behavior. Then gradually move to reinforcing only occasionally.

- Change tangible reinforcers into a related activity to use as reinforcement. For example, shift from rewarding with food to rewarding with a choice of foods at snacktime.

- Gradually shift from rewarding with tangible or activity-based reinforcers to providing a social reward with occasional tangibles or activity-based reinforcers.

- Gradually fade negative consequences so that they are more natural, easy to use in a variety of situations, allow for increased independence, are less intrusive, and carry a minimal risk of physical or psychological harm.

 **CAUTION!**

- Avoid totally fading out the use of structures, routines, rituals, visual prompts, and self-regulation strategies.

- Avoid abruptly ending the use of effective strategies.

- Avoid totally ending all reinforcers or consequences; instead gradually fade to a level usually provided to others in the same environment.

In addition to decisions regarding specific behavior intervention strategies used now, caretakers are faced with decisions regarding various treatment approaches and planning for future needs. When making these decisions, remember that what works for one individual may not work for another. Explore various options and combine interventions when appropriate. The ultimate test of an intervention's success is whether it improves the individual's quality of life.

 Informed decisions are critical to the success of interventions.

The study of autism is a growing field, with numerous interventions available. Increase the probability of making decisions that contribute to successful interventions by continually learning about autism.

 Intervention decisions are made based on a person's own:

- values and feelings;

- knowledge of autism;

- knowledge of the unique behaviors and personality of the individual targeted for behavior change;

- personal views and attitudes toward autism and behavior interventions; and

- knowledge of methods and approaches to working with persons with autism.

CHAPTER Twelve

Stress Management

Daily life in today's world is often highly stressful. Sharing life with a person with autism places unique challenges and responsibilities on caretakers. This can result in even higher stress levels.

Internal changes occurring within our bodies as a result of pressure from external circumstances or change are commonly referred to as stress. The daily challenges and responsibilities of sharing life with a person with autism require frequent changes and adjustments. This can lead to significantly high, unrelenting stress levels. Continuous or very high levels of stress can lead to "burnout". Burnout occurs when a person has stressors which are so serious, so numerous, or so continuous that the person feels unable to manage, feels helpless, or is out of control.

 To avoid burnout, it is critical for caretakers to:

- recognize signs of stress overload;

- reduce sources of stress;

- practice coping and stress management strategies; and

- avoid additional stress whenever possible.

Becoming aware of stress is a two step process. First, try to identify the situations in life that result in stress. These situations may be minor hassles, major lifestyle changes, or a combination of both. Once the causes of stress are recognized, focus on how your body reacts to stress.

 Physical signs of stress include:

- heart pounding,

- stomach ache distress,

- dizziness,

- high blood pressure,

- dry mouth,

- fatigue,

- sweating,

- back pain,

- muscle tension,

- shortness of breath,

- generalized aches and pains,

- circles under eyes,

- frequent or chronic illness, and

- headaches.

 CAUTION!

- Seek medical attention for any serious or persistent physical symptoms.

- Avoid the temptation to say "It's just stress."

- Stress results in real and sometimes serious physical conditions that may require professional treatment.

Not all people show physical signs of stress. Some people experience stress internally or psychologically. However, even when a person does not show outward, physical symptoms of stress, internal changes can be occurring as a result of stressful conditions.

 Psychological signs of stress include:

- depression,

- boredom,

- urge to cry,

- suspicion,

- nervousness,

- anxiety,

- negative thoughts or attitudes,

- a sense of loneliness,

- nightmares,

- feeling helpless,

- feeling confused,

- worry,

- feeling tired or lethargic,

- inability to concentrate, and

- desire to run away.

 Behaviors associated with stress include:

- tobacco use,

- increased use of medications,

- impulsivity,

- inappropriate crying,

- over- or under-eating,

- excessive initiative,

- isolation,

- manipulation of other people,

- increased alcohol intake or substance abuse, and

- nagging,

- being excessively critical,

- feeling overly cynical,

- exhibiting antisocial behavior,

- being quick to anger,

- being accident prone,

- acting overly argumentative,

- working ineffectively at work, school, or home, and

- being inflexible and uncooperative.

Once symptoms of stress overload are recognized, identify ways to reduce the sources of stress. It is also very important to learn healing and coping strategies for managing life's stresses that you cannot avoid.

 **Understanding the way in which stress effects your body can help you find ways to minimize the negative impact of stress.**

There are two types of stress: positive and negative. Positive stress can help you perform, concentrate, and work effectively. Once you've handled a stressful situation, your body automatically relaxes. This relaxation is the most important part of positive stress. It allows you to rest, gaining the physical and emotional energy needed to meet the next challenge. Positive stress basically consists of a series of arousal and relaxation responses that help you address the changes and challenges of daily life.

Negative stress starts the same as positive stress, but there is no actual relaxation between one stressful situation and the next one. Thus, your body remains in a stressful state, with no relief from the internal reactions such as muscle tension and increased heart rate and blood pressure. Some coping strategies that people often resort to, such as alcohol, drugs, smoking, or ventilating feelings by nagging and yelling, actually serve to worsen the negative impact of stress on the body.

When planning ways to decrease the negative impact of stress, it is important to understand that some strategies have a short-term impact, and need to be implemented on a regular basis for lasting effect. These short-term steps are called coping strategies.

 Coping strategies help a person relax, refocus, or ventilate, thus releasing the immediate pressure from stress.

Another way to address stress is by managing the stress, using strategies that actually create long-term change. Such strategies help to heal the conditions that are the main source of your reaction to the stressors.

 **Stress management strategies help a person resolve and change the physical, mental and emotional conditions that actively contribute to the negative impact of stress.**

Some commonly used *coping strategies* are listed below. Some coping strategies listed are those which people use that may worsen the situation or cause harm. It is important that people recognize both positive and potentially harmful behaviors they tend to use during stressful times.

 Potentially harmful coping behaviors are:

- blowing up,
- yelling,
- punching objects,
- kicking,
- nagging,
- complaining,
- alcohol abuse,

- drugs abuse, and

- slamming doors.

 Positive coping strategies for stress include:

- exercising,

- walking or jogging,

- aerobics,

- sports,

- dancing,

- gardening,

- hobbies,

- support groups,

- medication,

- relaxation training,

- deep breathing exercises,

- meditation,

- shopping,

- listening to soothing music,

- watching TV or movies,

- eating, and

- warm baths.

Coping strategies play a very important role in alleviating stress. They allow your body to experience the rest or relaxation states that occur with positive stress. However, using only coping strategies will not help reduce incoming stress. It will only help a person relax *after* experiencing the stress. *Stress management strategies* will help persons reduce the amount or intensity of stress experienced.

Stress management strategies have a long-term impact on stress levels. These strategies help reduce the amount of stress experienced, often by creating a more positive attitude and lifestyle. Such strategies include:

- setting aims, goals, and objectives;

- planning and prioritizing;

- accentuating the positive;

- developing a positive lifestyle;

- being tolerant and forgiving;

- being assertive instead of aggressive;

- building relationships;

- moderating habits;

- using problem-solving approaches;

- labeling and relabeling or changing the meanings of concepts, thoughts, or feelings;

- reducing or eliminating feelings of guilt, forgiving yourself;

- using imagination;

- developing commitment;

- increasing knowledge and understanding;

- improving self-understanding;

- participating in support groups;

- learning to separate the things you can change, control, or influence from those you can't;

- using conflict resolution;

- using time management;

- participating regularly in recreation; and

- communicating with an open mind.

If the source of a significant portion of your stress is a person with challenging behaviors, two of the most important stress reduction strategies you can use, are *planning and prioritizing* behavior interventions. Select the individual's misbehaviors that are the greatest source of stress for you and develop a behavior intervention plan that is reasonable to carry out. It is often highly appropriate to obtain assistance in prioritizing the behaviors to change, and in selecting strategies that are reasonable, yet effective. Once a plan is in place, *commit* to using it consistently and giving it time to work. Don't hesitate to obtain help as needed. Document progress toward your goals. Also, allow yourself, your loved ones and the people in your support system to be human. Take good care of yourself so that you can be there for your loved ones. They need you.

CHAPTER *Thirteen*

Final Gems

To conclude this book, we have some final reminders for your personal treasure chest about behavior change and autism.

 Behavior change takes time.

Although we want change to happen overnight, it seldom does. "It takes one month to change a behavior for every year it existed in its old form." (Cline & Fay, 1983, p. 61.). Don't give up. Keep on working. It won't change unless we do work at it. A common mistake made by many is giving up an intervention program before it has had time to work.

 Behavior change is not easy. Don't expect immediate success.

Although we sometimes see immediate results with medications or other treatments, behavioral interventions usually take time for change to occur. Don't stop the intervention because it hasn't produced immediate results. Collect data to make informed decisions about the success or failure of the intervention.

 Behaviors may get worse before they get better.

A common occurrence with behavioral change is a phenomenon called an *extinction burst*. This means that behaviors may get worse after a behavioral intervention is initiated before they get better. The person is used to certain responses by those in his environment. When responses change, the individual persists in the old behaviors, trying to elicit the previous responses. It may take a while to realize that you have really changed your responses. Until that connection is made, the person will persist in the old behavior.

Be aware of what you are reinforcing.

Don't inadvertently reinforce undesired behaviors. Don't be like the mom or grandma who takes her daughter into the grocery store. As they enter, she says, "We're just getting milk. You don't need anything else." By the time the mother and daughter are at the checkout stand, mom is also buying candy to end the temper tantrum that the child has thrown. What mom has reinforced is the tantrum behavior. The next time they are in the store, the child will be more likely to have another tantrum because she successfully got what she wanted with this tantrum.

 ## Don't make promises or threats that you can't enforce.

It is most important when working with individuals with autism that we respond consistently. They respond to rituals and routines. It is confusing to persons with autism when those around them are inconsistent. If you tell them a certain consequence will happen as a result of certain behaviors, be sure that those consequences happen. If you can't enforce the consequence, don't make the threat. There are times when you must assess the situation and back off.

As part of a school consultation, I went to a home to pick up a child who had not come to school. As soon as he saw me he ran into the woods. I followed him a short distance. There he was, standing in a clearing, swinging an 8 foot long two-by-four around his head. This fourth grader who happened to weigh about 175 pounds, was swinging the board round and round saying, "You ain't gonna take me to school." Assessing the situation, I determined that he was right. I asked him when his Dad would be home and told him I would be back then. By the time I got back to the house, his Dad had already taken him to school. The problem was resolved. Nothing would have been gained by my trying to wrestle him to school.

When withholding reinforcement, control all sources of attention or reinforcement.

If the individual is receiving reinforcement from other sources, your withdrawal or withholding of reinforcement will be meaningless.

 When selecting reinforcers, remember that it's not a good reinforcer if it doesn't consistently reward the person.

Andy, a ten-year-old, will usually work for a drink of juice or a soft drink. However, food is not a source of interest to him. When reinforced with potato chips, he just drops them on the floor. Use the Reinforcer Assessment in Appendix B to identify the best reinforcers for a specific person.

 Use logical consequences whenever possible.

Logical consequences are generally most meaningful. For example, while observing one young man playing basketball, it was noted he continually threw the ball into the bushes. He would then make noises and point until his mother went and got the ball. I suggested that she leave it there. Then he either had to go get it himself or suffer the logical consequence of not having the ball to play with.

 Don't overwhelm the individual with too many things at once.

Pick one or two behaviors that are most important. Work on those. Once those behaviors are under control, then look at another behavior to work on.

Survive the moment, but don't forget your long-term goals.

You'll always be in crisis if you don't also implement long-term supports and change your own responses to the behaviors that are troublesome. In working with one parent, it was obvious that she knew the appropriate ways to respond. However, she said "It's too hard. I just have to survive each day." Although that's true, it's much easier to manage the misbehavior of a four-year-old or an eight-year-old than it is to manage the problem behaviors of a person who is seventeen and larger than you are. The longer that you wait to implement appropriate behavior strategies, the more difficult it is to change the behaviors.

 Nothing is free. Behavior change takes effort.

As the saying goes, "If it sounds too good to be true, it usually is." Implementation of a behavioral change program takes lots of effort and consistency. It's hard to be consistent on good days and bad days. When we're feeling good, we're more likely to be lenient. Every time we are inconsistent in our responses, we increase the probability that the individual will exhibit the unwanted behavior.

We all need support. Find a support group or a good friend. Work with other parents implementing behavioral programs. Work with your school staff. Learn all you can. Find someone you can call when you're really down. If you don't have a support group in your area, start one. To quote a line from a child's book, *Becca and Sue Make Two,*

"Different people do things in different ways, but together we're better."

Appendices

Appendix A
Behavior Intervention (Management) Plans

This appendix includes behavior intervention plans for three students. The plans are based upon sample forms from the Texas Education Agency. Although the sample forms use checklists, these were done in a narrative form to better meet the unique needs of these three students. The students were selected to give an indication of plans for different ages and levels of severity.

The first student, Jessie, is a child who is just turning five years old. He received services this past year in a Preschool Program for Children with Disabilities (PPCD) classroom. He exhibits characteristics similar to children with moderate levels of functioning.

Evan, the second child, is twelve years old, and is functioning at the severe level. He is nonverbal, communicating with gestures and some objects. He still needs total assistance with basic self-help skills including toileting.

John, a 16 year old, is completing his freshman year of high school. His behavior management plan is representative of an older student who functions at a higher level. A list of present competencies is included with John's behavior intervention plan to illustrate links between statements of competencies, goals and objectives, and intervention strategies listed on the behavior intervention plan.

Although these plans meet Texas and federal guidelines for behavior intervention plans, it is not necessary to use this format. There are many formats of behavior intervention plans that can be used. Most states that require a behavior intervention plan also provide sample forms for individuals in their state to use. These plans are provided for the reader's information and reference.

IEP SUPPLEMENT

BEHAVIOR MANAGEMENT PLAN

Student: Jessie   **Date of Meeting: April 30, 1997**

Program: Preschool Program for   **Age: 5 years**
Children with Disabilities

Based on current data, the IEP committee considering this student's educational programming and placement has made the following determinations regarding this student's IEP and discipline management.

1.   The student does not have the capacity to understand school rules as outlined in the district's code on conduct.

2.   The student does not have the capacity to follow school rules in the district's code on conduct.

3.   Due to the student's disability, special behavior management techniques are necessary.

Jessie's school instruction should focus on compliance behavior, extending his communication system, and developing daily living skills and appropriate social behaviors, including finding appropriate activities in which he can independently participate.

Behaviors reported by parents:

Temper tantrums and biting when angry

Behaviors reported by teachers and counselors:

General noncompliance

Temper tantrums used to indicate his displeasure with something

Self-scratching and scratching of others when angry

Throwing objects and chairs

Kicking

What happens before the behavior occurs?

The teacher/staff/parents request or direct him to do something.

He is being redirected from an inappropriate activity.

Another student either takes something or is playing with something that he wants.

The following behaviors which have occurred during the past year are related to the student's disability.

Leaving class or campus (He will run out the door to the outside if allowed the opportunity).

Violation of class rules (noncompliance or not following directions).

Fighting when he is angry.

Destruction of school property when angry.

Goals and objectives for increasing positive behaviors and decreasing negative behaviors are included in his IEP.

Describe reinforcers (activities, people, tangible items, privileges, token economies, etc.) that have been attempted during the past year and their effectiveness.

Reinforcer	Effectiveness
Verbal Praise	Somewhat effective
Activity reinforcers such as puzzles	Usually effective
Teacher attention	Somewhat effective
Special toys	Somewhat effective
Premack Principle	Somewhat effective

Describe consequences (parent conference, loss of privileges, detention, etc.) that have been applied during the past year and their effectiveness.

Positive and negative reinforcers.

Time-out.

Physical restraint (i.e. holding of hands to prevent throwing of objects).

Restitution (picking up mess made when angry).

Loss of privilege.

They are generally effective when the behavior is responded to early. Loss of privilege is generally not effective because he doesn't appear to understand the concept.

Identify reinforcers or consequences that have not been tried but might be effective:

Carol Gray's Social Stories.

Hierarchy of Consequences.

1. Tell him, "No, Do . . ." in a calm, firm voice.

2. State consequences. "If you do _____, _____will happen."

3. Redirect to appropriate task with visual cues.

4. Demonstrate task.

5. Tell him, "Do this."

6. If he continues with inappropriate behavior, use TOOTS (time-out on the spot).

7. At the end of time-out, redirect to the same task so he learns temper tantrums do not get him out of the task.

8. If behaviors continue, remove him to time-out away from the classroom (no longer than 5 minutes).

9. Use a visual object to indicate time-out (such as a three-minute timer).

10. When he has calmed, allow him to re-enter the classroom and redirect to the same task.

Specific Procedures for Temper Tantrums.

1. Tell him, "No, Do . . . ." in a calm, firm voice.

2. Redirect to an appropriate incompatible task.

3. Physically prompt him to a chair if necessary.

4. Physically prompt to a sitting position in the chair with hands in lap.

5. Every time he makes a sound, tell him, "Sit quietly" in a firm voice.

6. When he has calmed, redirect him to the task.

7. If the tantrum behavior continues, remove him from the classroom for a short time.

8. When he has calmed, allow him to reenter the classroom and redirect him to the same task.

This IEP committee agrees that corporal punishment is not appropriate for this student.

Person(s) responsible for carrying out the behavior management plan and reviewing this plan with the student (if not present at IEP committee meeting).

Special Education staff,

Principal, and

Special Education Support personnel.

ASSURANCES

The IEP committee assures that the requirements of statutory and constitutional due process and due process under the Individuals with Disabilities Education Act (IDEA) have been met.

IEP SUPPLEMENT

BEHAVIOR MANAGEMENT PLAN

Name: Evan   **Date: May 1, 1997**

Program: **Self-contained Special Education   Age: 12 years**

Based on his current assessment and identification as a student with autism, the IEP committee considering this student's educational programming and placement has made the following determinations regarding this student and discipline management.

1.   The student does not have the capacity to understand school rules as outlined in the district's code on conduct.

2.   The student does not have the capacity to follow school rules as outlined in the district's code on conduct.

3.   Due to the student's disability of autism, special behavior management techniques may be necessary.

His school instruction should focus on compliance behavior, extending his communication system through gestures and objects, and developing daily living skills and appropriate social behaviors, including finding appropriate activities in which he can independently participate.

Behaviors reported by parents:

temper tantrums,

yelling, and

wanting to be outdoors all of the time.

Behaviors reported by teachers and other support personnel:

The behavior which is currently interfering most with his education is his desire to go to the door and outside. The door to the early childhood classroom is most distracting to him.

General noncompliance.

Temper tantrums which are used as a form of communication to indicate his displeasure with something.

Attempts to teach him more appropriate methods of indicating displeasure have not succeeded at this time.

Making loud noises.

The behavior of falling and dropping to the ground to indicate displeasure is somewhat better and he is walking to more places around the campus.

What happens before the behavior(s) occur?

The teacher/staff/parents request or direct him to do something.

He is being redirected from an inappropriate activity.

Sometimes, there appears to be no obvious precipitating events.

The following behaviors which have occurred during the past year are related to the disability.

Leaving class or campus (He will go out the door to the outside if allowed the opportunity.).

Violation of class rules (Noncompliance or not following directions).

Destruction of school property. (This is accidental when it occurs, not purposeful).

Goals and objectives for increasing positive behaviors:

Behaviors	Mastery Criteria
He will comply with a request with 2 or less prompts within 1 minute of a request.	50%
Evan will sit for 10 minutes.	60%
Evan will attend to the same work task for 10 minutes.	60%
Evan will indicate that he is listening to a story for 8 minutes by sitting in his chair or desk and looking at the person reading or telling the story.	60%
He will interact with peers in social situations.	40%

Reinforcers for Special Education Classes: Verbal praise, attention, activity reinforcers such as short walks, and tangible reinforcers such as drinks.

Reinforcers for General Education Classes: Verbal praise, attention, activity reinforcers, other tangible reinforcers.

Interventions:

Continue with implementation of the TEACCH program.

Consistently provide instruction in compliance skills.

Use frequent verbal and non-verbal reinforcement.

Use social stories with visual cues to reinforce appropriate behaviors.

Continue to implement the object swap system for communication.

Reinforce completion of work tasks with 2 to 3 minutes break time.

A weighted vest has also been used and other deep pressure activities for promoting a state of calmness.

Goals and objectives for decreasing negative behaviors:

Behaviors	**Mastery Criteria**
Evan will decrease temper tantrums.	20% decrease
Evan will decrease falling and dropping to the ground,	40% decrease
Evan will decrease screaming and loud noises.	40% decrease

Sp. Ed. Consequences:
Use the Procedure for Temper Tantrums and the Hierarchy of Consequences outlined below as interventions for decreasing negative behaviors. Use social stories, routines, and structure in the classroom.

Reg. Ed. Consequences:
Use the specific procedures for mainstreaming described below.

Interventions:
Consistently implement the procedures as described.

Describe reinforcers (activities, people, tangible items, privileges, token economics, etc.) that have been attempted during the past year and their effectiveness:

Food	Not consistently effective.
Drinks	Not consistently effective.
Short walks outside	He usually responds to short walks outside, but they sometimes present a problem when it is time to go in.
Hugs	He responds to deep pressure and he really likes "bear hugs."

Verbal Praise   Somewhat effective.

Teacher attention   Somewhat effective.

Describe consequences (parent conference, loss of privileges, detention, etc.) that have been applied during the past year and their effectiveness.

Time-out and a hierarchy of consequences have been used. They have not been consistently effective. Positive rewards have also been used with inconsistent results.

Identify reinforcers or consequences that have not been tried but might be effective.

None. It is recommended that funtional analysis be used to determine an effective reinforcer.

Hierarchy of Consequences

1. Establish a consistent, structured routine through implementation of structured teaching principles.

2. Use visual cues (objects) when giving him commands and directives.

3. Set well defined limits and rules and consistently enforce the rules and apply consequences.

4. Set well defined task expectation with visual cues for the task. Always present the tasks in a left to right or top to bottom sequence.

5. Provide frequent verbal and non-verbal reinforcement for appropriate behaviors.

   a. Utilize tasks he enjoys for rewards. For example, after he has completed a task, let him go outside for a short walk or to get a drink.

   b. Use verbal praise as often as possible for appropriate behaviors.

6. Redirect him into appropriate activities as needed.

7. Continue with implementation of the compliance training procedures a minimum of five times per day.

8. Use time-out (no longer than 5 minutes for inappropriate behaviors) only when other consequences have not worked.

9. When he can calmly reenter the room, he may be allowed to return to his activity.

Hierarchy of Consequences (Responses).

1.   Tell Evan, "No, Do . . . . ." in a calm, firm voice.

2.   State consequences, "If you do _____, _____ will happen."

3.   Redirect to appropriate tasks with visual cues.

4.   Demonstrate the task.

5.   Tell him, "Do this."

6.   If he continues with inappropriate behavior, place him in time-out (no longer than 3 minutes) within the classroom. Use a visual object to indicate time-out (such as a three-minute timer).

7.   At the end of time-out, redirect to the same task so that he learns temper tantrums do not get him out of the task.

8.   If behaviors continue, return him to time-out within the classroom (no longer than 5 minutes).

9.   When he has calmed, redirect him to the same task.

Specific Procedures for Temper Tantrums

1.   Tell Evan, "No, Do . . . ." in a calm, firm voice.

2.   Redirect to an appropriate incompatible task.

3.   Physically prompt to a chair if necessary.

4.   Physically prompt to a sitting position in the chair with hands in lap or to safe area for calming down.

5.   Every time Evan makes a sound, tell him, "Sit quietly" in a firm voice.

6.   When he has calmed, redirect him to the task.

7.   If the tantrum behavior continues, repeat chair procedure.

8.   When he has calmed, redirect to the same task.

The IEP Committee recommends that corporal punishment should not be used.

Person(s) responsible for carrying out the behavior management plan are:

Classroom teachers,

Paraprofessionals,

Educational Diagnostician,

Related service personnel, and

Behavior management specialist

This plan will not be reviewed with the student due to the cognitive functioning level of the student. However, implementation of consistent routines and structure will communicate the plan to the student in a very positive way.

Specific Procedures for Mainstreaming:

These procedures will vary according to the type of class into which he is mainstreamed. For the computer time this spring, it has been effective to take him into the classroom about 15 minutes before the other students come in so that he is used to the setting before they get there. However, these procedures may vary for other settings. This should be decided by instructional staff with consultation from Special Education Support Staff and parents.

Goals and objectives for increasing positive behaviors and/or decreasing negative behaviors have been included in the IEP.

ASSURANCES

The IEP committee assures that the requirements of statutory and constitutional due process and due process under the Individuals with Disabilities Education Act (IDEA) have been met.

IEP SUPPLEMENT

Behavioral Competencies for John as Included in his IEP

Name: John   **Date: May 1, 1997**

School: High School   **Grade: 9th**

John exhibits the following competencies in the behavioral area:

1.   He maintains a clean, well-groomed appearance.

2.   He compliments or offers help to others.

3.   He remains on task and completes classroom assignments during class time.

   a. He demonstrates on task behavior by sitting quietly, looking at material, and performing the task.

   b. He completes a task before going on to the next task.

   c. He uses the time provided to work on assigned tasks.

   d. He remains on task long enough to complete the task.

   e. He remains in his seat during the work period.

4.   He maintains appropriate eye contact.

   a. He maintains eye contact when listening to oral directions.

   b. He makes eye contact with adults when the adult speaks his name.

5.   He is able to state the consequences of given behaviors.

John exhibits difficulties in the following behavioral areas:

1.   Using appropriate language when upset or angry.

2.   Touching self or others in inappropriate ways/maintaining an appropriate personal space (an arm's length away).

3.   Manipulating/touching the physical property of others without permission.

4.   Acting impulsively without considering the consequences of behaviors.

In general, his behaviors have improved considerably during the spring semester, and the behaviors he is exhibiting now are not as major as they previously were.

IEP SUPPLEMENT

BEHAVIOR MANAGEMENT PLAN

Name: John   Date: May 1, 1997

School: High School   Grade: 9th

John is currently completing his freshman year at High School. He is residing at a special group home placement within the School District geographical area. At the beginning of the current school year, he was served in a self-contained special education setting with a paraprofessional providing specialized support. He was sent home several times during the fall because of behavioral difficulties.

Based on current data, the IEP committee considering this student's educational programming and placement has made the following determinations regarding discipline management.

1.   The student has the capacity to understand the school rules as outlined in the district's code on conduct.

2.   The student does not have the capacity to follow school rules as outlined in the district's code on conduct.

3.   Due to the student's disability, special behavior management techniques may be necessary.

Behaviors reported on previous assessments of this student:

He inappropriately seeks hugs and violates the personal space boundaries of others.

Social awareness is significantly impaired.

He exhibits an immature approach to social interactions.

He exhibits impulsive behavior.

He exhibits cognitive disintegration of thinking, i.e., illogical associations, and interconnections of things.

Under high arousal, he exhibits significant deterioration in emotional self-control.

Behaviors exhibited in the school environment reported by teachers:

1.   Difficulty accepting criticism or correction.

2.   Talking out inappropriately in class (i.e., using inappropriate language).

3.   Inappropriate touching of self and others/violation of personal space.

4.   Arguing with adults when given a direction.

5.   Acting impulsively without thinking about the consequences of his behavior.

It must be noted that since December, John is making good choices on his own. His general behavior has been much better. There have been no major problems at school during the spring semester.

Behaviors/rules which the group home enforces.

1.   Keeping an arms length space from others at all times (no hugging, patting, or arm around the shoulder),

2.   Nothing in the mouth unless it is to be eaten - no pencils, rulers, or paper.

3.   Following directions on the first request, and

4.   Not handling other people's belongings - touching without asking.

The following behaviors have occurred during the spring semester and are related to the student's disability.

1.   Inappropriate language,

2.   Put stars at the top of his papers,

3.   Calls his agriculture teacher the "Queen of Ag",

4.   Violation of personal space and inappropriate hugging of others.

Reinforcers which have been tried during the past year:

1.   Verbal praise,

2.   Tangible reinforcements (food, candy, money, tokens, etc.),

3.   Activity reinforcers, and

4.   Premack Principle,

    Describe the effectiveness of these reinforcers:
    These reinforcers are generally effective. He particularly likes time on the computer to play solitaire.

Consequences that were applied during the past year:

1.   Student/teacher conference.

2.   Premack Principle (If you do _____, you may do _____.).

3.   Loss of privileges.

4.   Isolation in area by himself away from other students.

5.   Time-out for cooling off.

6.   Conference with teacher, principal, and student.

7.   Conference with principal, teacher, and parent.

8.   Sent home for calming down.

9.   Stopped him and asked him to reconsider his choices.

10.   Gave him wait time to allow him to process information and make the right decision.

> **Describe the effectiveness of these consequences:**
> # 6 and # 7 are not effective; they are a privilege for him. # 9 and 10 are effective.

Reinforcers or consequences that have not been tried but might be effective:

None have been identified.

The IEP Committee agrees that corporal punishment would not be appropriate for this student.

Person(s) responsible for carrying out the behavior management plan and reviewing this plan with the student (if not present at IEP committee meeting.

Instructional staff and parents.

Other school staff and special education support personnel will be available to assist the teacher and paraprofessionals with carrying out the behavior management plan.

Goals for increasing positive behaviors: (Mastery criteria in italics)

John will:

1.   Be able to identify the facial gestures and voice inflections associated with different emotional states.   (60%)

2. Accept criticism by looking at the person and listening without getting angry. (60%)

3. Accept praise by looking at the person and thanking the person for the compliment. (75%)

4. Demonstrate an understanding of the consequences of behavior by practicing alternative responses in role play situations. (50%)

5. Move from one activity to another in a reasonable amount of time with no more than three prompts. (60%)

6. Respond appropriately to authority figures by talking to them in a conversational voice and performing requested task with no more than three prompts. (60%)

7. Respond to peers by talking to them in social situations (i.e., greeting with hello when entering class; working with a buddy or in a cooperative group in mainstream classes). (70%)

8. Maintain an arm's length of space when interacting with others. (85%)

9. Follow directions on the first request. (50%)

Goals for decreasing negative behaviors:

John will:

1. Refrain from asking to leave the room to avoid doing assignments. (80%)

2. Refrain from arguing, using a harsh tone of voice, yelling, etc., when angry. (70%)

3. Refrain from using curse words when he is angry. (50%)

4. Refrain from using hugs as a form of greeting to anyone other than family members. (60%)

5. Refrain from using another's personal space without invitation. (60%)

6. Refrain from putting inedible substances (pencils, rulers, straws, paper, etc.) in mouth. (70%)

7. Refrain from touching other people's belongings without asking. (60%)

Reinforcers which will be used by special education personnel include:

tangible reinforcers,

activity reinforcers, and

extra privileges.

The vocational education teacher will use the same reinforcers and consequences.

Recommended Interventions:

1. Establish consistent routines.

2. Structure the classroom space to minimize distractions.

3. Set well defined limits and rules and reinforce or consequent them immediately.

    Visibly post rules in the classroom.

4. Set well defined tasks expectations using precision requests and adequate wait time speaking in a low voice tone. (Direct statements reflecting the desired action.) For example, "John, please take out your spelling folder."

5. Ignore minor inappropriate behaviors, whenever possible.

6. Provide frequent verbal and nonverbal reinforcement for appropriate behaviors.

    Praise statements should exceed reprimand statements by a 4 to 1 ratio.

7. Provide many opportunities for success.

8. Use the Premack Principle. (If you do _____, you may do _____).

9. Encourage John to communicate his feelings/needs/wants, etc. in an appropriate manner at appropriate times.

10. Redirect John into appropriate activities as needed (shape appropriate behaviors with reinforcements and ignore or redirect inappropriate ones).

11. Use visual cues and supports to cue him into more appropriate behaviors.

12. Implement a social skills training program which will provide opportunities for him to practice appropriate, prosocial behaviors in a nonthreatening situation.

13. Implement hierarchy of consequences whenever inappropriate behaviors are exhibited.

Hierarchy of Consequences:

1. Redirect to assigned task.

2. Allow one minute of wait time.

3. Reminder of rules/restatement of instruction.

4. Redirect to appropriate activities and behaviors.

5. Warning (state verbal limits and options).

6. State Premack Principle (If you do _____, you may do _____).

7. Time-out from teacher/adult attention (5 minutes) in the classroom.

8. Redirect to a task.

9. Time-out from teacher/adult attention (10 minutes) in room.

11. Loss of privilege.

12. Take to principal's office for principal/teacher/student conference.

13. If John remains out of control, he may be removed from the class and sent home for a "calming down" period. This is usually for the remainder of the day.

   Anytime that John is sent home for three "calming down" periods, an IEP Committee Meeting must be held to evaluate the current IEP.

14. When John comes back to school, he must conference with his teacher. This conference would include having John apologize for his behavior, practice appropriate behavior, and request permission to come back to school.

The goals and objectives will be evaluated at least once per six week period. A report detailing IEP progress will be sent to the parents.

Other comments from the IEP Committee:

ASSURANCES

The IEP committee assures that the requirements of statutory and constitutional due processes and due process under the Individuals with Disabilities Education Act (IDEA) have been met.

Appendix B
Data Collection Forms

CHECKLIST FOR DEVELOPING BEHAVIORAL INTERVENTIONS

INSTRUCTIONS: When developing behavioral intervention plans, use a 4 to indicate the completion of each step.

- ❑ 1. Identify the behavior to change.
- ❑ 2. Complete a functional analysis of the behavior.
- ❑ 3. Complete a reinforcer assessment.
- ❑ 4. Measure the frequency, intensity, and/or duration of the behavior.
- ❑ 5. Develop effective communication strategies.
- ❑ 6. Develop strategies for meeting sensory needs.
- ❑ 7. Identify appropriate social skills to teach.
- ❑ 8. Develop antecedent control strategies.
- ❑ 9. Develop self-regulation strategies.
- ❑ 10. Develop strategies for teaching new behaviors.
- ❑ 11. Develop strategies for reinforcing desired behaviors.
- ❑ 12. Outline negative reinforcers for unacceptable behaviors, if needed.
- ❑ 13. Develop a crisis plan if needed.
- ❑ 14. Determine procedures for measuring progress.
- ❑ 15. Review progress on a regular basis.
- ❑ 16. If progress is satisfactory, continue using the intervention program.
- ❑ 17. If progress is unsatisfactory, refer to the checklist titled "Guidelines for Troubleshooting Unsatisfactory Progress".
- ❑ 18. Develop procedures for generalization training.
- ❑ 19. Fade reinforcers.
- ❑ 20. Take care of yourself! Use coping and stress management strategies.

FUNCTIONAL ANALYSIS

INSTRUCTIONS: Answer each question regarding the behaviors targeted for change.

Behavior	Where did it occur?	When did it occur?	With whom did it occur?	How long did it last?	What happened after it occurred?

Comments:_____

_____

_____

REINFORCER ASSESSMENT

Name:_____   **Date:**_____

INSTRUCTIONS: Use a check mark (✔) to indicate the items preferred.

SOCIAL AND SENSORY REINFORCERS

❑ Adult attention

❑ Attention from specific adults.   List preferred adults:_____

❑ Being left alone

❑ Time spent with peer   List preferred peers:_____

❑ Freedom from interference from adults

❑ Freedom from interference from peers

❑ A positive note to give to person of choice		❑ Stim time
❑ Hugs	❑ Praise	❑ Eye contact
❑ Private praise	❑ Public recognition	❑ Public praise
❑ Being rocked	❑ Being held	❑ Applause
❑ OK sign	❑ Back rub	❑ Tickles
❑ Sit in adult's lap	❑ Thumbs up sign	❑ Shake hands
❑ High five sign	❑ Pats	❑ Twirl around
❑ Swinging	❑ Being brushed	❑ Jumping
❑ Vibrator	❑ Lotion	❑ Powder
❑ Roll up in blanke	❑ Smiles	❑ Motor lab
❑ Blowing bubbles	❑ Shoes off	❑ Cologne

❑ List other _____

❑ List other _____

❑ List other _____

❑ List other _____

❑ List other _____

❑ List other _____

REINFORCER ASSESSMENT

Name:_____   Date:_____

INSTRUCTIONS: Use a check mark (✔) to indicate the items preferred.

ACTIVITY REINFORCERS

❑ Music, List preferred music _____

❑ Playing with toys, List preferred toys _____

❑ Puzzles	❑ Computer	❑ Water play
❑ Outside play	❑ Snack time	❑ Free time
❑ Playing with pets	❑ Riding toys	❑ Books, stories
❑ Going for a walk	❑ Making choices	❑ Helping adult
❑ Drawing	❑ Painting	❑ Being read to
❑ Job responsibilities	❑ Wearing cosmetics	❑ Visiting
❑ Wearing jewelry	❑ Special seat	❑ Balloons
❑ More independence	❑ Riding bikes	❑ Cooking

❑ List preferred materials_____

❑ Computer

List preferred programs_____

_____

❑ Social activities

List preferred types_____

_____

❑ Leisure activities

List preferred types_____

_____

REINFORCER ASSESSMENT

Name:_____   Date:_____

INSTRUCTIONS: Use a check mark (✔) to indicate the items preferred.

TANGIBLE ITEMS

❑ Chips
List preferred types_____

❑ Cookies
List preferred types_____

❑ Candy
List preferred types_____

❑ Fruit
List preferred types_____

❑ Cereal
List preferred types_____

❑ Snacks
List preferred types_____

❑ Drinks
List preferred types_____

❑ Other preferred foods
List preferred types_____

❑ Stickers
List preferred types_____

❑ Toys
List preferred types_____

❑ Games
List preferred types_____

❑ Other
List preferred types_____

REINFORCER ASSESSMENT

Name:_____   Date:_____

INSTRUCTIONS: Use a check mark (✔) to indicate the items preferred.

AREAS OF INTEREST

❑ Animals

List preferred types_____

❑ Weather	❑ Trucks	❑ Trains
❑ Dinosaurs	❑ Cars	❑ Science
❑ Math	❑ Numbers	❑ Shapes
❑ Machines	❑ Tools	❑ Clothes
❑ Outdoors	❑ Sports	❑ Computers

❑ List favorite TV programs   _____

❑ List favorite celebrities   _____

❑ List favorite colors   _____

❑ List favorite movies   _____

❑ List favorite songs   _____

❑ List favorite places to go   _____

❑ Other   _____

❑ Other   _____

❑ Other   _____

MISCELLANEOUS INFORMATION

❑ List foods disliked   _____

❑ List noises disliked   _____

❑ List activites disliked   _____

❑ List places does not like to go   _____

❑ List materials disliked   _____

❑ List animals disliked   _____

❑ List any other dislikes   _____

❑ List any known fears   _____

BEHAVIOR CHART FOR HIGH FREQUENCY BEHAVIORS

Name:_____   **Date:**_____

INSTRUCTIONS: List times or activities for monitoring behavioral performance. List one desired behavior in each box. Add pictures if needed to depict desired behaviors. For each time period, circle the approximate number of times the behavior occurred.

Time or Activity	Behavior #1	Behavior #2	Behavior #3	Behavior #4	Signature
	0 1-3 4-7 8-10 More than 10	0 1-3 4-7 8-10 More than 10	0 1-3 4-7 8-10 More than 10	0 1-3 4-7 8-10 More than 10	
	0 1-3 4-7 8-10 More than 10	0 1-3 4-7 8-10 More than 10	0 1-3 4-7 8-10 More than 10	0 1-3 4-7 8-10 More than 10	
	0 1-3 4-7 8-10 More than 10	0 1-3 4-7 8-10 More than 10	0 1-3 4-7 8-10 More than 10	0 1-3 4-7 8-10 More than 10	
	0 1-3 4-7 8-10 More than 10	0 1-3 4-7 8-10 More than 10	0 1-3 4-7 8-10 More than 10	0 1-3 4-7 8-10 More than 10	
	0 1-3 4-7 8-10 More than 10	0 1-3 4-7 8-10 More than 10	0 1-3 4-7 8-10 More than 10	0 1-3 4-7 8-10 More than 10	

Comments:_____

Copyright 1996. All rights reserved. Maria Bird-West Wheeler
Permission to copy granted for use with individual behavior change programs.

BEHAVIOR CHART FOR HIGH FREQUENCY BEHAVIORS

Name:_____   **Date:**_____

INSTRUCTIONS: List times or activities for monitoring behavioral performance. List one desired behavior in each box. Add pictures if needed to depict desired behaviors. For each time period, circle the approximate number of times the behavior occurred.

Time or Activity	Behavior #1	Behavior #2	Behavior #3	Behavior #4	Signature
	0 1-5 6-10 11-15 16-20 More than 20	0 1-5 6-10 11-15 16-20 More than 20	0 1-5 6-10 11-15 16-20 More than 20	0 1-5 6-10 11-15 16-20 More than 20	
	0 1-5 6-10 11-15 16-20 More than 20	0 1-5 6-10 11-15 16-20 More than 20	0 1-5 6-10 11-15 16-20 More than 20	0 1-5 6-10 11-15 16-20 More than 20	
	0 1-5 6-10 11-15 16-20 More than 20	0 1-5 6-10 11-15 16-20 More than 20	0 1-5 6-10 11-15 16-20 More than 20	0 1-5 6-10 11-15 16-20 More than 20	
	0 1-5 6-10 11-15 16-20 More than 20	0 1-5 6-10 11-15 16-20 More than 20	0 1-5 6-10 11-15 16-20 More than 20	0 1-5 6-10 11-15 16-20 More than 20	
	0 1-5 6-10 11-15 16-20 More than 20	0 1-5 6-10 11-15 16-20 More than 20	0 1-5 6-10 11-15 16-20 More than 20	0 1-5 6-10 11-15 16-20 More than 20	

Comments:_____

Copyright 1996. All rights reserved. Maria Bird-West Wheeler
Permission to copy granted for use with individual behavior programs.

BEHAVIOR CHART FOR HIGH DURATION BEHAVIORS

Name:_____   **Date:**_____

INSTRUCTIONS: List times or activities for monitoring behavioral performance. Use one column for each behavior to be measured. If a behavior tends to occur more than one time in the indicated time frames, then measure each episode of the same behavior in a separate column. For each time period, circle the approximate length of time each episode of the behavior lasted.

Time or Activity	Behavior #1		Behavior #2		Behavior #3		Behavior #4		Signature
	↓ 1 1-3 4-7 8-10 10-15 ↑15		↓ 1 1-3 4-7 8-10 10-15 ↑15		↓ 1 1-3 4-7 8-10 10-15 ↑15		↓ 1 1-3 4-7 8-10 10-15 ↑15		
	↓ 1 1-3 4-7 8-10 10-15 ↑15		↓ 1 1-3 4-7 8-10 10-15 ↑15		↓ 1 1-3 4-7 8-10 10-15 ↑15		↓ 1 1-3 4-7 8-10 10-15 ↑15		
	↓ 1 1-3 4-7 8-10 10-15 ↑15		↓ 1 1-3 4-7 8-10 10-15 ↑15		↓ 1 1-3 4-7 8-10 10-15 ↑15		↓ 1 1-3 4-7 8-10 10-15 ↑15		
	↓ 1 1-3 4-7 8-10 10-15 ↑15		↓ 1 1-3 4-7 8-10 10-15 ↑15		↓ 1 1-3 4-7 8-10 10-15 ↑15		↓ 1 1-3 4-7 8-10 10-15 ↑15		
	↓ 1 1-3 4-7 8-10 10-15 ↑15		↓ 1 1-3 4-7 8-10 10-15 ↑15		↓ 1 1-3 4-7 8-10 10-15 ↑15		↓ 1 1-3 4-7 8-10 10-15 ↑15		

Comments:_____

Copyright 1996. All rights reserved. Maria Bird-West Wheeler
Permission to copy granted for use with individual behavior programs.

KEY: ↓ = less than
      ↑ = greater than
      time = # of minutes

BEHAVIOR CHART FOR HIGH DURATION BEHAVIORS

Name:_____   **Date:**_____

INSTRUCTIONS: List times or activities for monitoring behavioral performance. Use one column for each behavior to be measured. If a behavior tends to occur more than one time in the indicated time frames, then measure each episode of the same behavior in a separate column. For each time period, circle the approximate length of time each episode of the behavior lasted.

Time or Activity	Behavior #1	Behavior #2	Behavior #3	Behavior #4	Signature
	↓1 1-10 10-30 30-45 45-60 ↑60	↓1 1-10 10-30 30-45 45-60 ↑60	↓1 1-10 10-30 30-45 45-60 ↑60	↓1 1-10 10-30 30-45 45-60 ↑60	
	↓1 1-10 10-30 30-45 45-60 ↑60	↓1 1-10 10-30 30-45 45-60 ↑60	↓1 1-10 10-30 30-45 45-60 ↑60	↓1 1-10 10-30 30-45 45-60 ↑60	
	↓1 1-10 10-30 30-45 45-60 ↑60	↓1 1-10 10-30 30-45 45-60 ↑60	↓1 1-10 10-30 30-45 45-60 ↑60	↓1 1-10 10-30 30-45 45-60 ↑60	
	↓1 1-10 10-30 30-45 45-60 ↑60	↓1 1-10 10-30 30-45 45-60 ↑60	↓1 1-10 10-30 30-45 45-60 ↑60	↓1 1-10 10-30 30-45 45-60 ↑60	
	↓1 1-10 10-30 30-45 45-60 ↑60	↓1 1-10 10-30 30-45 45-60 ↑60	↓1 1-10 10-30 30-45 45-60 ↑60	↓1 1-10 10-30 30-45 45-60 ↑60	

Comments:_____

Copyright 1996. All rights reserved. Maria Bird-West Wheeler
Permission to copy granted for use with individual behavior programs.

KEY: ↓ = less than
↑ = greater than
time = # of minutes

BEHAVIOR CHART FOR RATING INTENSITY
OF LOW FREQUENCY BEHAVIORS

Name:_____   **Date:**_____

INSTRUCTIONS: List times or activities for monitoring behavioral performance. Use one column for each behavior to be rated. If a behavior tends to occur more than once in the indicated time frame, then rate each occurrence of the same behavior in a separate column. Rate the severity of each episode of the behavior by circling the best descriptor. Refer to the following key to indicate the severity of the behavior observed.

ML   =   MILD; the behavior was offensive or inappropriate, but did not disrupt ongoing activities.

MOD   =   MODERATE; the behavior interrupted ongoing activites, but there was no significant potential for harm.

SV   =   SEVERE; the behavior included significant potential for harm.

0   =   The behavior did not occur.

Time or Activity	Behavior #1	Behavior #2	Behavior #3	Behavior #4	Signature
	ML MOD SV 0	ML MOD SV 0	ML MOD SV 0	ML MOD SV 0	
	ML MOD SV 0	ML MOD SV 0	ML MOD SV 0	ML MOD SV 0	
	ML MOD SV 0	ML MOD SV 0	ML MOD SV 0	ML MOD SV 0	
	ML MOD SV 0	ML MOD SV 0	ML MOD SV 0	ML MOD SV 0	
	ML MOD SV 0	ML MOD SV 0	ML MOD SV 0	ML MOD SV 0	
	ML MOD SV 0	ML MOD SV 0	ML MOD SV 0	ML MOD SV 0	

Comments:_____

Copyright 1996. All rights reserved. Maria Bird-West Wheeler
Permission to copy granted for use with individual behavior change programs.

YES / NO BEHAVIOR CHART

Name:_____   **Date:**_____

INSTRUCTIONS: List times or activities for monitoring behavioral performance. List one desired behavior in each box. Add pictures if needed to depict desired behaviors. If the behavior occurred consistently during the time or activity indicated, circle "yes" in the correct box. If the behavior did not occur consistently during the time or activity indicated, circle "no". When completed, count and record the number of "yeses" circled. Color that many boxes on the Bar Graph Chart.

Time or Activity	Behavior #1	Behavior #2	Behavior #3	Behavior #4	Signature
	YES NO	YES NO	YES NO	YES NO	
	YES NO	YES NO	YES NO	YES NO	
	YES NO	YES NO	YES NO	YES NO	
	YES NO	YES NO	YES NO	YES NO	
	YES NO	YES NO	YES NO	YES NO	
	YES NO	YES NO	YES NO	YES NO	
	YES NO	YES NO	YES NO	YES NO	
	YES NO	YES NO	YES NO	YES NO	
	YES NO	YES NO	YES NO	YES NO	
	YES NO	YES NO	YES NO	YES NO	
	YES NO	YES NO	YES NO	YES NO	
	YES NO	YES NO	YES NO	YES NO	
	YES NO	YES NO	YES NO	YES NO	
	YES NO	YES NO	YES NO	YES NO	
	YES NO	YES NO	YES NO	YES NO	

Total Number of "Yeses" Cirlcled:_____

Comments:_____

Copyright 1996. All rights reserved. Maria Bird-West Wheeler
Permission to copy granted for use with individual behavior change programs.

YES / NO BEHAVIOR CHART BAR GRAPH

INSTRUCTIONS: Color one box for each "yes" earned, moving up each column, from bottom to top. When you reach the top of the column, you earn a reinforcer. To continue, start at the bottom of the next column.

☺	☺	☺	☺	☺	☺

BEHAVIOR INTERVENTIONS:
GUIDELINES FOR TROUBLESHOOTING UNSATISFACTORY PROGRESS

YES	NO	
❏	❏	Is the behavior stated in specific, observable, and measurable terms? *If no, restate the behavior using these terms.*
❏	❏	Does the behavior need to be measured differently? *If yes, consider measuring frequency, intensity, and duration.*
❏	❏	Is the intervention plan being implemented consistently? *If no remove the barriers that interfere with consistent implementation, or develop strategies that can be implemented effectively.*
❏	❏	Is the individual still engaging in misbehavior that gives sensory stimulation? *If yes, examine and address the individual's sensory needs.*
❏	❏	Is the individual communicating effectively? *If no, provide communication strategies which the individual can access and use in all settings.*
❏	❏	Are cues and conditions in the environment structured in a way that triggers desired behaviors? *If no, include antecedent control strategies in the intervention plan.*
❏	❏	Are reinforcers used consistently, and do they actually increase the behaviors they follow? *If no, develop an effective menu of reinforcers and use them consistently.*
❏	❏	If negative consequences are used, do they actually decrease the behaviors they follow? *If no, identify negative consequences that are reasonable and naturally or logically related to the misbehavior.*
❏	❏	Has the plan been implemented long enough for the person to consistently connect with consequences on numerous occasions? *If no, allow more time for the person to experience consequences.*
❏	❏	Is the individual showing signs of increased agitation or anxiety, since the implementation of the intervention? *If yes, re-examine the demands being placed on the individual, making sure expectations are clear, and not too high or too low. Make sure the demands are logical and meaningful to the person. Re-examine the negative consequences being used, making sure they are not too harsh, lengthy, severe, unpredictable, or illogical.*

HOME-SCHOOL COMMUNICATION CHECKLIST

Name:_____   **Date:**_____

PARENT: Please complete the checklist below and send this to school with your child each day. Thank You!!

YES	NO	
❑	❑	Student slept through the night. If no, please comment _____
❑	❑	Student ate meals with no unusual problems. If no, please comment _____
❑	❑	Student took all medications as prescribed. If no, please comment _____
❑	❑	Have there been any behavior changes or significant events that may impact the student? If yes, please comment_____

TEACHER: Please complete the checklist below and send home with this student each day. Thank you!!

YES	NO	
❑	❑	Student participated in scheduled activities. If no, please comment _____
❑	❑	Student ate meals with no unusual problems. If no, please comment _____
❑	❑	Student took all medications as prescribed. If no, please comment _____
❑	❑	Have there been any behavior changes or significant events that may impact the student? If yes, please comment_____

Appendix C
Resources

Authors' Note: This is a list of resources we have found to be usable with the autism population. However, it is not a complete list of resources that are available. Inclusion in no way implies that we endorse a particular product or program. It simply provides the reader with other avenues of information and an idea of the types of resources that are available.

Children's Books about Autism

Amenta, C. A. (1992). *Russell is Extra Special*. New York, NY: Magination Press.

This book begins with an introduction for parents about autism. The story begins with a photograph and description of Russell. This is followed by explanations of Russell interacting with his family in various situations at home. Photographs of Russell and family members serve as illustrations for the book. This book was written as a book to help parents talk to their children about autism. I have also used it in school settings to help peers of children with autism understand more about their classmate. Age Group: Approximately 4 to 8 years as a read aloud book and can be used with older elementary children for individual reading.

Katz, I., & Ritvo, E. (1993). *Joey and Sam*. Northridge, CA: Real Life Storybooks.

This book is a story about autism, a family, and a brother's love. Joey, the sibling, describes a day in his and Sam's life from waking up in the morning through the school day. He talks about how difficult it is to have a brother with autism, but ends the short story with "I love you the way you are!" Age Group: Approximately 4 to 8 years as a read aloud book and can be used with older elementary children for individual reading.

Messner, A. (1994). *Captain Tommy*. Arlington, TX: Future Horizons, Inc.

This book is about John, a special boy at a day camp for children. Told by one of the children at the camp, the others creatively draw John into activities with the other children. The story teller is assigned the role of space-ship captain with the task of bringing in a floating spaceship that represents John, the camper with autism. Age Group: Elementary.

Nolette, C. D. (1985). *Having a brother like David*. Minneapolis, MN: Minneapolis Children's Medical Center.

This book is designed to be read with siblings of children with autism. It discusses characteristics of David, the brother with autism, as well as the perspective of Marty, the sibling. Age Group: It can be read to children from 4 to 8 years. Older elementary age children may be able to read it without assistance.

Simmons, Karen L. (1996). *"Little Rainman."* Arlington, TX: Future Horizons, Inc.

According to the author, this book was written to help parents, teachers, and siblings of children with autism understand as early as possible the real "world of autism." It is also designed to help children with autism understand more about their disability. The events in the story are true events from her son Jonathan's life. The story is written as if Jonathan were talking to the reader about how he feels, thinks, and acts. Age Group: Appropriate for all age levels as a general awareness book about the characteristics of autism.

Thompson, M. (1996). *Andy and his yellow frisbee*. Bethesda, MD: Woodbine House, Inc.

This story begins with Andy spinning his yellow frisbee during recess on the playground at school. This book shows concern by Rosie, Andy's sister, about her brother with autism. In the story, Sarah, a new girl at school, tries to befriend Andy. Although he doesn't respond, the story ends with Sarah and Rosie playing together. The last page of the book has a short explanation about autism. Age Group: The reading level is listed as grades Kindergarten through fifth grade.

Watson, E. (1996). *Talking to angels*. New York, NY: Harcourt Brace & Co.

Illustrated by the author with very unique pictures, this book is a quick and easy book describing Christa, a child with autism. With only 17 sentences in the book, it would be good for young children because it can be read very quickly. Text pages with one to two sentences per page alternate with full-page illustrations. Age Group: Preschool and primary.

Children's Books about Related Topics

Authors' Note: Many of the books on this list are more appropriate for higher functioning children with autism or children with Asperger's Syndrome. However, since we frequently don't know to what extent many nonverbal children with autism understand, it wouldn't hurt to use them with any young child. Certain books were selected because children with autism sometimes have other disabilities, and they need information about their other problems too.

Anger Control

Aborn, A. (1994). *Everything I Do You Blame on Me!* King of Prussia, PA: The Center for Applied Psychology.

This book is about Eddie, a child who is angry at everyone. The story tells how Eddie learned new coping strategies for anger which resulted in people changing his nickname to "Steady Eddie." On the back side of this book, there is an upside down book called *Why Should I? It's not my Birthday!* This is a book about an angry kid. The book offers a choice of solutions to problems. The reader must select one of the solutions. Once the solution is selected, the reader turns to the appropriate page to read how that solution turned out. Age Group: Elementary School

Attwood, T. (2004). *Exploring Feelings: Anger.* Arlington, TX: Future Horizons, Inc.

A clinical psychologist from Brisbane, Australia, Dr. Attwood brings over 30 years of experience with individuals with autism/Asperger's/PDD. Dr. Attwood is recognized and respected internationally for his leadership in the field. Dr. Attwood has helped several thousand individuals, from infants to octogenarians, along the full range of the autism spectrum, from profoundly disabled to university professors. His book and videos on Asperger's Syndrome and High-Functioning Autism are recognized as the best offerings ever in the field.

Crary, E. (1992). *I'm Frustrated.* Seattle, WA: Parenting Press, Inc.

This book can be used to help children develop different ways to cope with frustration. The goal of this book is to help children learn social skills by letting them make decisions for the characters and then see the consequences. This is part of a whole series designed to teach social skills published by Parenting Press, Inc.. (Phone: 800-992-6657) Other books that might be of interest are *I Want It, I Can't Wait,* and *My Name is not Dummy.* Age Group: 5-12 years.

Crary, E. (1992). *I'm Mad.* Seattle, WA: Parenting Press, Inc.

This book teaches how Katie learned to deal with anger in appropriate ways such as doing something physical and talking about her feelings instead of having a temper tantrum and yelling. Age Group: 5-12 years.

Duncan, R. (1989). *When Emily Woke Up Angry*. Hauppauge, NY: Barron's Educational Series, Inc.

This is about Emily, a young girl, who woke up angry and didn't know how to deal with her anger. She encountered many animals and tried their methods of dealing with anger until she found one which worked for her. Then, she wasn't angry anymore. Age Group: Kindergarten through 6th grade.

Ludwig, T. G. (1994). *Terry's Temper*. Warminster, PA: Mar-Co Products, Inc.

Terry, a young girl who can't control her temper, gets into trouble at school and at home because of her temper. Through the text and activities, children can learn that tempers can be controlled. The book includes reproducible activity sheets at the back of the book. There are also suggestions for involvement activities which require no writing by the students. Age Group: Grades 1 through 4.

Moser, A. (1994). *Don't Rant and Rave on Wednesdays!* Kansas City, MO: Landmark Editions, Inc.

This delightful book provides strategies for children to use to control their anger. Age Group: This is a great book for counselors, parents, and teachers to use with young preschool through primary grade children.

Shapiro, L. E. (1995). *Sometimes I Like To Fight, But I Don't Do It Much Anymore*. King of Prussia, PA: The Center for Applied Psychology, Inc.

This is about a young boy who likes to fight. It is told from his perspective. He discusses his fighting, going to counseling, and how he has changed as a result of learning to manage his anger in better ways. Age Group: Elementary School

Asthma

Ostrow, W., & Ostrow, V. (1989). *All about Asthma*. Morton Grove, IL: Albert Whitman & Co.

William, a young boy with asthma, tells the reader what it is like to have asthma. The book not only describes how asthma makes william feel, but it gives the young reader information about asthma and how to cope with it. Age Group: Elementary and Junior High.

Attention Deficit Disorder

Galvin, M. (1988). *Otto Learns about His Medicine. A Story about Medication for Hyperactive Children*. New York, NY: Magination Press.

This book is about a small car named *Otto*. His engine is too "revved up" and he has to visit a special mechanic who prescribes medicine to control his hyperactive behavior. Although medication is prescribed, personal responsibility for behavior is still emphasized. The mechanic says, "Medicine can't make you behave. It can help you to choose to behave." Age Group: 4-10.

Gehret, J. (1991). *Eagle Eyes. A Child's Guide to Paying Attention*. New York, NY: Verbal Images Press.

This book about Ben, a young boy with attention deficit disorder, helps readers of all ages understand this disorder. It also provides practical suggestions for organization, social cues, and self calming. Age Group: Elementary School

Korman, C. & Trevino, E. (1995). *Eukee, the Jumpy, Jumpy Elephant*. Plantation, FL: Specialty Press.

This book about Eukee, a bright, hyperactive, young elephant, helps children understand why he is so jumpy and hyperactive. It shows how he learns to help himself and improve his self-esteem. Age Group: 3 to 8 years.

Moss, D. (1989). *Shelley, the Hyperactive Turtle*. Bethesda, MD: Woodbine House.

This book tells the story of Shelley and his family as they face the challenges presented by his hyperactivity. It explains hyperactivity for children with ADHD as well as for siblings and friends. Age Group: 4 to 8 years.

Nadeau, K. G., & Dixon, E. B. (1993.) *Learning to Slow Down and Pay Attention*. Revised Edition. Annandale, VA: Chesapeake Psychological Publications.

This book helps your child identify problems and explains how parents, doctors, and teachers can help him or her to function more successfully. The book addresses paying better attention, managing feelings, getting more organized, and learning to problem-solve. Age Group: 6 to 14 years.

Parker, R. N. (1992). *Making the Grade. An Adolescent's Struggle with ADHD.* Plantation, FL: Impact Publications.

Jim Jerome's difficulties with self-control and inattention create problems for him as he enters junior high school. His parents, teachers, and health professionals assist him in learning about ADD and in developing strategies to help himself. This book is also available in a Spanish edition, Como Pasar De Grado. Age Group: 9 to 14 years.

Parker, R. N. (1993). *Slam Dunk: A Young Boy's Struggle with ADD.* Plantation, FL: Impact Publications.

This book uses Toby, a fifth-grade student with problems paying attention, to discuss classroom accommodations and behavioral and medical interventions. The fictional story is followed by a Questions and Answer section by Harvey C. Parker. Age Group: 8 to 12 years.

Quinn, P. (1991). *Putting on the Brakes, A Young People's Guide to with ADHD.* New York, NY: Magination Press.

This book attempts to give children sense of control and a feeling that they can learn to control their behavior. Age Group: 8-12 years.

Shapiro, L. (1993). *Sometimes I Drive My Mom Crazy, But I Know She's Crazy About Me.* King of Prussia, PA: The Center for Applied Psychology, Inc.

This story, about a young boy with attention deficit hyperactive disorder, addresses the difficult issues children like him confront every day. It presents behavior programs, educational management, and medication information by featuring a young boy who has developed a sense of self-worth through effectively dealing with his problems. Age Group: 5 to 10 years.

Depression

Dubuque, N., & Dubuque, S. (1996). *Kid power tactics for dealing with depression.* King of Prussia, PA. The Center for Applied Psychology, Inc.

Nicholas, the first author of this book, is an 11 year old boy who experiences depression. The book begins with a short description of what depression is followed by causes and treatments for depression. Following that, the book provides 15 tactics for depression. Age Group: This book would be most appropriate for 5th through 9th grade students.

Divorce

All of the books listed under this topic help the child to understand why parents get divorced provide some strategies for coping with the feelings they might have.

Balter, L. (1989). *The Wedding*. New York, NY: Barron's.

Brown, L. K., & Brown, M. (1986). *Dinosaurs Divorce. A Guide for Changing Families*. Boston, MA: Joy Street Books. Little Brown and Company.

Evans, M. D. (1986). *This is Me & My Two Families. An Awareness Scrapbook/Journal for Children Living in Stepfamilies*. New York, NY: Magination Press.

Field, M. B., & Shore, H. (1994). *My Life Turned Upside Down, But I Turned it Rightside Up. A Self-esteem Book About Dealing with Shared Custody*. King Of Prussia, PA: The Center for Applied Psychology, Inc.

Girard, L. W. (1987). *At Daddy's on Saturdays*. Morton Grove, IL: Albert Whitman & Company.

Hogan, P. Z. (1980). *Will Dad Ever Move Back Home?* Milwaukee, WI: Raintree Childrens Books.

Sanford, D. (1985). Please Come Home. *A Child's Book About Divorce*. Hong Kong: Multinomah Press.

Epilepsy

Moss, D. M. (1989). *Lee, the Rabbit with Epilepsy*. Bethesda, MD: Woodbine House.

This book is about Lee, a rabbit with absence seizures (formerly called petit mal seizures). The book begins with a description of the seizure and takes the reader through the diagnosis and medication phases. It ends with Lee realizing that she can still participate in many activities even though she has epilepsy. Age Group: It is most appropriate for 4 through 8 years.

Pridmore, S., & McGrath, M. (1991). *Julia, Mungo, and the Earthquake.* New York, NY: Magination Press.

This book is about tonic-clonic seizures, formerly known as grand mal seizures. It describes from a child's perspective what is like to have this kind of seizure disorder. Characteristics of this form of seizure and the feelings of the individual with the seizure disorder are described. It also ends with Julia being a class hero and other children in her room realizing that basically, she is just like everyone else. Age Group: Elementary through Junior High School.

Swanson, S. (1994). *My Friend Emily.* Boise, ID: Writer's Press Service.

This excellent book about tonic-clonic seizures not only describes the seizure, but also describes what peers can do to help children who have a seizure when no one else is around. It focuses on a friendship between Emily and Katy. While giving excellent information about seizures, it also emphasizes the importance of being a good friend. Age Group: Pre-kindergarten through 3rd grade.

Feeling Different

Cosgrove, S. (1987). *Fanny.* Los Angeles, CA: Price Stern Sloan.

This book, a favorite of mine, is part of the "Serendipity Series." Fanny is a three-legged cat who lives on a farm where none of the animals will talk to her. They think because she is handicapped, she has nothing to say. Ruby, a small dog who loves to kiss and lick, took a dare from one of the other animals and kissed Fanny. Ruby found out that Fanny had lots to say. They became fast friends. The book ends with this sentence, "As you walk, hop, hobble, or wheel meeting people of different kinds, remember that being handicapped is only a state of mind." Age Group: Elementary.

Feelings

Cain, B. S. (1990). *Double-Dip Feelings. Stories to Help Children Understand Emotions.* New York, NY: Magination Press.

This book is about ambivalent feelings. Have you every felt joyful and sad at the same time? Can you love and hate at the same time? This book helps children to understand that we can have confusing feelings - that sometimes we can be mad at people and still love them. The book uses significant childhood events to explored having two different feelings at the same time for each childhood event. Age Group: Elementary.

Conlin, S., & Friedman, S. L. (1989). *Let's Talk About Feelings: Ellie's Day*. Seattle, WA: Parenting Press, Inc.

This book explores family relationships and the feelings that result from family interactions. The book addressed being excited, proud, sad, grumpy, sorry, scared, rejected, worried, and happy. Age Group: Elementary.

Doleski, T. (1983). *The Hurt*. Mahwah, NJ: Paulist Press.

This book is about a boy, Justin, whose friend called him a "pig-faced punk." He got his feelings hurt and went home to "nurse" his feelings. Justin's hurt got bigger and bigger until his Dad helped him to let his hurt go. Once he let his hurt go, he and Gabriel were able to be friends again.

Friendship

Hart, P. (1994). *Caleb Finds a Friend*. Boise, ID: Writer's Press Service.

This is a story about a hilarious bear who looks and looks. He finally realizes that his friend is the bear who has been helping him search for a friend. The book ends with grandpa, the storyteller saying, "Sometimes we look very hard for the things we already have." He then adds, "Caleb looked and looked for a friend, when his friend panda was there helping him all the time." Age Group: Pre-kindergarten to Grade 3.

Grief Management

Moser, A. (1996). *Don't despair on Thursdays!* Kansas City, MO: Landmark Editions, Inc.

The author talks about the losses that might cause bad feelings and provides strategies for feeling better. Dr. Moser explains the grief process as a normal response that may last a few days or weeks. Age Group: This is a great book for counselors, parents, and teachers to use with young preschool through primary grade children.

Learning Differences

Cummings, R., & Fisher, G. (1991). *The Survival Guide for Kids with LD*. Verbal Images Press.

Although written specifically for students with learning disabilities, it has good information for students with attention deficit disorders. Appropriate sections include dealing with feelings, getting along better in school, reacting to teasing, tips for making friends and getting along at home. Age Group: 8 to 12 years.

Cummings, R., & Fisher, G. (1993). *The Survival guide for teenagers with LD*. Minneapolis, MN: Free Spirit Publishing Inc.

Gehret, J. (1990). *The Don't-give-up Kid*. Fairport, NY: Verbal Images Press.

This book is about Alex, a child with a learning disability, who realizes that his hero, Thomas Edison, faced similar problems. Like Edison, he learns to try new solutions until he succeeds at his dream of creating things that no one ever thought of before. This is a great book which deals with learning disabilities in a very positive way - emphasizing the things the child can do. Age Group: Elementary

Kinicher, J. (1990). *Psychology for Kids. 40 Fun Tests that Help You Learn About Yourself*. Minneapois, MN: Free Spirit Publishing.

This book helps children learn about themselves through a series of easy to use checklists. It provides information about interests, abilities, and what makes the child different from everyone else.

Root, A., & Gladden, L. (1995). *Charlie's Challenge*. Temple, TX: U.S.A. Printmaster Press.

Charlie can design an award-winning castle, but has difficulty reading and spelling. The readers find out about Charlie's strengths and weaknesses and how he meets the daily challenges in his life. This book is a very good tool for helping children with learning disabilities understand their disability.

Stern, J., & Ben-Ami, U. (1996). *Many Ways to Learn. Young People's Guide to Learning Disabilities*. New York. NY: Magination Press.

This book helps children with learning disabilities to understand what it means to have a learning disability. The theme running throughout the book is "your strengths will be what carry you through." Age Group: Upper Elementary through High School. The book is also available on audiotape for students who can't read.

Mental Retardation

Phillips, G. (1995). *Becca and Sue Make Two*. Boise, ID: Writer's Press.

This book is about Sue, a young girl with Down syndrome. However, it conveys a message to all persons about disabilities. It shows how Becca and Sue become friends. They even play the piano together in the talent show. In the course of the story, it also gives information about Down syndrome. Age Group: 4 years to 9 years.

O'Shaughnessy, E. (1992). *Somebody called me a retard today. . . and my heart felt sad.* New York, NY. Walker and Company.

Although this book is designed for children, I use it with all ages. I think it says a lot in a minimum number of words. The little boy says "When somebody called me a retard today, I cried." He then goes on to say what his Dad tells him about all the things that he can do. He tells about his abilities. He ends with a heartwrenching admission, "But I'll tell you a secret. . .when somebody called me a 'retard' today. . .my heart felt sad." Age Group: Pre-kindergarten through Elementary.

Miscellaneous

Hoke, S. (1995). *My Body is Mine, My Feelings are Mine.* King of Prussia, PA: The Center for Applied Psychology, Inc.

This book about body safety is a great way to teach young children how to protect themselves from the possibility of sexual abuse. The author talks about appropriate kinds of "touching" and what is not appropriate. The author also provides helpful guidelines for adults summarizing the major points that parents and professionals should know about body safety for their children. Age Group: Pre-school and Elementary School.

Lobby, T. (1990). *Jessica and the Wolf. A Story for Children Who Have Bad Dreams.* New York, NY: Magination Press.

The parents in this story help Jessica solve her problem about a bad dream. Jessica learns that her parents are there to help her when she needs help. Age Group: Pre-school and Elementary.

Martin, A., Rivers, R., & Tannenbaum, M. (1988). *Safety in the home.* New York, NY: Grolier Limited.

This book is part of a safety series. It goes through all of the areas in the home pointing out the potential dangers. The main characters are animals, the Badgerson Family. Age Group: Designed for young children, it is an excellent book to promote discussion about potential dangers in the home. Age Group: Preschool, first, and second grades.

Help Me Be Good Books. Grolier Books.

This is a series of books for children which deals with the various behavior problems that young children exhibit. Titles include: *Bad Sport, Being Bossy, Being Bullied, Being Careless, Being Destructive, Being Forgetful, Being Greedy, Being Lazy, Being Mean, Being Messy, Being Rude, Being Selfish, Being Wasteful, Breaking Promises, Cheating, Complaining, Disobeying, Fighting, Gossiping, Interrupting, Lying, Overdoing It, Showing Off, Snooping, Stealing, Tattling, Teasing, Throwing Tantrums, and Whining.* Age Group: 4 to 8 years.

Self-Esteem

Kaufman, G., & Raphael, L. (1990). *Stick Up for Yourself! Every Kid's Guide to Personal Power and Positive Self-Esteem.* Minneapolis, MN: Free Spirit Publishing.

This book tells children how to stick up for themselves with other kids, siblings, and even parents and teachers It discusses feelings, using power in relationships, and learning to like yourself. A teacher's guide is also available.

Moser, A. (1991). *Don't feed the monster on Tuesdays!* Kansas City, MO: Landmark Editions, Inc.

The author provides children with information that will help them understand the importance of their self-worth. Practical strategies and suggestions are provided so that children can evaluate and strengthen their sense of self-esteem. Age Group: This is a great book for counselors, parents, and teachers to use with young preschool through primary grade children.

Payne, L, M. (1994). *Just Because I Am. A Child's Book of Affirmation.* Minneapolis, MN: Free Spirit Publishing.

The author of this book, designed to strengthen and support a child's self-esteem, says, "Little ones learn that they are special 'not because of things I do, not because of what I look like, not because of what I have. . . just because I am.'" This book provides the child with positive, affirming messages. Age Group: Pre-kindergarten through Elementary. *A Leader's Guide* is also available which provides a complete introductory course on self-esteem for young children.

Stress Management

Hipp, E. (1985). *Fighting Invisible Tigers. A Stress management Guide for Teens.* Minneapolis, MN: Free Spirit Publishing.

This book provides strategies for adolescents to use in surviving and thriving in the world today It includes information about the fight-or-flight response, crashing and burning, self-monitoring, fears and misconceptions, distractions, procrastination, relaxation techniques, asserivteness and humor. A leader's guide for teachers is also available.

Moser, A. (1988). *Don't pop your cork on Mondays!* Kansas City, MO: Landmark Editions, Inc.

This entertaining book explores the causes and effects of stress and provides children with practical approaches for dealing with stress in their daily lives. Age Group: This is a great book for use with young preschool through primary grade children.

Resources for Adults

Autism - General

Janzen, J. E. (1996). *Understanding the nature of autism. A practical guide.* San Antonio, TX: Therapy Skill Builders. A division of The Psychological Corporation.

This book lives up to the title - it is a practical guide. The author provides many useful forms that can be used with individual students.

Siegal, B. (1996). *The world of the autistic child. Understanding and treating autistic spectrum disorders.* New York, NY: Oxford University Press.

This is a very comprehensive text on autism.

Behavior Materials

Burke, R. V., & Herron, R. W. *Common Sense Parenting. A Practical Approach from Boys Town.* Boys Town, NE: Ather Flanagan's Boys' Home.

This book contains helpful information that all parents can use with their children. It is easily understood and provides information on how to give effective praise and encourage positive behavior.

Clark, L. (1985). *SOS! Help for Parents.* Bowling Green, KY: Parents Press.

This is an excellent guide for providing solutions to parents of all young children. It provides basic, easy to read information about rewards, punishment, and time-out.

Gillingham, G. (1995). *Autism: Handle with care!* Arlington, TX: Future Education, Inc.

This is a great book for the beginner who knows nothing about autism. It's great to give to your child's new teacher.

Jenson, W. R., Rhode, G., & Reavis, H. K. (1996). *The tough kid tool box*. Longmont, CA: Sopris West.

This book of forms is designed to accompany *The Tough Kid Book*.

Johns, B. H., & Carr, V. G. (1995). *Techniques for managing verbally and physically aggressive students.* Denver, CO: Love Publishing Co.

This book which was written for school staff provides methods for managing students who are physically and verbally aggressive in the classroom. Although some of the techniques may also be used by parents, the focus is on the educational setting.

Maurice, C., Ed. (1996). *Behavioral intervention for young children with autism.* Austin, TX: Pro-Ed.

This book comprehensively covers behavioral interventions for young children with autism.

McIntyre, T. (1989). *A resource book for remediating common behavior and learning problems.* Boston, MA: Allyn and Bacon.

This book contains lists of interventions for over 350 different behavior and learning problems. It is a wonderful resource guide when you just need some quick ideas about what to do for a specific problem. From 10 to 100 interventions are listed for each of the problems discussed.

Rhode, G., Jenson, W. R., & Reavis, H. K. (1993). T*he tough kid book. Practical management strategies.* Longmont, CO: Sopris West

This book provides practical strategies for management of behavior. It is an easy-to-read book with very good behavioral strategies for parents and educators.

Schopler, E., & Mesibov, G.(Ed.) (1994). *Behavioral issues in autism.* New York, NY Plenum Press.

This book provides comprehensive coverage of behavioral issues and the methods that are used in North Carolina in the TEACCH Program.

Simpson, R. L., & Regan, M. (1988). *Management of autistic behavior.* Austin, TX: Pro-Ed.

This book provides suggestions for specific problems such as head banging, scratching, and other problem behaviors.

Communication Materials

Frost, L. A., & Bondy, A. S. (1994). PECS. T*he picture exchange communication system. Training Manual.* Cherry Hill, NJ: Pyramid Educational Consultants, Inc.

This manual provides detailed instructions for implementing the Picture Exchange Communication system with nonverbal individuals.

Goossens', C. & Crain, S. S. (1992), *Utilizing switch interfaces with children who are severely physically challenged. An emphasis on communication strategies.* Austin, TX: Pro-Ed.

This book provides detailed instructions for the use of switches. It also provides the reader with simple to follow instructions and illustrations for making switches to adapt toys and other devices such as radios and tape recorders.

Hodgdon, L. (1995). *Visual strategies for improving communication.* Troy, MI: QuirkRoberts.

This book provides excellent information with illustrations about the use of visual strategies for promoting and improving communication. It provides specific information about structuring the environment, making visual tools, and integrating visual strategies into communication and education.

Korsten, J. E., Dunn, D, K., Foss, T. V., & Francke, M. K. *Every move counts.*

This book presents sensory-based activities in a framework designed to facilitate communication development. It is designed for all individuals unable to communicate their wants and needs regardless of the cause.

Korsten, J. E., Dunn, D, K., Foss, T. V., & Francke, M. K. *Every move counts. Parent's Guide.*

The parent's guide to *Every Move Counts* examines the types of stimulation most likely to elicit a response.

Mayer-Johnson Company, P. O. Box 1579, Solana Beach, CA 92075-1579. Phone: 619-550-0084.

This company specializes in materials for nonverbal individuals. *The Picture Communication Symbols, Books I, II, and III* are standards in most classrooms serving individuals who cannot speak. Simple, clear drawings are available in book form. *The Boardmaker Program* is also available from Mayer-Johnson. It is the computerized version of the picture symbols and now comes in either Mac or IBM format. Other products in the catalog are support products such as other instructional materials that use the picture symbols, computer programs, various types of wallets for carrying and displaying picture communication symbols, and communication books.

Quill, K. A., (Ed.) (1995). *Teaching children with autism. Strategies to enhance communication and socialization.* New York, NY: Delmar Publishers Inc.

This book describes teaching strategies and instructional modifications which promote communication and socialization in individuals with autism. Chapters in the book are written by Temple Grandin, Charles Hart, Barry Prizant, Diane Twachtman, Carol A. Gray, Nancy J. Dalrymple, Linda Hodgdon, and others.

Miscellaneous Materials

Adderholdt-Elliot, M. (1987). *Perfectionism. What's Bad About Being Too Good?* Minneapolis, MN: Free Spirit Publishing.

This book, written for children and adolescents, helps the person find out if he or she is a perfectionist and it explores some possible reasons for perfectionism. Useful strategies for dealing with perfectionist tendencies are provided.

Falvey, M. A., Forest, M., Pearpoint, J., & Rosenberg, R. L. (1994). *All my life's a circle. Using the tools: Circles, MAPS, & PATH.* Toronto, Ont. Canada: Inclusion Press.

This booklet provides step by step instructions for implementing 3 common strategies to facilitate inclusion. They are circles (identifying the individual's circle of friends); MAPS (making action plans): and PATH (planning alternative tomorrow's with hope).

Fouse, B. (1996). *Creating a Win-Win IEP for students with autism.* Arlington, TX: Future Horizons, Inc.

This book provides comprehensive information about the child centered process for education beginning with referral and assessment and ending with placement. The information about related services and IEP goal development may be of particular interest to parents of school-age children.

Foxx, R. M., & Azrin, N. H. (1973). *Toilet Training the Retarded.* Champaign, IL: Research Press.

This book describes a toilet training program which can be used with individuals with developmental disabilities.

Perske, R. (1988). *Circles of friends.* Nashville, TN: Abingdon Press.

This book describes the concept of "circles of friends" which may be used to include individuals with disabilities in the home, school, and community.

Ziegler, R. G., & Ziegler, P. (1992). *Homemade Books to Help Kids Cope.* New York, NY: Magination Press.

This book shows parents how to create personalized books for and with their children about special problems or situations with which they must cope.

Sensory Integration Materials

Anderson, E., & Emmons, P.(1996). *Unlocking the mysteries of sensory dysfunction.* Arlington, TX: Future Horizons, Inc.

This book provides readers with basic information about sensory dysfunction. The authors offer the unique perspective of parents of children with Sensory Integrative Dysfunction. The authors also provide information about how to access services.

Ayres, A. J. & Robbins, J. (1979). *Sensory integration and the child.* Los Angeles, CA: Western Psychological Services.

This is a classic text about sensory integration written by the founder of the sensory integration movement. The text describes sensory integration and addresses specific components of sensory integrative dysfunction. The book also includes a section about what parents can do.

Fink, B. E., OTR. (1989). *Sensory-motor integration activities.* Tucson, AZ: Therapy Skills Builders. A division of Communication Skill Builders.

This book explains the sensory systems and provides specific activities for remediation of sensory dysfunctions. The activities are appropriate for elementary age children.

PDP Products, 12015 N. July Ave., Hugo,MN 55038. Phone: 612-439-8865.

This company sells sensory integration products such as the silent whistles and other touchy, feely toys discussed in the book. It also sells brushes that are used in brushing therapy. The company also provides continuing education workshops related to sensory integration needs and activities.

Sensory Integration International. (1991). *A parent's guide to understanding sensory integration.* Torrance, CA: Sensory Integration International.

This booklet provides an explanation of the different sensory systems and how they work together for sensory integration. It also tells parents what to expect from therapy and provides a glossary of terms related to sensory integration.

Therapy Skill Builders

This company provides many materials in the area of communication and sensory integration.

Trott, M. C., & Laurel, M. K., & Windeck, S. L. (1993). *SenseAbilities. Understanding sensory integration*. Tucson, AZ: Therapy Skill Builders.

This booklet explains sensory integration, praxis, and alertness. It also discusses the individual sensory systems, therapy sessions, and provides suggestions and activities for home and school use.

Social Skills Materials

Baker, Jed, (2003). *The Social Skills Picture Book*. Arlington, TX: Future Horizons, Inc.

Seeing is learning. Dr. Jed Baker embraces this philosophy in The Social Skills Picture Book, a dynamic teaching tool that engages the attention and motivation of students who need extra help learning appropriate social skills by demonstrating nearly 30 social skills such as conversation, play, emotion management and empathy. Through his work with autistic and disabled students, Dr. Baker has proven that students of all ages learn more effectively when pictures are used to supplement verbal descriptions and instructions.

Carledge, G., & Milburn, J. F.. (1986). *Teaching social skills to children.* Innovative approaches, Second ed. New York, NY: Pergamon Press.

This book is a basic guide for teaching social skills. It provides an overview of social skills instruction. The *Think Aloud Program* is explained. One chapter deals with social skills through leisure instruction for students with severe disabilities and another chapter deals with social skills instruction for peer interactions.

Center for Applied Psychology, Inc., P. O. Box 61587, King of Prussia, PA 19406, USA. Phone: 800-962-1141.

This company sells books and materials for counseling. Many of the book listed in the children's section of resources are available through this company. A subdivision of this company, Childswork/Childsplay, specializes in the materials and games for children.

Dowd, T., & Tierney, J. (1992). *Teaching social skills to youth. A curriculum for child-care providers.* Boys Town, NE: Boys Town Press.

This book gives an overview of social skills training and provides excellent information about teaching specific skills. The basic skills group includes following instructions, greeting others, and accepting "no" answers. Some of the skills at the intermediate level following rules and initiating, maintaining, and closing conversations. At the advanced level, a few of the topics are dealing with fear, frustration, failure, rejection, and anger. This is an excellent resource for parents and teachers to use as a guide when deciding what social skills need to be taught.

Research Press, Dept. 961, P. O. Box 9177, Champaign, IL 61826.

This company sells a variety of social skills instructional programs. One widely known series, The Skillstreaming Series is produces by this company. This series includes Skillstreaming in Early Childhood, Skillstreaming the Elementary School Child, and Skills Streaming the Adolescent. Other products available through this company include The Prepare Curriculum; Skills for Living; Thinking, Feeling, Behaving; Connecting with Others; ICPS. I Can Problem Solve; Life Lessons for Young Adolescents; Growing up on Purpose; and Viewpoints.

Pro-Ed. 8700 Shoal Creek Boulevard.

Although this company specializes in assessment materials, professional books are also available. Social skills curricululms available through this company include *The Walker Social Skills Curriculum (The ACCEPTS Program and The ACCESS Program), The Culture and Lifestyle Appropriate Social Skills Intervention Curriculum (CLASSIC), The Waksman Social Skills Curriculum,* and *I Can Behave.*

Sarget, L. (1991). *Social Skills in the School and Community.* Reston, VA: Council for Exceptional Children.

This curriculum provides practical social skills lessons for elementary, middle, and secondary school students. Skills addressed include getting along with peers, teachers, and people in the community.

Schab, L. M. (1996). *The coping skills workbook.* King of Prussia, PA: The Center for Applied Psychology, Inc.

This book is designed to for children to help them learn nine essential skills for dealing with crisis. The skills include asking for help, relaxing, discovering choices, etc.

Shapiro, L. E. (1997). *Don't be difficult*. King of Prussia, PA: The Center for Applied Psychology, Inc.

This book is designed to help children, age 7 to 12, consider the consequences of both positive and negative choices.

Williams, M. S. (1994). *"How Does Your Engine Run?" A Leader's Guide to The Alert Program for Self-Regulation*. Albuquerque, NM: Therapy Works, Inc.

This gook provides a way for parents, teachers, and therapists to help children learn about themseles. It helps students to moitor the signals that indicate an internal level of readiness to work, play, listen, attend, and participate in the activities of life.

Publisher Information

Abingdon Press, 201 Eighth Avenue South, Nashville, TN 37203.

Arena Press, (an imprint of Academic Therapy Publications), 20 Commercial Boulevard, Novato, CA 94949-6191.

Center for Applied Psychology, Inc., P. O. Box 61587, King of Prussia, PA 19406, USA. Phone: 800-962-1141.

Doubleday, (a division of Bantam Doubleday Dell Publishing Group, Inc.), 1540 Broadway, New York, NY 10036.

Future Education, Inc. is now Future Horizons, Inc.

Future Horizons, Inc., 720 North Fielder, Arlington, TX 76012. Phone: 800-489-0727.

Keats Publishing, Inc., 27 Pine Street, Box 876, New Cannaan, CT 06840-0876.

Landmark Editions, Inc., PO Box 4469, 1402 Kansas Ave., Kansas City, MO 64127. Phone: 816-241-4919.

Magination Press, 19 Union Square West, 8th Floor, New York, NY 10003.

Oxford University Press, 198 Madison Ave., New York, NY 10016.

Potential Unlimited Publishing, the PUP Foundation, P. O. Box 218, Stratham, NH 03885-0218. Phone: 603-778-6006.

Price Stern Sloan, Customer Service Dept., 390 Murray Hill Parkway, East Rutherford, NJ 07073.

Pro-Ed, 8700 Shoal Creek Blvd., Austin, TX 78758-6897.

Pyramid Educational Consultants, Inc., 5 Westbury Drive, Cherry Hill, NJ 08003. Phone: 609-489-1644; 888-732-7462 (Toll Free).

QuirkRoberts Publishing, P. O. Box 71, Troy, MI 48099-0071. Phone: 810-879-2598. FAX: 810-879-2599.

Sensory Integration International, Inc. 1402 Cravens Ave., Torrance, CA 90501-2701.

Teacher's College Press, 1234 Amsterdam Ave., New York, NY 10027

Therapy Skill Builders. A division of The Psychological Corporation. 555 Academic Ct. San Antonio, TX 73207 502-323-7500.

Therapy Works, Inc., 4901 Butte Place N. W., Albuquerque, NM 87120.

Verbal Images Press, 19 Fox Hill Drive, Fairport, NY 14450. Phone: 716-377-3807. Fax: 716-377-5401.

Western Psychological Services, 12031 Wilshire Blvd., Los Angeles, CA 90025.

Woodbine House, 6510 Bells Mill Rd., Bethesda, MD 20817. Phone: 800-843-7323.

Writer's Press Service, 5278 Chinden Blvd., Boise, ID 83714, Phone: 800-574-1715 or 208-327-0566.

Glossary

A-B-C is a common abbreviation used to refer to antecedent, behavior, and consequence.

Agitation refers to a state of extreme excitement, irritation, or alarm.

Aggression is an unprovoked attack or hostile behavior, generally directed toward other people or objects. Aggression may be either verbal or physical.

Activity reinforcers, a form of positive reinforcement, may include favorite activities, use of preferred objects, or increased responsibilities.

Alert, when used as a verb, refers to signaling or warning the body to be ready to respond. When used as a noun, it refers to a state of awareness or vigilance.

Alerting refers to raising the individual's level of awareness and attentiveness.

Allergen refers to a foreign substance that enters the body causing some form of reaction. Common allergens include dust, molds, foods, animal hairs, and various plant pollens.

Allergy refers to an overreaction of the individual's immune system to an ordinarily harmless substance that results in skin rash, sneezing, asthma, or other physical or behavioral changes.

Alternative communication system generally refers to a different way (other than verbal) for an individual to communicate. It may be by use of gestures, objects, picture symbols, or other specialized equipment.

Antecedent refers to an event that immediately precedes a behavior.

Antecedent control is the manipulation of cues or conditions in the environment in an effort to trigger a different behavior.

Antidepressant(s) refers to a class of medications which are used to relieve mental depression. In individuals with autism, antidepressants may also reduce hyperactivity, anxiety, and the frequency and intensity of obsessions and compulsions.

Anxiety is a general feeling of uneasiness that may result in physical characteristics including increased muscle tension and heart rate, fidgeting, or generally increased levels of arousal.

Applied behavior analysis refers to the direct application of the principles of behavior modification in natural environments such as home, school, and community. It is using behavioral principles to improve the individual's performance in various situations.

Arguing is an attempt to change the conditions that have been presented.

Arousal level refers to the individual's state of reactiveness which may be underreactive, normal, or overreactive. Persons may exhibit high arousal (excited) levels or low arousal (calm) levels.

Asperger syndrome (or Asperger's Disorder), a disorder closely related to higher functioning autism, is characterized by differences in responses to sensory stimuli, impaired language or communication, and persistent difficulty in understanding social situations. Although individuals with Asperger syndrome usually have average or above average intelligence, they may also have learning disabilities in specific areas and difficulties in turn taking or perspective taking.

Assistive technology refers to special items or pieces of equipment which are used to increase, maintain, or improve the functioning abilities of individuals. Commercially produced assistive technology devices include calculators, computers, pencil holders, food and utensil holders, specialized switches for environmental control, etc.

Assistive technology services refers to assisting any child with a disability in the selection, acquisition or use of an assistive technology device.

Audiokinetron is the name of specialized equipment that modulates sound frequencies. It is used to provide auditory integration training to individuals with autism or other developmental disabilities.

Auditory integration training (AIT) refers specifically to a treatment developed by Dr. Guy Berard (France) which uses special equipment, the audiokinetron, to treat hypersensitive or painful hearing through modulation of sound frequency. The recommended treatment is 20 thirty minute sessions (two sessions twice a day for thirty minutes each.)

Auditory modality refers to the channel of learning in which information is received through the sense of hearing.

Auditory processing disorders (problems) refer to difficulties within the brain that prohibit normal processing of information that is heard.

Auditory training should not be confused with auditory integration training. Auditory training is a technique used by speech pathologists and educators of the deaf. It uses specific techniques to teach individuals better use of any hearing ability they may have.

Augmentative communication is a form of supplementary communication for persons who have no control over their body. It may be a simple paper communication board or a sophisticated device producing sound output for nonverbal individuals.

Autism is a developmental disability that typically appears during the first three years of life resulting from a neurological disorder that affects brain functioning. Although characteristics vary greatly, essential features include difficulties in communication and language, social interaction, cognitive processes, and a restricted repertoire of activities and interests.

Autism Society of America (ASA) is the national support group organized for the purpose of supporting individuals with autism and their families and caretakers. In addition to the national organization, there are state and local chapters.

Aversive refers to a condition that the person tries to avoid or escape.

Avoidance behavior (reaction) refers to a protective behavior that an individual uses to escape a disliked experience such as withdrawal or a rocking behavior done to calm the person.

B$_6$ and magnesium refers to a specific vitamin therapy recommended by Dr. Bernard Rimland designed to reduce inappropriate behaviors and increase desired behaviors.

Backward chaining is breaking a skill into small steps that are then taught in a sequence, starting with the *last step* in the sequence *first*. It is commonly used for teaching self-help skills such as putting on and taking off pants.

Bargaining or negotiating refers to attempts by the person to change established conditions.

Baseline refers to the level or frequency of a behavior prior to the implementation of an instructional strategy or technique that will be evaluated at a later date.

Behavior intervention plan, also called a *behavior management plan*, is a written document that becomes part of the IEP (individual educational plan). This plan identifies problem behaviors; goals for decreasing unwanted behaviors and increasing desired behaviors, and specifies intervention strategies to use when specific behavioral events occur.

Behavior management is a general procedure for changing behaviors through consistent application of consequences.

Behavior management plan is another name for the behavior intervention plan. See behavior intervention plan.

Behavior modification refers to a model of behavioral change that is used to change behavior by applying the principles of reinforcement learning or operant conditioning.

Behavioral momentum, a differential reinforcement approach, refers to ignoring and redirecting misbehavior by guiding the problem behavior into a more appropriate response. The force that is driving the behavior is used to direct the person's energy and efforts toward a more appropriate response.

Behavior reduction procedure(s) refer to strategies whose primary purpose is to decrease unwanted behaviors. Behavior reduction procedures may include positive reinforcement strategies, extinction, redirection, or punishment.

Behavioral supports are supports within the environment such as visual cues, social cues, or physical prompting which increase the likelihood that the individual will exhibit appropriate behaviors.

Body language refers to physical gestures, nods, glances, facial expressions, position of body, etc., that a person uses to transmit messages without speaking.

Brushing therapy is an occupational therapy method developed by Patricia and Julia Willbarger. Therapists use a soft surgical brush to brush the arms, legs, and back of individuals who exhibit tactile defensiveness.

Cadence refers to how fast or slow an individual speaks. Fast speech usually indicates anger or excitement. Slow tone typically indicates calmness. In dealing with angry people, an appropriate response is to lower the voice and speak slower. Faster, louder speech has a tendency to escalate the other person's anger.

Catastrophic reaction, also called a *meltdown*, is a reaction exhibited when the person is overwhelmed by stimulation from the environment, people, tasks, sensory input, or emotions. The individual generally displays a loss of control resulting in screaming, aggression, runaway, panic attacks, tantrums, or severe withdrawal.

Central auditory processing disorder refers to a problem which exists when, despite normal hearing and adequate environmental stimulation, an individual has difficulty acquiring, understanding, or using language appropriate for the individual's age and intellectual level.

Chaining is sequencing the steps of an activity or skill and putting the individual steps together for the individual to learn new, complete skills.

Communication board refers to an object persons can hold in their hands that generally has pictures, words, or symbols that can be pointed to in order to express a want, feeling, or desire.

Communication system refers to any form of communication (gestures, signs, objects, pictures, or words) that provides a way for the individual to express wants, needs, thoughts, and feelings across a variety of settings, persons, and tasks.

Communicative function refers to the intent of the behavior used to express wants, needs, thoughts, and feelings; the purpose the behavior was exhibited.

Communicator refers to the nonverbal individual who is receiving physical support from another person in order to be able to point to letters on a communication board.

Compliance training is used to increase the amount of instructional control over an individual. It refers to teaching the individual to follow another person's directions through planned practice sessions in which various simple cues are given. The learner's response is followed by consistent, preplanned consequences. This is also a form of *discrete trial training*.

Compulsions refer to a ritual or activity done in response to an obsession to give the individual a feeling of safety. Examples include constant washing of hands, having to have everything in the house or on a particular shelf arranged in a specific order, the need to follow a specific routine every time something is done, having to go the same way to work or school everyday, etc.

Concrete thinking refers to thoughts that can be related to specific or actual objects, acts, behaviors, or feelings. This is in direct contrast to abstract thinking which expresses a quality apart from any specific object or instance.

Conjoint therapy refers to the simultaneous delivery of two related services or therapies. For example, some therapists provide speech therapy and occupational therapy as one integrated therapy. The purpose is to enhance functioning in speech and language as a product of participation in sensory integrative activities.

Consequence refers to conditions that follow a behavior and affects the frequency of future behavior.

Contingent observation, a form of time-out, involves moving the person 1 to 3 feet away from the activity or people for a short period of time during which time the person still faces the ongoing activity.

Crisis management involves short-term strategies such as physical restraint or removal of stimulation that enable caretakers to get behaviors under control so that other prevention techniques may be implemented.

Cueing procedures refers to the use of some form of cue or reminder that a certain behavior is expected. The cue must be clearly understood and the individual must be capable of performing the task. Effective cues are clear, concise, logical, and meaningful.

Daily schedule refers to a visual picture or written list that shows the daily sequence of activities or subjects that the individual is to participate in. Daily schedules usually are visually depicted in a left-to-right or top-to-bottom sequence for individuals with autism.

Deep breathing exercise(s) refer to the use of taking deep breaths or sequences of breaths to assist the individual with self-regulation by interrupting an irritating stimulus and providing a focus for attention.

Deep pressure therapy involves the use of deep pressure for calming purposes. Activities which provide deep pressure sensations include: jumping, bouncing, skipping, hopping, pushing, pulling, digging, squeezing, and "sandwiching" between mats. Joint compression, weighted vests, and quilts are also used to provide deep pressure sensations.

Delayed echolalia is a characteristic exhibited by some individuals with autism in which a sentence, phrase, or partial phrase is repeated over and over, generally some time after hearing it. Delayed indicates that the repetition may occur several hours later; or days, weeks, months, or even years later.

Delayed time loss is used when time-out is not feasible. A symbol indicating time-out is provided as a reminder that time-out or time loss will take place at a later time during the same day.

De-stim area, also referred to as a *safe area*, is a physically defined place with obvious visual boundaries and lowered stimulation that is used to manage overstimulation. The individual may go to the de-stim or safe area to calm down.

De-stimulation is removing potentially stimulating people, objects, activities, and events from the person's environment allowing them to calm down or preventing escalation of overstimulation.

Differential reinforcement uses positive reinforcement for acceptable behavior while ignoring misbehaviors.

Differential reinforcement of alternative behaviors (DRA) refers to reinforcing a target behavior (hand raising and waiting for a response) while ignoring the misbehavior (calling out).

Differential reinforcement of incompatible behaviors (DRI) refers to rewarding a student for a behavior (staying in his seat) that cannot occur simultaneously with the unwanted behavior (walking around the room).

Differential reinforcement of other behaviors (DRO), also referred to as *differential reinforcement of the omission of the behavior*, refers to rewarding a student for not exhibiting a specific behavior, regardless of other behaviors that occur during the time period. For example, reinforcing the individual for not hitting during recess even though other inappropriate behaviors were exhibited.

Direct defiance is an overt refusal to comply to a request from an authority figure.

Direct instruction is a teaching approach in which lessons are goal-oriented and structured by the teacher. Skills are divided into small, specific steps consisting of concrete, observable behaviors with instruction provided for each sequential step.

Discrete trial learning is another term for compliance training. One method of discrete trial learning involves isolating and teaching a specific task to an individual by repeatedly presenting the same task to the person. Responses are recorded for each trial and each successful response is usually rewarded with tangible reinforcers.

Discipline plan refers to a written document which describes discipline procedures that are to be used when certain behaviors are exhibited by the individual.

Distractibility refers to difficulty in focusing or maintaining attention.

Distracting noncompliance occurs when the person tries to direct attention away from the expected response.

DMG (dimethylglycine) is a natural food substance recommended by Dr. Bernard Rimland. According to Rimland, DMG may be helpful for individuals with autism.

Duration of behavior refers to how long the behavior lasts.

Dysfunctions refers to any type of problem that an individual might have with a particular body system not working in the way it is supposed to. A brain dysfunction means the brain is not working the way most brains work. A sensory system dysfunction means that one of the sensory systems is not functioning as it is supposed to. You may also have things that dysfunction. A computer system dysfunction generally means the computer didn't do what it was supposed to do.

Echolalia is continued repetition of the speech of others. The word or phrases may be the exact same words or phrases or a slight modification of the words and phrases that were heard.

Exclusionary time-out, the most restrictive form of time-out, consists of removing persons to an area where they are totally excluded from peers and ongoing activities.

Expressive communication/language refers to the ability of the individual to express wants, needs, desires, feelings, etc., through nonverbal or verbal methods.

Extinction refers to eliminating or decreasing a behavior by removing reinforcement from it.

Facilitated communication (FC) is a communication method. A *facilitator* provides physical support to a *communicator* while the person is typing messages. The typing may take place on a typewriter, computer, or paper alphabet board.

Facilitator refers to a person who provides physical support to a nonverbal person that enables the individual to be able to point to letters on a communication board.

Fade, in behavioral terms, refers to the gradual removal of cues or supports in specific behavioral situations or settings.

Fading is the process of gradually changing the conditions or gradually removing conditions related to a student's response.

Frequency of behavior refers to how often a behavior occurs.

Frequency of sound refers to the number of cycles per unit of time or wave.

Frustration tolerance refers to the level of discomfort that an individual can tolerate before losing control of behavior.

Functional analysis of behavior refers to a procedure used to examine behaviors to determine what happens before, during, and after behaviors occur. Behaviors are examined in terms of the purposes and functions that the behavior serves for the individual exhibiting the behavior.

Galactosemia is a condition commonly associated with mental retardation in which the individual is unable to metabolize lactose appropriately. When lactose is ingested, toxins are formed which cause brain injury.

Generalization(s) refers to the ability to take a skill learned in one setting, such as the classroom, and use it in another setting like the home or community. It may also be taking a specific skill and using it in a slightly different way. For example, a person might learn to use a vending machine at school, and be able use the same skill at a vending machine at Wal-mart that operates slightly differently. Another example would be learning to use a washer and dryer at school and being able to use the washer and dryer at home.

Gravity refers to how comfortable people are with their heads in various positions.

Gravitational insecurity refers to a an unusual fear of movement which changes position of the head. A child may be afraid to walk without the support of a wall or person.

Gustatory refers to the sense of taste.

Hierarchy of responses refers to the technique of using several consequences to weaken an individual's behavior. The consequences are generally presented from least to most aversive or restrictive.

High tech refers to assistive technology that indicates that greater levels of technology are required for the development or use of the equipment.

Hyperactivity is a condition characterized by extreme restlessness and short attention span relative to others of the same age.

Hyperarousal refers to a state of high stimulation or overreaction to stimuli that might result in behavioral changes.

Hypersensitivities are characterized by an elevated or higher than normal reaction to sensory input. Hypersensitivity to sound may indicate painful hearing at certain frequencies. Individuals generally exhibit more acute reactions to sensory input than others who are not hypersensitive.

Hypoarousal refers to a state in which the individual appears to make no response or limited responses to the world around them. This may also be referred to as a low arousal state.

Hyposensitivities are characterized by a lack of response to incoming information or stimuli significantly impacting the person's ability to participate in the environment. The individual may appear to be unaware of sensory stimuli from visual, auditory, tactile (touch), kinesthetic (movement), olfactory (smell), and gustatory (taste) sources. One hyposensitivity exhibited by some individuals with autism is the lack of response to pain. Some individuals respond to sound as if they are deaf; i.e., a lack of response to sound.

Idiom(s) refers to an expression or group of words that has a different meaning from the actual literal translation of the words. For example, "blow your socks off" doesn't really mean that someone is going to get down on their knees and try to "blow" your socks off. It means that whatever you're talking about is really good. A Dodge® commercial says "This car will really blow your socks off." Chrysler Corporation really meant "This car is wonderful!"

Immediate echolalia refers to words that an individual speaks right after the individual hears the words or phrases. If the parent says, "Chris, do that.", he immediately repeats or parrots "do that."

Impulsive runaways refers to a type of runaway behavior that might be exhibited by an individual. The person generally leaves the area of supervision as a result of overstimulation, agitation, or an impulsive reaction to novel cues.

Impulsivity refers to acting without stopping to think about the consequences of the behavior.

Inflection refers to modulation of the voice such as raising or lowering the pitch.

Inaccuracy refers to inaccurate attempts by the person to follow the direction.

Isolated time-out involves sending the person to an isolated spot, removed from peers and activities, but still in the same room or general area.

Level systems refers to a system where students are moved from one level to the next based upon improvements in their behavior. Each higher level usually involves increased privileges and responsibilities for the student.

Literal interpretations of language is interpreting the meaning of phrases and sentences based upon the exact meaning of the words within the phrase. For example, "He's the top dog." doesn't really mean the person is a dog on top. It means, "He's very important." (See idiom.)

Logical consequence refers to what happens following the behavior that naturally occurs as a result of the behavior. For example, if the child throws a toy out the car window, the toy will not be available for play. If an individual gets mad and throws an appliance across the room, the individual will not be able to use that appliance because it is broken.

Lovaas method is an intensive method of behavioral therapy. Dr. Lovaas recommends that children with autism receive forty hours per week of direct instruction. Discrete trial formats are used as a method of providing intensive behavioral therapy.

Low arousal state refers to a state of being in the individual in which the person's state of alertness is very low. The individual is extremely unreactive to stimuli within the environment.

Low-tech refers to assistive technology or aids and services that do not require sophisticated equipment. For example, a pencil grip would be considered a low tech device. A home-made switch used to turn a toy, radio, and tape player on or off might also be considered to be a "low tech" device. It does not take a lot of technical knowledge to make or use the particular object.

Manipulation refers to a situation in which the individual tries to change environmental conditions by interaction with the individual in charge or person giving the instructions or directives.

Masturbation refers to stimulation of the genitals, sometimes to the point of orgasm.

Megavitamin therapy refers to the use of extremely large doses of vitamins to improve behavior.

Meltdown, also called a *catastrophic reaction*, is a reaction exhibited when the person is overwhelmed by stimulation from the environment, people, tasks, sensory input, or emotions. The individual generally displays a loss of control resulting in screaming, aggression, runaway, panic attacks, tantrums, or severe withdrawal.

Modeling is providing the person with a visual, verbal, and/or manual representation of the behavior you want him or her to engage in.

Monitoring is observing and recording behavior.

Mono-channel refers to a state in which individuals can only attend to sensory input from one sensory system at a time. They cannot look and listen. They must look or listen.

Monotone refers to a very flat, even way of speaking, with no rises or drops in pitch or volume.

Motor planning is what allows individuals to create, use, and combine various motor skills to perform new, more complex acts.

Motor planning difficulties refer to difficulties in creating or using various motor skills to perform new, more complex acts.

Multi-channel means that an individual needs sensory input from more than one source or modality in order to process incoming information accurately.

Negative consequences are actions which follow a behavior and serve to decrease that behavior while including a teaching component. While they may cause some discomfort, negative consequences increase the probability that the person will choose an appropriate response in the future by pairing punishment with cues for appropriate behavior.

Negative reinforcement refers to the effect of removing a disliked experience or event following a behavior to strengthen the behavior.

Neurobiological disorder refers to a disorder which has its origin in the neurological or biological functioning of the individual.

Neuroleptics refer to a class of medications (antipsychotic) that are used to suppress or prevent symptoms of psychosis. Major tranquilizers are considered to be neuroleptic medications.

Neurological refers to functioning of the central nervous system which includes the brain, spinal cord, and nerves.

Noncompliance is a failure to follow an instruction.

Noncompliant behavior is refusal to follow an instruction. Noncompliant behavior may be exhibited in direct defiance or refusal to do a specific command or request or because the individual doesn't understand what is requested.

Nonverbal communication refers to any form or attempt at communication that an individual makes. The communication may take the form of temper tantrums, gestures, pointing, leading another person to a door, etc.

Nonverbal social cues refer to looks, smiles, frowns, other facial expressions, and positions of the body to communicate certain information without the use of speech.

Obsessions are silly or frightening thoughts that an individual can't get out of his mind. Some individuals are obsessed by the need to have a specific object such as a book or video tape with them. Others are obsessed by a specific topic such as wheels, numbers, Disney movies, etc.

Object board is one form of communication board. The objects (cup, spoon, toilet tissue, small ball, slinky, etc.) are used to communicate the needs or desires of the individual.

Object swap refers to a form of communication in which the individual exchanges an object for something desired or needed.

Operant refers to any voluntary behavior such as walking, talking, reading, etc., that produces an effect on the environment.

Operant conditioning is a form of learning popularized by B. F. Skinner in 1938 which forms the basis of behavior modification. The Lovaas program is an example of a program that uses operant conditioning as a method of instruction.

Oral-motor activities include blowing, licking, sucking, chewing, crunching, and mouthing of objects.

Oral-motor defensiveness refers to a state in which the individual rejects food or other touches to the mouth because taste, texture, etc. are irritating or uncomfortable.

Oral-motor stimulation refers to activities such as blowing, sucking, and chewing, that tend to reduce oral-motor defensiveness and organize and calm the individual.

Orienting response refers to a reflex reaction that involves physiological arousal and turning the head to perceive the new stimulus.

Overcorrection is a form of punishment that requires the individual to make restitution and practice an exaggerated form of an incompatible behavior. For example, if a student called another student a name, restitution would involve apologizing to the student. Practice would involve paying a compliment to every student in the classroom.

Overreaction refers to a behavior (reaction) that appears to be excessive compared to the irritating agent. For example, a young boy with autism may go into a rage because the teacher tells him that it is time for work.

Overstimulation refers to a state of being in which some individuals become so overwhelmed by sensory stimuli that acting out behaviors such as screaming, aggression, self-abuse, or tantrums occur in reaction to the stimulation. Other individuals with autism may withdraw or "shut down" as a method of reacting to overstimulation.

Panic attack refers to a serious episode of anxiety in which the individual experiences a variety of symptoms including palpitations, dizziness, nausea, trembling, etc. These symptoms are not caused by medical problems.

Passive noncompliance refers to actions by an individual indicating the person is unaware the directive has been presented.

Paraverbal refers to how fast or slow a person speaks; the loudness or softness of the speech; and the tone of speech.

Peer buddy refers to a person of approximately the same age who has been assigned or requested to be an individual's companion during work and play activities. A peer buddy may coach the person with autism in appropriate work and play behaviors or actually tutor or assist the individual with specific work or play tasks.

Peer group refers to a group of individuals of approximately the same age or grade level who have been assigned or have volunteered to be companions to the person with autism during school and/or home activities. Peer groups may be a club group, a school organization, or a *Circle of Friends.* Typically, the purpose of the peer group is to provide social interaction for the individual with autism.

Peer mentor(s) are generally older than the individual with autism and may be an adult with expertise in a specific field of interest. The mentorship experience may involve the individual with autism in a possible career area or it may be used to facilitate social interaction and friendships.

Perceptual distortion refers to a situation in which incoming sensory information is seen or heard accurately, but is interpreted differently or is distorted during the processing of the information. Although the person hears what is said, the message may not be understood because of auditory processing difficulties occurring in the transmission of stimuli from the ear or from dysfunctions within the auditory processing center of the brain.

Perseverative noises refer to vocalizations and other sounds made through body movements that are continually repeated without change. This usually lasts over a period of time with no alteration in the quality of noise.

Pervasive developmental disorder (PDD) is a term used by the *Diagnostic and Statistical Manual, 4th Ed. (DSM-IV)* to refer to a "severe and pervasive impairment in the development of reciprocal social interaction or verbal and nonverbal communication skills; or when stereotyped behavior, interests, and activities are present." (APA, 1994, p. 77-78.) This category is also used to describe atypical autism.

Phenylketonuria (PKU) is an inherited disorder that usually results in severe retardation. However, if detected at birth through a simple blood test, a special diet can reduce the serious complications associated with this condition.

Physical aggression is any physical act applied to a person or object with the potential to inflict harm or damage. It includes behaviors such as kicking, hitting, biting, pinching, and self-injurious behavior.

Picture swap system refers to a form of communication in which the individual exchanges a picture for a desired object or activity.

Picture symbols are pictures that are used instead of words to convey information by individuals who do not understand words.

Pitch refers to the height or depth of a tone or sound (i.e., the highness or lowness of a voice). See *voice pitch*.

Planned ignoring refers to ignoring a misbehavior (removing attention for the misbehavior) for the purpose of increasing the targeted behavior.

Positive intervention techniques refer to strategies for changing behaviors that emphasize teaching acceptable responses while minimizing discomfort to the individual.

Positive practice requires the person to practice a behavior that is an appropriate alternative to the misbehavior.

Positive reinforcement refers to any object or activity following a behavior which strengthens the behavior.

Premack principle is also referred to as "Grandma's rule." If you eat your vegetables, you can have cookies and ice cream for dessert. In this principle, receiving a high frequency behavior (eating ice cream and cookies) is made contingent on completion of a low frequency behavior (eating vegetables).

Preteaching is reminding the person of the task, routine or behavioral expectations immediately prior to the experience occurring.

Proprioceptive refers to the body system that provides us with unconscious information from the muscles and joints. Through proprioception, we know where each part of the body is and how it is moving - where we are in relation to the world around us.

Props refers to objects or activities that may be used to facilitate relaxation in the safe area. Some props which can have a calming effect include soft pillows, music, sensory toys, objects for deep pressure, weighted clothing, or books.

Prosocial behaviors are actions that show respect and caring for others.

Psychoactive medications are used to treat symptoms of autism. They are used to change moods or mental states and include antidepressant medications, stimulant medications, and neuroleptic medications.

Punishers are objects, activities, or events (consequences) that weaken the behaviors (or operants) they follow.

Punishment follows an unwanted behavior and causes enough discomfort that the person avoids engaging in the behavior. Punishment refers to an experience that follows the behavior that results in the behavior occurring less often, for shorter periods of time, or with less intensity.

Put-in tasks refers to a simple type of task in which the person is required to pick up an object from one container or the table top and drop it in or release it into another container.

Receptive communication/language refers to the individual's interpretation or perception of the language that is actually heard. Does the person understand what he or she is hearing?

Reciprocity refers to a give and take between individuals. If I do something for you, you will do something for me. In conversation, it refers to turn-taking. You say something, I say something, then you say something again. The term implies that the individual monitors and adjusts behaviors when responding to others.

Reinforcement is providing consequences, activities, or other reinforcers that will increase the probability that a person will do the task or skill again.

Reinforcers are consequences that strengthen behaviors they follow. They may take the form of tangible reinforcers (generally food or toys), social reinforcers (smiles), or activity reinforcers (listening to music).

Relaxation training refers to techniques in which individuals are trained to monitor and control muscle tension. The person develops an awareness of muscle tension and can respond to anxiety or stress at an early stage by practicing relaxation exercises, muscle stretching, or other calming strategies.

Response cost involves removal of something the individual likes because of misbehavior. Response cost can also entail loss of a valued object or activity.

Reward is a consequence that follows a behavior that is intended to increase the behavior.

Ritualistic behaviors refer to complex, unique patterns of motor movements.

Routines refer to a customary or regular sequence of procedural steps such as following a daily schedule or going through the steps for dressing each morning.

Safe area, also referred to as a *de-stim* area, is a physically defined place with obvious visual boundaries and lowered stimulation that is used to manage overstimulation. The individual may go to the de-stim or safe area to calm down.

Satiation occurs when a reinforcer loses its reinforcement value. For instance, if cookies are reinforcing, the child become *satiated* when he or she is no longer hungry. Therefore, the cookies are no longer reinforcing.

Schedules refer to plans or procedures listing a sequence of events.

Scotopic Sensitivity Syndrome refers to a condition in which the eyes react negatively to certain reflections of light. This condition is generally treated with the use of colored glasses known as *Irlen lenses*.

Self-concept refers to the person's perception of his or her own strengths and weaknesses.

Self-control strategies are techniques used by an individual to monitor personal reactions and manage resultant responses.

Self-esteem refers to the person's feeling of self-worth.

Self-injurious behaviors (SIB) refers to a form of aggression that is directed against the person exhibiting the behaviors. Examples are biting oneself, slapping your head, etc.

Self-management refers to the ability of individuals to manage their own behavior. With individuals with autism, this also implies the ability to recognize when they are becoming overstimulated and initiate activities, places, or events that will enable them to calm down.

Self-monitoring refers to strategies used by an individual to increase awareness of personal reactions and resultant responses.

Self-regulation refers to a strategy used by individuals to monitor and manage their own behavior.

Self-stimming is a term commonly used to refer to self-stimulation.

Self-stimulation includes many varieties of verbal and motor stereotyped behaviors such as arm-flapping, rocking, hand-flicking, and verbal repetition of words, songs, numbers, etc.

Sensory-based toys are toys that provide stimulation from sound, taste, smell, sight, movement, or touch.

Sensory diet refers to an activity plan that includes specific activities designed to satisfy the individual's sensory requirements in order to develop and maintain optimal functioning levels.

Sensory dysfunctions refers to impairment in the functions of or response to stimulation from sound, taste, smell, sight, movement, or touch.

Sensory integration is a "process by which the brain organizes sensory information for appropriate use." (Ayres, 1979).

Sensory integrative dysfunction refers to an impairment in the ability of the brain to organize information from sight, sound, taste, smell, movement, or touch and to respond appropriately to that information.

Sensory integrative therapy is a program of treatment used by occupational therapists to promote development of sensory integration in individuals who have sensory integrative dysfunction.

Sensory overload refers to a state of being in which some individuals become so overwhelmed by information from sound, taste, smell, sight, movement, or touch that inappropriate responses occur.

Sensory stimuli is information received from sound, taste, smell, sight, movement, or touch.

Shaping is using small steps combined with feedback to help learners reach goals. The term is frequently used interchangeably with successive approximation.

Short term reactive strategies are interventions which are necessary to respond to the behavior of the moment, such as crisis intervention.

Shut down is a withdrawal reaction in which an individual significantly decreases responses to the environment or cues.

Simple refusal refers to a situation where the individual is aware of the directive, but simply does not follow the directive.

Social cues refer to looks, smiles, frowns, other facial expressions, and positions of the body to communicate certain information without the use of speech.

Social diet provides for social interactions on a scheduled basis and when the individual requests social interaction.

Social skills training describes instruction used to develop acceptable behaviors such as sharing, greeting people appropriately, accepting no for an answer, etc.

Social reinforcers meet an individual's social-emotional needs such as smiles, compliments, or praise.

Social rules are unwritten and unspoken principles or regulations for governing social conduct.

Social Stories® refers to two books of stories by Carol Gray that describe social situations in terms of relevant social cues, and often define appropriate responses.

Sound sensitivity refers to extreme reactions to normal sounds because the sounds are irritating or painful to the listener. Most persons with sound sensitivity hear much better than the typical person.

Speak and spin refers to giving a directive using effective cues, then immediately turning and walking away.

Spectrum disorder refers to a disorder that is expressed through a broad range of characteristics and functioning. In autism, individuals functioning at the low end of the spectrum exhibit many challenging behaviors. Persons at the higher end of the spectrum tend to be very intelligent and verbal.

Stims is another term that is used to refer to self-stimulation.

Stimulant medications are used to alter functioning in the brain, thus allowing the individual to better control responses. Therefore, as a result of better behavioral control, an individual may exhibit less hyperactivity and more focused attention.

Stress refers to psychological changes that take place as a result of stressors (stimuli) from the environment.

Stressors refers to events in the person's life that tend to produce anxiety or stress. For the individual with autism, this can be sensory experiences, social interaction, uncertainty, changes in routine, etc.

Structured teaching refers to an approach to instruction that uses visual and environmental cues, schedules, routines, direct instruction, and environmental or instructional adaptations to facilitate learning and independence. An example of a program that uses structured teaching is Project TEACCH.

Successive approximation refers to reinforcing responses that are close to the expected behavior. As the individual improves performance, closer approximations or performances of the task are required for reinforcement to occur. (See shaping.)

Symbolic communication refers to the use of symbols and objects to represent concepts when communicating thoughts, feelings, or desires.

Symbolic object refers to a concrete object used to represent something. For example, a small ball might be used to indicate playtime.

Tactile refers to the sense of touch.

Tactile defensiveness refers to an avoidance reaction to touch because touch is offensive or uncomfortable.

Tactile/kinesthetic involves the use of information from touch and movement.

Tangible reinforcers are physical objects such as food, toys, books, etc. that are presented following a behavior to increase the probability that the behavior will occur again.

Task analysis is the process of breaking a skill down into smaller steps.

Temper tantrums are sudden bursts of ill temper, usually consisting of highly disruptive displays of aggressive or inappropriate behaviors.

Theory of mind is a concept that addresses the ability of an individual to understand the perspective of others.

Three-step prompting is a form of cueing in which three basic steps are presented. The caretaker provides a verbal prompt supplemented with a visual prompt such as a picture, gesture, or symbol, followed by a physical prompt, if necessary.

Time-out is a period of time, generally not to exceed one minute per year of age, when a person cannot receive reinforcement.

Time-out on the spot (TOOTS) consists of a short, mild time-out which is performed without moving the person to another area.

Token system is a system of reinforcement in which an object or visual symbol is provided following a desired behavior.

Tolerance thresholds refer to the levels of discomfort a person can endure before losing control of behavior.

Transition refers to changing from one activity to another. Transition also refers to moving from one stage of life to another such as early childhood to elementary school, junior high school to high school, or high school to the world of work, and other postsecondary options.

Transition area is an area of the classroom where a student goes to check his or her schedule before moving on to the next activity.

Turn-taking refers to alternating positions. In games, you take a turn, then I take a turn. In conversation, I say something, then you respond. After you respond, it's my turn again.

Underreactions refers to a behavior or response that appears to be insufficient compared with the incoming stimulus or expected response.

Verbal aggression occurs when someone directs name calling, profanity, or verbal threats toward another person.

Vestibular refers to the provision of unconscious information from the inner ear to the brain about the body's movement and position in space. It integrates the neck, eye, and body adjustments to movement and helps the head in relation to gravity and movement.

Visual cue(s) refers to anything which can be seen that elicits a behavioral response.

Visualization refers to the ability to see or imagine visual pictures or imagery in the mind without seeing the actual object or view.

Visual stims provide a way for individuals to meet visual sensory needs. Examples include flicking their hands in front of their eyes, blinking their eyes, staring at a crystal chandelier, etc.

Visual supports refer to any type of visual cues, schedules, or signs that increase the probability of successful functioning.

Visual thinking means that the individual visualizes ideas and concepts in terms of images and pictures as opposed to words.

Vitamin therapy refers to the use of vitamins to improve behavior.

Voice tone refers to how a person's voice sounds. Is the tone loud and angry, lilting and happy, sad, etc.? Generally, tone is conveyed through the speed of talking (cadence), the volume (loud or soft), and body language accompanying the message.

Voice pitch refers to the highness (soprano) or lowness (bass) of speech.

Work schedule refers to a visual picture or written list that tells the individual how much work he or she must do and when the work will be finished. Work schedules are generally visually depicted in a left-to-right or top-to bottom sequence for individuals with autism. Each visual picture, symbol, or word indicates a work task. A reinforcer symbol is generally used after the last task in the sequence to tell the individual when and what kind of a reward he or she will receive when the work tasks are completed.

References

Autism Society of America. (1997). What is autism? *The Advocate.* 29 (2), 3.

Ayres, A. J. (1979). *Sensory integration and the child.* Los Angeles, CA: Western Psychological Services.

Berard, G. (1993). *Hearing equals behavior.* New Canaan, CN: Keats Publishing, Inc.

Biklen, D. (Oct., 1992). *Advanced Facilitated Communication Trainers' Workshop,* Huntsville, TX.

Biklen, D. (1993). *Communication unbound.* New York, NY: Teachers College Press.

Condon, R. (1992). *Toilet training children with deaf-blindness/multiple disabilities: Issues and strategies.* Conference Handout. Texas School for the Blind and Visually Impaired Deaf-Blind Outreach., Austin, Tx, July 25, 1992.

Crossley, R. (1994). *Facilitated communication training.* New York, NY: Teachers College Press.

Crossley, R., & McDonald, A. (1984). *Annie's coming out.* New York, NY: Penguin Books.

Donnelly, J. (Organizer and Moderator) (Speakers). (1995). *Speaking for ourselves: Young adults with autism panel.* (Cassette Recording, ASA National Conference on Autism. July 12-15, 1995, Greensboro, NC.)

Donnelly, J., Grandin,T., Bovee, J., Miller, S., & McKean, T. (Speakers). (1996). *With a little help from my friends: People who have opened doors for me.* (Cassette Recording No. ASA-601-96). EARS, P. O. Box 2200, Athens, TX 75761. 1-800- 782-7961.

Foster, C., & Fay, J. M. (1983). D*iscipline with love and logic.* Evergreen, CO: Institute for Professional Development, Ltd.

Frost, L. A., & Bondy, Λ. S. (1994). PECS. *The picture exchange communication system. Training Manual.* Cherry Hill, NJ: Pyramid Educational Consultants, Inc.

Grandin, T. (1995). *Thinking in pictures.* New York: Doubleday.

Grandin, T., & Scariano, M. M. (1986). *Emergence labeled autistic.* Novato, CA: Arena Press.

Gray, C. (Ed.). (1993). *The original social story book.* Arlington, TX: Future   Education.

Gray, C. (1994). *Comic strip conversations.* Arlington, TX: Future Education.

Gray, C. (Ed.). (1994). *The new social story book.* Arlington, TX: Future Education.

Gray, C. (Speaker). (1996). S*ocial Stories and Comic Strip Conversations. Unique methods to improve social understanding.* (Videotape). (Available from Future Horizons, Inc., 720 North Fielder, Arlington, TX 76012. 1-800-489-9727).

Green, G. (1996). Evaluating claims about treatments for autism. In C. Maurice, G. Green, & Luce, S. (Eds.), *Behavioral interventions for young children with autism. A manual for parents and professionals* (pp. 15-28). Austin, TX: Pro-Ed.

Hayward, A. (Producer). (1994). *Eye to Eye with Connie Chung.* (An interview with Donna Williams). New York: CBS.

Hodgon, L. A. (1995). *Visual strategies for improving communication.* Troy, MI: Quirk Roberts Publishing. 810-879-2598.

Houston Dispute Resolution Center. (1990). *Mediation training.* Houston, TX: H o u s t o n Dispute Resolution Center.

Individuals with Disabilities Education Act of 1990. *Federal Register.* 57, (189), Sept. 29, 1992.

1994 Amendments to the Technology-Related Assistance for Individuals with Disabilities Act of 1988.

1997 Amendments the Individuals with Disabilities Education Act .

McKean, T. (1994). *Soon will come the light. A view from inside the autism puzzle.* Arlington, TX: Future Education, Inc.

McKean, T. (1996). *Light on the horizon. A deeper view from inside the autism puzzle.* Arlington, TX: Future Horizons, Inc.

Mesibov, G. (July, 1995) *TEACCH* Training Workshop at Chapel Hill, NC.

Miller, S. (1993). Some insights into autism. *The Advocate.* 25 (4), 7-8.

Miller, S. (1996). Interpreting behaviors: An autistic review of the movies. *The 1996 Autism*

Society National Conference Proceedings. Madison, WI: Omnipress, 202-306.

Perske, R. (1988). *Circles of friends*. Nashville, TN: Abingdon Press.

Prizant, B. M., & Wetherby, A. M. (1987). Communicative intent: A framework for understanding social-communicative behavior in autism. *Journal of the American Academy of Child Psychiatry*. 26, 472-479.

Rimland, B. (1991a). *ARI recommendations on treatments for autistic and other mentally and neurologically handicapped children*. ARI Publication 49. Revised 3/91.

Rimland, B. (1991b). F*orm letter regarding high dosage vitamins B6 and Magnesium therapy for autism and related disorders*. San Diego, CA: Autism Research Institute (ARI). 2/91 Revision.

Rimland, B. (1994). An interview with Bernard Rimland. *The Advocate.*

Rimland, B., & Edelson, S. (1994). The effects of auditory integration training on autism. *American Journal of Speech-Language Pathology*. 3 (2), 16-24.

Sensory Integration International. (1991). *A parent's guide to understanding sensory integration*. Torrance, CA: Sensory Integration International.

Siegel, Bryna. (1996). *The world of the autistic child. Understanding and treating autistic spectrum disorders*. New York: Oxford University Press.

Trott, M. C., & Laurel, M. K., & Windeck, S. L. (1993). SenseAbilities. *Understanding sensory integration*. Tucson, AZ: Therapy Skills Builders.

Veale, T. (1994). Auditory integration training: The use of a new listening treatment within the profession. *American Journal of Speech-Language Pathology*. 3 (2), 12-15.

Willbarger, P., & Willbarger, J. L. (1991). *Sensory defensiveness in children, age two to twelve: An intervention guide for parents and other caretakers*. Santa Barbara, CA: Avanti Educational Programs.

Williams, D. (1995). The lived experience of Irlen Filters. *The Advocate*. 27 (6), 7.

Williams, D., (1996). A*utism - An inside-Out approach*. Bristol, PA: Jessica Kingsley.

Williams, M. S., & Shellenberger, S. (1994). *"How does your engine run?" A leader's guide to the alert program for self-regulation*. Albuquerque, NM 87120.